Advance Praise

"In *Connections Over Compliance* Dr. Desautels redefines the educational process with an innovative neuroscience-informed and compassionate perspective. This transformative volume provides a glimpse into the optimistic future of education and radically dispels strategies vested in antiquated behavioral models of learning that have been engrained in education dogma. Through a transdisciplinary approach, we gain a deep respect for the behaviorally challenged child's attempts to survive in a threatening world, we become aware that learning is dependent on a neurophysiological state that is only efficiently and effectively available when the child has trusting relationships with teachers, and we learn how these relationships can be leveraged to enable the child to feel sufficiently safe to dampen threat reactions and to spontaneously become social and cognitively available to learn. In this accessible book, Dr. Desautels provides tools and exercises to restructure the classroom environment to effectively meet the needs of the most vulnerable and behaviorally reactive children to feel safe in the classroom and to leverage these feelings into cognitive and social successes."

— DR. STEPHEN PORGES, Neuroscientist, Author, and Creator
of the Polyvagal Theory

"Dr. Lori Desautels explores and interrogates the beliefs systems under-girding long-accepted discipline systems and invites readers to reimagine our interactions with children and youth. As a parent and educator, the book inspired me to recommit to relational and responsive discipline in my home and in my work with educators."

— BROOKE KANDEL-CISCO, Ph.D., Dean, College of Education,
Butler University

"I have worked alongside Dr. Lori Desautels for the past 8 years. As our collaboration grows and changes, I continue to use these resources for meaningful and researched ways to support young people, teachers, families, and myself. The unique path they have paved for engaging educators and having worked alongside them, has opened doors and minds to this critical work of educational neuroscience. I look forward to adding *Connections Over Compliance* to my bookshelf along with all of her other books."

— DEANNA NIBARGER, Social and Emotional Behavior Coach,
Metropolitan School District of Washington Township

"*Connections Over Compliance* is a gift for teachers, principals, university professors, state and federal departments of education, and for parents. Even more importantly, it is a blessing for all the students whose teachers, support staff, administrators, and parents read, understand, and apply the wealth of information, insight, and practical suggestions contained within the book. Dr. Desautels does an excellent job of translating complicated neuroscience concepts into immediately accessible language. She makes the information real and applicable through the provision of examples and a wealth of resources."

> —BETH TOLLEY, Director of Educational Advocacy, Alliance Against Seclusion and Restraint, Board Member, NAMI Virginia (National Alliance on Mental Illness), Board Member, Early Childhood Mental Health Virginia

"This book is an important read for educators or parents who want to understand how to make positive connections with children. It is giving us a much-needed perspective on discipline and how we must build relationships and trust with children. We learn that as adults, we must focus on self-regulating and staying in a calm brain state so that we can best help our children. The calming strategies in this book can be used immediately to have a positive impact on everyone around us. Thank you, Lori, for your expertise and sharing this information at such a critical time."

> — SANDY BRYANT, Curriculum Coordinator, St. Mary's Child Center

"In *Connections Over Compliance* Dr. Lori Desautels provides educators powerful science-based insights, built on years of study and practical application, to enhance their understanding of themselves as teachers and the effectiveness with which they connect with affected students in supporting their growth into adulthood."

> —JAMES P. BIEN, MD, MPH, FAAP, Chief Medical Officer, VP Quality and Patient Safety, Pediatrician, Indiana University Health Arnett

"By giving language to co-regulated ways of being, Dr. Lori Desautels continues to catalyze a new reality in school communities. Her translational fusion of embodied sciences and the art of education practices provides a prescient and essential guide for honoring our shared human journey amid our complex times."

> — SHEILA DENNIS, PhD, MSW, Senior Lecturer, Indiana University School of Social Work

"It is my honor and privilege to write about my support for *Connections Over Compliance*. With the support of renowned therapeutic researchers, Dr. Desautels identifies key elements that should be a part of any school's approach to discipline and professional development. As she wrote the book, the most serious pandemic in history, COVID-19, threw our world into a new reality previously unexperienced. This experience shed new light on issues for which are unknown and for which we are unprepared.

How will schools cope with the pandemic's impact on children's fears, violence, and a loss of a safe place of well-being when the schools abruptly closed and the remaining trepidation of our new unknown reality? Dr. Desautels' book is attempting to provide a backdrop on these issues and a lens for us to see the future.

Schools and school personnel are in the relationship business. Relationships provide the oxygen for connections. With those relationships and connections severed by schools closing. Dr. Desautels outlines how this detachment could manifest itself in behaviors previously unseen. She gives us insight into the possibilities of a new paradigm for operationalizing the effects of adverse childhood experiences."

—J. T. COOPMAN, ED. D., Executive Director IAPSS

"Dr. Desautels has a passion for leading educators on the journey to understanding brain functions provides the knowledge, tools and hope to better understand the impact of adversity when understanding student behavior. It is an honor to partner with Dr. Desautels in providing professional development and support for our students. She continues to amaze me with the latest research and practical implementation of strategies that best serve our children."

—DR. FLORA REICHANADTER, Superintendent, Metropolitan School District of Pike Township, Indianapolis

"*Transformational!* This book sets a brilliant new standard for the urgently needed paradigm shift in education. Based in relational neuroscience, *Connections Over Compliance* shows educators how to respect and nurture natural brain functions to maximize learning potential and resilience for all students. It should be required reading for everyone who works with students and the systems that serve them."

—MONA DELAHOOKE, Ph.D., Author of *Beyond Behaviors: Using Brain Science and Compassion to Understand & Solve Children's Behavioral Challenges*

"Dr. Desautels created a must read by combining relational neuroscience with practical application. Read this book if you are starting or already embarking on your trauma-informed journey!"

—MATHEW PORTELL, Principal, Fall-Hamilton Elementary, Facilitator, Paradigm Shift Education

"Dr. Desautels has put together a compilation of current neuroscience that will bring any reader to a foundational knowledge of interpersonal neurobiology as well as explain current evidence-based practices that will help heal and guide those youth that come from difficult backgrounds and may struggle with challenging behaviors. Dr. Desautels' work goes beyond just presenting the data, as her compassion for children in need shines through while she shares from her own life of living the model inside and outside of the classroom. This book is truly an essential tool for any teacher or direct caregiver that wants to understand behavior and know how to help children connect, heal, and move into a positive life trajectory."

—SCOTT E. LEPOR, D.O., Medical Director of Texas Juvenile Justice Department, Trauma Informed, Trust Based Relational Intervention (TBRI®) Practitioner/Educator

"Punitive school discipline and zero-tolerance approaches are not working for our schools. The cycle of suspension, expulsion, corporal punishment, restraint, and seclusion are leading our children down the school-to-prison pipeline. In *Connections Over Compliance*, Dr. Desautels provides a roadmap and resources to help educators move to a brain-aligned preventive discipline model based on modern neuroscience. Dr. Desautels explains that regulation, control, empathy, and kindness are skills that need to be taught and modeled just like math and reading. We know better and must do better for our children."

— GUY STEPHENS, Founder and Executive Director, Alliance Against Seclusion and Restraint

Lori L. Desautels, Ph.D.

Award-winning author of *Eyes Are Never Quiet* and *Unwritten*

Connections
Over Compliance

Rewiring Our Perceptions of Discipline

Wyatt-MacKenzie Publishing

DEADWOOD, OREGON

Connections Over Compliance
Rewiring Our Perceptions of Discipline

Lori L. Desautels, Ph.D.

Hardcover Edition ISBN: 978-1-954332-19-5
Softcover Edition ISBN: 978-1-948018-89-0
eBook Edition ISBN: 978-1-948018-91-3

Library of Congress Control Number: 2020942539

Edited by Alan K. Lipton

Cover illustration ©Garry Killian I iStock
Black & White Illustrations ©Regan Desautels

Wyatt-MacKenzie Publishing
DEADWOOD, OREGON

TABLE OF CONTENTS

FOREWORD

by

Michael McKnight

"Children are the most honest barometers of the health of our communities. Their disruptive behavior is a call to action to all of us— to tend to the broken links and suffering with compassion and wisdom."
TRAUMA INFORMED POSITIVE BEHAVIOR SUPPORT WEBSITE

As I sit to write this opening of *Connections Over Compliance, Rewiring Our Perceptions of Discipline*, at the beginning of May 2020, our schools in America remain closed due to the coronavirus pandemic. The United Nations state that this pandemic is the most challenging crisis the world has faced since World War II. Over 65,000 people in the United States have died, and there is no clear end in sight. Within the general public, including those who never acquire the virus, the over-all lifestyle change and the fear that we are managing on a daily basis, will lead to a massive collective trauma response. We are all experiencing a global trauma, and researchers are warning that the coronavirus pandemic could inflict long-lasting emotional trauma on an unprecedented global scale. There is no question that when our schools reopen, we will see an enormous increase in children and youth who are carrying toxic levels of stress into our school. This new book becomes even more important at this time.

Dr. Lori Desautels and I first met in 2012. We believe it was on Facebook or LinkedIn. What immediately drew my attention was the photograph on the cover of her first book, *How May I Serve You? Revelations in Education,* published that same year. The photo is of an adolescent young woman with words inscribed on her troubled face— LOSER, NOBODY, FAILURE, DESPERATE—that vividly describe her inner state. That photo impacted me emotionally before I ever talked to Lori, now my very good friend and colleague. Albert Bandura, professor emeritus at Stanford University, says that fortuitous events have more to do with what happens in our lives than with formal plans or normal processes, and stumbling into Dr. Lori's first book was one of those major events in my life.

i

Anyone who knows Lori knows how fast she moves. Shortly after contacting her, I was invited to speak at Marian University, where she was teaching at that time. We have been great friends and collaborators ever since, writing two books together and often co-teaching as we share what we learn with other educators.

The overarching theme in Lori's first three books speaks to creating deep connections with all students, and creating touch points in the lives of the students we teach. Lori is passionate about changing the way schools view children and their behavior. In *How May I Serve You?*, she speaks about creating a compassionate presence. In *Unwritten, The Story of a Living System: A Pathway to Enlivening and Transforming Education*, you will hear Lori speak about how deep learning is profoundly relational as she frames it as an essential part of schools that are living systems rather than machines. And in *Eyes Are Never Quiet: Listening Beneath the Behaviors of Our Most Troubled Students*, her voice speaks to the integration of neuroscience, psychology, and pedagogy into our efforts toward supporting our most challenging children and youth. It has been a pleasure watching the evolving nature of her passion to change the way we educate our young. For me, there is no more important work.

With her fourth book, *Connections Over Compliance: Rewiring Our Perception of Discipline*, Lori now takes a deep dive into the essence of school and classroom culture: school discipline systems. These systems, working best for students who need them the least and working poorly for students who we think need them the most, are at the heart of how schools treat our young. We take many of the current school discipline practices as something that schools have always done, and we rarely get to see a clear vision of what these practices do and what they could become. A school cannot call itself "trauma responsive" without an overhaul of this behavior management system. In this new book, Lori literally rewires our perception of school discipline.

Through her use of the term "relational discipline," she shifts the entire way that most people think about discipline, moving the focus away from student punishment and toward the expectations—and, indeed, the brain states—of the adults tasked with teaching them.

Lori aligns her model of relational discipline with applied educational neuroscience that gives educators the tools needed to begin this shift. She firmly situates this new view of discipline in our current understanding of neuroanatomy and neuroscience. Discipline shifts away from consequences and punishments, and toward our ability to regulate our students—beginning with regulating ourselves.

This book will give educators, parents, guardians, and any other adult tasked with looking after our young a foundation for understanding that students showing disrespect, defiance, disobedience, disinterest, and depression may actually be struggling with regulation. By aligning relational discipline with what we know about neurobiology, Lori offers a wealth of resources for concrete, brain-aligned discipline strategies. You'll be able to learn and immediately deploy many of these easy-to-use classroom and school strategies. You'll also learn how to teach children and youth about their own neuroanatomy to help them gain a deep understanding about their emotions and behaviors, leading them toward the valuable life skill of self-regulation.

Beneath all the brain-aligned strategies and ideas you'll encounter in *Connections Over Compliance,* you'll discover the foundation that has been at the heart of every book Lori has written: connections. Lori calls them "touch points." Everything in this book rests on the foundational skill of adults creating connections with the students they serve. These brain-aligned strategies ask us to focus on our own internal states, allowing us to intentionally build connections, even with our most troubled students. A favorite Nelson Mandela quote resonates with both of us: "Let us build communities in which our children and youth, especially our most troubled, can belong."

As our schools reopen after the coronavirus pandemic and as our students come back to us struggling with regulation issues, possibly in greater numbers than we've ever seen, this book offers us the tools we so desperately need to begin to actualize this vision of connections over compliance in our schools, classrooms, and communities.

somewhere safe.

#1

A Pandemic Crisis Calls for a Re-Envisioning and an Opportunity in Our Educational Systems

"We are not here to see through one another,
but to see one another through."
ANNE LAMOTT

I am completing this book during our global COVID-19 pandemic. It has been a challenging, heartbreaking, thought-filled, and soul-searching endeavor as I watch from both the outside and inside. What am I observing? A living collective organism, our world, trying to discover and grasp ways to make sense and meaning through the vast unknown of this disease and the time that its spread has both taken from us and given to us. And yet, life has always been plagued with the unknown. We have always managed to work through challenging and extraordinary historical periods, as traditional ways of living start to break apart, and the emergent "new" is met with resistance, grief, confusion, innovation, and sometimes resolve.

As I write these words, the United States has more confirmed cases of and deaths from this current virus than any other nation. The traumatic conditions of isolation, chronic unpredictability, and physical/emotional restraint are affecting all of us at some level. And although this is a learning experience that nobody wants, perhaps we can now understand how these conditions of "trauma" are what so many families, children, and communities live with daily.

The existing adversities of poverty, racism, mental illness, crim-inalized addiction, healthcare inadequacies, and marginalized living conditions all contribute to extreme levels of depression, anxiety, and other mental health challenges for youth who must cope with them every day. These societal adversities correlate highly to adverse childhood experiences—and we now face an additional layer of pandemic trauma on top of all this existing trauma and adversity. COVID-19 is producing a growing "viral fear" throughout the world, and our youth and children feel it all! CNN reported that nine of the 20 largest metropolitan police departments reported "double-digit percentage jumps" in domestic violence 911 calls or cases in March, 2020, compared to last year or the months of January or February 2020.[1] "Domestic violence is rooted in power and control, and all of us are feeling a loss of power and control right now," Katie Ray-Jones, the CEO of the National Domestic Violence Hotline, told CNN.[2] I share these statistics because many of our children and youth are being impacted by the fears, violence, and loss of a felt-safe place of connection when schools abruptly closed in March of 2020.

Our students and educators across the country and the world walked out of school on a Friday afternoon ... and many will not return for several months, with possible additional extensions. We did not have the closure we normally expect at the end of a school year. Many students lost their safe place and their meals. They didn't get to say goodbye. They missed that needed, predictable, safe closure with the adults whom they trust and who are their lifelines through challenging times.

How do children and youth express their feelings of abandonment, loss, grief, and confusion? How do adults express these same feelings? Often, our behaviors tell our stories, signaling the pain we can barely speak of or understand. Our behaviors are always communicating our needs, our feelings, and quite possibly our fears that feel too big to contain. And how does the world receive and tolerate these expressions?

In this book, we will explore what is beneath the behaviors we observe as we attune and address those embodied, implicit emotions and sensations creating the words, actions, and scenarios that often feel so disrespectful and disruptive. Through our postures, gestures, and facial expressions, our bodies can shed light on the behavioral landscape that feels so unreachable. Our bodies are our greatest teachers.

Psychiatrist and author Dr. Iain McGilchrist shares that when there is a serious jolt to the world community and landscape, much like a global pandemic, a crisis develops alongside a turning point. He refers to this type of event as a "meaning crisis." A meaning crisis communicates a common cause and a call to bring out the best in one another, giving us an opportunity to belong, to shift our perspectives, and to reframe these benign developments.

I am addressing this conceptual shift in the introduction of this book because our perceptions, thought processes, and current actions with regard to school and home discipline protocols have left many learning and home environments stalled in the outdated mindsets of punishment, harsh consequences, and behaviorism, and often completely out of touch with current research. We continue to act and react upon past belief systems with discussions, guidelines, and policies that exclude the sciences of attachment, adverse childhood experiences, and the effects on developing brain architecture.

In this time, we have been plunged into a state of global uncertainty. And as we try to comprehend our best responses on the scale of human interaction with these uncertainties, starved for anything that feels familiar, safe, and nonthreatening, we may find ourselves subconsciously forcing outcomes. Sadly, this response is all too familiar. We have often unintentionally—through educational preparation, professional developments, extensive teacher trainings, and histories of unexamined, patterned, and repetitive ways of being and doing—created experiences of recycled discipline and behavioral policies that resemble an outdated rulebook for order and obedience. We have grasped fixes while forgetting that human behaviors are always communicating a desire to connect, feel better, and recalibrate toward equilibrium.

In writing this book at this time, I believe we are presented with a "hermeneutic circle" challenge. Hermeneutics is defined by the understanding and interpretation of an experience through contextual dependency. For example, if you begin to see the world as a machine, everything in your interpretation of this view becomes machine-like, and the elements of a machine become a model of your personal understanding based on your angle of vision. Our visions hold our belief systems, private logic, and cultural values.

If you see the world as a fluid, interpersonal, dynamic entity, then your experiences and angle of vision begin to show you many events, relationships, and conditions through this relational context. Whenever any of us pursue knowledge, it is context dependent, leading us to take the unfamiliar and subconsciously infuse what we know and believe as we weave it into a new model. How do our current discipline protocols mirror our hermeneutic circles? How do our belief systems, cultural heritage, and generational tales affect our vision and biases regarding traditional discipline protocols? It feels as if we have repackaged similar behavior management models, systems, and practices with new labels and fancy terms.

Traditional discipline programs and practices have often embraced the concepts of right, wrong, logic, consequence, reward, punishment, exclusion, pain, discomfort, disobedience, noncompliance, and correction, all with a singular focus on student behavior. We now are called to explore and redefine discipline protocols from a place of crisis and opportunity with the initial perceptual shift on *adult behaviors*—that is to say, the behavior of the adults interacting with the students.

Our world systems do not operate separately, and this is also true for the systems within our learning environments. The school-to-prison pipeline is an example of how improperly blended systems can and have distorted, stifled, and compromised human growth and development while intimately impacting a pathological evolution that affects the well-being of children, adolescents, adults, and eventually communities as a whole. We see this now. We are living this pathology now. But the human organism is built for resiliency. We are created to bend, wobble, heal, and repair, *and this calls for an emphasis on relational discipline frameworks through a brain-aligned lens.* When we begin to deeply understand that all experiences build brain architecture, we will uphold our ordinary experiences as sacred and tangible teaching moments that support and prioritize safety and connection throughout our children's lives.

Our nervous systems are constantly asking, "Who can I trust and are you with me?" Trauma therapist Bonnie Badenoch shares that a felt sense of safety is at the core of healing trauma and compensating for adversities, and it is in this safe, warm, stable, responsive space between educator and student, or parent and child, where the aching desire to feel heard, seen, and felt is at the heart of embodied relational discipline practices.[3] When we hold this silent receptive space for another person, we enable repair and healing.

All children and youth experience several small potential traumas during each day and, as Bonnie Badenoch describes, "these shards of these accumulating experiences that linger in our muscles, belly, hearts, brains, and body systems gradually shape our perceptual systems and how the world looks."[4] Referring to these events as "small traumas" is not intended to diminish or disrespect the horrific experiences so many youth carry into our schools. This research helps us to understand that when we hold the sacred space of co-regulation for our children and youth, we are helping them, through the safety of our own regulated nervous system, to digest and integrate the dysregulating experiences they have amassed. Our brains are complex historical organs, and they have the inherent capacity to self-organize and self-regulate, but in many cases, it requires a relational experience to fully realize this state. Each moment with a child is a potentially therapeutic moment. As Dr. Stephen Porges states so beautifully, "We wear our hearts on our faces and in our voices, as our nervous systems influence our body's moment-to-moment expression, automatically offering a sense of safety or danger on one another."[5]

Our current understanding of relational interpersonal neurobiology brings us to a crossroads where this body of knowledge is at the core of how we can re-envision discipline practices and protocols in our schools. Recent research emphasizes that true discipline for our students begins with an adult brain that feels safe, calm, and still. The behaviors to which we should give the most attention are the behaviors that we want to sprout and flourish. This intentional attention begins with adults who are willing to dive into their uncontested and possibly unexplored perspectives and belief systems—individual, familial, communal, and generational. These are the perspectives and belief systems that we have unintentionally carried into this moment, and that we should examine with the intention of doing what is best for our students.

May you find personal and professional grace within this book, written to acknowledge and share the new focus on adult well-being as the cornerstone to this discipline shift that we hope to see in the educational arena, in our homes, and in our communities. This is the discipline shift that will inform our future, brain-aligned, and relational discipline policies. May you find connection to your inner source of well-being, and may you share the contagion of this discovery with every student and colleague that you encounter! It is said that the greatest gift we can give our children and youth rests with the care we give ourselves.

In the compelling words of Dr. Bruce D. Perry: "The most traumatic aspects of all disasters involve the shattering of human connections. And this is especially true for children. Being harmed by the people who are supposed to love you, being abandoned by them, being robbed of the one-on-one relationships that allow you to feel safe and valued and to become humane—these are profoundly destructive experiences. Because humans are inescapably social beings, the worst catastrophes that can befall us inevitably involve relational loss. As a result, recovery from trauma and neglect is also all about relationships—rebuilding trust, regaining confidence, returning to a sense of security, and reconnecting to love. Of course, medications can help relieve symptoms and talking to a therapist can be incredibly useful. But healing and recovery are impossible—even with the best medications and therapy in the world—without lasting, caring connections to others."[6]

✦

As this book was being sent to press, more devastating events have occurred across this nation, and its pain is felt throughout the world. All 50 states and 18 countries have joined together to fight racism across this nation and the world. The 2020/2021 school year will be filled with many unknowns, heightened emotions, and a variety of behaviors masked with heart-felt sadness.

Difficult discussions, reflections, and opportunities will be shared across our communities, and our children and youth will be significantly impacted by these events, unrest, and the suffering that has taken place over the past several months. Our emotional and social school cultures and climates will matter much more than the content and academics being taught!

We will need to address the COVID-19 pandemic: the chronic unpredictability, isolation, and the physical and emotional restraint that so many communities, families, and youth have experienced. Additionally, the viral effects and contagion of the blatant racism that has compromised the lives of so many of our black and brown families, students, and communities requires our sustained attention, deepened learning, and our active engagement and action.

Racism is embedded in the fabric of our country as well as our educational systems. Black students are four times more likely to be suspended from school with a significant correlation of poorer health outcomes. Black students are three times more likely to be referred to police for something happening on the school grounds and three and a half times more likely to be arrested for school-related incidents. Data from 32 million students in 96,000 K- 12 schools across the United States found the discipline gap between black and white students was much larger in counties with more racial bias. The study was taken from 1.6 million respondents from The National Academy of Sciences. These are not brand-new statistics, but our collective awareness has been magnified by the on-going and recent national corruptive injustices to our black communities!

Systems of oppression can be disrupted in our schools as educational environments can become the fertile, emergent, and sacred places of felt safety, co-regulation, and inclusive practices of the teaching and learning processes that are founded on social justice, equity, and systemic tolerance that have been missing for over 400 years. This occurs when discipline practices are seen as preventive, relational, and brain aligned! Our discipline protocols must be in place inside our procedures, routines, morning meetings, and rituals with open discussions and reflections of current events, feelings, and sensations as we bring our lived experiences into our classrooms and schools. This is the adult shift that we must lead for our disciplinary practices to be equitable, non-biased and steeped in social justice for all students. These protocols are not scripted social and emotional curriculums or after-thoughts; rather, they are living practices that are embedded in every moment of our school day.

All brains learn deeply and experience well-being when we feel safe and connected to one another, and these conditions must be created and prioritized in our classrooms and schools for the critical discussions of social justice and equity to occur. Considering the recent COVID virus and racial traumas alongside the tenuous national brokenness, we are going to be challenged with escalating emotions, and therefore survival behaviors from our students and staff who carry in significant amounts of hopelessness. Layered traumas can create chaos, pain, and much dysregulation, and these traumatic conditions will be challenging.

As educators, we will be called to first and foremost create a safe, stable, and emotionally available space for our children and youth with an adult who has taken the time to calm his or her own nervous system. Emotions are contagious and brain-aligned relational discipline will need to begin with the adults.

The way in which we are each attended to shapes the relational moment and possibilities. In other words, when we shift the focus of our attention, those within our focus will intimately sense the change. When we attend to a disorder, a disability, a disturbance, our students intuit this negative focus. It calls forth that disorder, disturbance, that fragile and developing identity that subconsciously whispers, "something is wrong with me." Being perceived as having a disorder, a behavioral challenge, or being a liar, a troublemaker, an addict, an alcoholic, or a **variance** of any kind indirectly states that there is something wrong that needs to be fixed! This creates further separation in the possibility of relationships and feels disrespectful! There is a felt sense of judgment and disconnection! Kids and adults in stress already believe they are damaged goods. When we label, judge, and assess based upon our own thoughts, perceptions, and stories, we unintentionally disrupt and rob the fragile ground of safety!

#2

Our Brain's Development and the Impact of Implicit Bias and Racial Disparities and Discipline Gaps in Our Schools

"Try again, fail again, but fail better."
SAMUEL BECKETT

Human brains begin developing in utero from the brain stem to the cortex (back to front), and from the inside out. Brains are social-, historical-, and experience-dependent organs and survival is the priority of the brain. Since the time of our evolution the major predators of humans are humans[7] and we witnessed this on television and social media for eight minutes and 46 seconds on May 25, 2020. Hate, power, aggression, and violence are steeped in fear. Fear wears many masks establishing in and out groups, control over, power over, isolation, rejection, humiliation, taking, killing, and attacking people and their lives. Racism is a social disease.

Brains are also built for resiliency as are our communities and world systems, but differences scare people. The truth is that diversity in living systems create stronger systems if that diversity is recognized, celebrated, and deeply integrated into our cultures and communities for personal and collective growth and resiliency. Diversity promotes creativity and innovation. Systemically in this time, we are still embracing diversity and differences as a personal and collective predatory threat to overcome ... leaving our nation's systems in a survival and inflammatory state of functioning.

Our brains are creating one million synapses, or connections, per second during the first 1000 days of life, which is the greatest time in human brain development, and our brains, bodies, and stress response systems continue evolving throughout young adulthood. Our brains grow by organizing, disorganizing, and reorganizing based upon the experiences we encounter in our young lives. As our brains evolve, the right hemisphere develops during the first year of life holding visual images, emotion, and our unfolding sense of mind-body-core self. Traumatic experiences leave emotional scars on our bodies and brains, and trying to live through moments of felt danger and threat feels like one is running on injured knees! Trauma and adversity are nervous system challenges. The right hemisphere embraces a stronger connective pathway or pathways to the body. In this early developmental time, we are capable of sensation, feeling, and perception. Our right brains are communicating through reading facial expressions, gestures, body postures, and listening and learning from vocal expressions. When adversities and trauma happen in these developing early years, they are often held in sensations and are fragmented with little to no narrative for cohesive explicit understanding. We have not acquired language in this time, but we soak up our social and emotionally felt environments like digital recorders, feeling the pain and suffering and positive emotion of our caregivers, family, and those around us. Without words and their meanings, trauma and adversity are sensed and felt, becoming embodied implicit memories. The left hemisphere comes on board in the second year when language begins to develop. In these first few years of life our communication systems are nonverbal and felt through our sensory, emotional, perceptual, and motor systems as we learn about our world. What type of world did we inherit? What meaning are we making of our historical and generational experiences in the present moment?

We have a brain for many reasons and in order of priority, lies survival. We are wired with a negative bias because of survival. Implicit bias and implicit racial bias are a significant part of the unconscious collections of thoughts, beliefs, and attitudes about groups of people that influence and impact our brain states, emotions, behaviors, perceived stressors, and our decision-making processes. Emotions are contagious and so we feel and sense danger and safety around us in all moments, subconsciously stumbling upon our own felt sensory and emotional maps of lived experiences.

For humans to be able to reason, regulate, problem solve, empathize, collaborate, and discern, we must be able to access the cortex, the newest part of the brain where we have the reasoning and clarity to think clearly, pause, reflect, and be in the present moment. Our perceptions of experiences are critical to our survival and well-being, as we constantly cart around our personal journals and maps of felt experiences that are a part of our unconscious history, often, without awareness. In turn, we have created unconscious implicit biases. In moments of these lived experiences, all information is constantly compared and associated with information that is already in our brains and bodies. If our brains are never able to process these experiences in the cortex, the reasoning region in the brain, these experiences may consistently activate and dominate lower filters or brain regions in our fight, flight, and shut down subcortical pathways. We find ourselves living in a stream of survival reactions which create elevated and dysregulated stress response systems, based on our subconscious interpretations and perceptions of past and present experiences and events. Dr. Mary Hellen Imordino-Yang shares that brains are grown by how we feel and think, and these become the patterns of our lives. We construct knowledge in the space of our relationships and this knowledge and our experiences teach us what to expect in the world. Brain development is not just genetically coded but needs epi-genetic-like social experiences!

We create catalogs and memory-associated file folders, sorting and sifting safe or dangerous experiences with our analogies, associations, and predictions. Every experience is helping us to predict other experiences and our nervous systems are always predicting how experiences will play out.

Just as our brains grow and develop from organizing, disorganizing, and reorganizing, so do our systems in this world. The educational system is going through a huge growth spurt as I write these words: there is a disorganization in this moment as this system is trying to reorganize in ways to adapt to changing times, and it is rough. More people have become gravely ill with COVID-19—and death rates are higher—in counties with a relatively larger black population. From the time COVID-19 took hold in the United States and community spread of the virus became evident, communities of color have been disproportionally hampered by the disease.[8]

Racism has been a part of our collective humanity for hundreds of years, operating on an institutional level through systems that treat people as superior or inferior in ways that produce outcomes of increased inter-generational, historical, and man-made trauma and adversity! Many of our systems, including our educational system, are experiencing a collective inflammation of systemic brain body functioning and this heated, swollen, pain-filled deeply rooted disease can no longer be managed with a band-aid. We must reach for the roots of this inflammation; it begins with each of us and our attention, awareness, and action. I am learning that our schools can provide the cultural humility that our students, families, and colleagues need. This cultural humility says, "I do not know everything, but I want to learn and listen!" Attachment builds our nervous systems and is the carrier of brain development. Attachment occurs through moment-to-moment touch points and the human rhythms of rupture and repair. Human communication is critical for mental, emotional, and physiological well-being and occurs through a lifetime of ruptured and repaired moments. Knowing that ruptures are a daily occurrence in all our relationships, when we experience this break in communication, followed up by patterned repetitive attempts to repair, we are building pathways for individual and collective resiliency.

As we address the impact of implicit biases and racism weaving silently and sometimes screaming throughout our schools and communities, trauma responsive and restorative practices, begin with our own subconscious and deeply held biases, histories, and lived experiences. When we begin within, we can connect with the lived experiences of our students that hold an agenda-less presence, and feel safe, stable, and emotionally available. Many of our students carrying in significant trauma and adversity have only experienced rupture after rupture after rupture with little to no opportunity to ever repair. Young brains have more plasticity and malleability than older brains in creating and establishing thought, emotional, and behavior patterns that are antiracial and inclusive. When we provide opportunities to discuss cultural strengths, share our lived black and brown experiences, while exploring personal biases, we will begin taking the small steps, while sitting beside our students, to rebuild an unconditional ethos of love and belonging.

The following questions are for educator self-reflection because when we self-reflect, questioning our historical beliefs and habits of thoughts, we are better prepared to meet our students and staff where they are addressing the individual, generational, racial, and collective traumas and adversities of past and present.

1. Am I deeply aware of the rich and complex neural streams flowing throughout our bodies and brains?

2. Do I question, hold, or resist the belief that we and our students are adaptive rather than disordered?

3. Am I able to appreciate the opportunity to connect and learn from every student's lived experiences?

4. Am I hopeful that my own implicit biases can change with growing understanding and questioning that is patterned, repetitive felt safety and connection?

5. Am I open to language shifts knowing that as words change, so do perceptions? For example: are we wanting to fix, remediate, intervene, grasp, or are our words embracing connection and support, such as curious, wondering, process, trusting, and listening?

6. As we observe the racial discipline and racial achievement gaps, along with the traumas carried in by so many students, can we move away from a judgmental, analytical, disembodied perspective, to a more open curious, connected focus on the lived experiences of our students and ourselves? How do these collide? How do these reshape us? How have they affected our adversities and traumatic experiences in the past, present, or foreseeable future?

7. Can we create leadership that is shared by students and adults in our buildings and districts, reshuffling the power for equitable and deep learning and well-being?

8. What is your story? Am I willing to share my story? Can we create spaces where shared stories feel safe for the vulnerabilities that desire to be unconditionally accepted and revered?

9. Can I redefine or shift my role from "teacher" to include mentor/facilitator? If this feels uncomfortable, why?

10. Can I help to reset the desire to learn and hold a calm presence based on the trauma and adversity form the past several months where many of our students lost connection and safety?

11. Instead of the focus on numerical gaps, can we explore, discuss, and challenge one another with the racial discipline, motivation, relationship, and engagement gaps?

12. Am I unconditionally asking my parents, students, and staff for their rich traditions, love languages, felt hurts and pain, through intentional times during the day that begin to rebuild community and deepen connection?

The child who is not embraced by the village
will burn it down to feel its warmth.

AN AFRICAN PROVERB

"I am who I am because somebody loved me."
CORNELL WEST

CHAPTER 1

A Journey Through Discipline

"Discipline has come a long way since its original association with disciple.
It now means 'punishment' ... To return to punitive control is to admit
that we have failed to solve a central problem in education."

B.F. SKINNER

I have learned that words mean very little when attempting discipline from a place of dysregulation and agitation, and that my calm presence can be the real anchor for relational brain-aligned discipline. What if we perceived discipline through a lens of connection? What if we began to collectively think about *replacing* the behaviors we see as harmful or negative rather than just stopping them? What if we quit talking so much about behaviors and focused on one another's brain and body state and the miraculous power of neuroplasticity? What if our discipline goal was just as much about our own brain and body states as it is about the students we are sitting beside? As I write the opening chapter of this book, I know that, knowing what I know about brain development, adversity, and resiliency, I would have been a different mom, sister, friend, daughter, and spouse than I was years ago! I would have shared this brain, attachment, and neuroscience research with my students, and I would have paid very close attention to my own regulation and brain state before I uttered a word to my own children or to my students.

I open this chapter with a story I have shared a thousand times in presentations and talks. This story is an integral part of the "new lens for discipline." This story changed me. It changed my son. It shares the power of relationship during conflict and chaos. Looking back on this time, I was not a conscious parent or educator—and I carried my own agenda and belief system into every experience with my children, my students, and more than likely with many if not all the

1

relationships in my life. I was coming from a space and place of desiring conformity. I was solution oriented and wanting the best for my children and students, but I was forgetting that *my* view and "best" was probably not *their* best. As humans, we place our personal agendas and belief systems within the context of every relationship because we are social creatures whose existences rely on one another and emotions are contagious. Educator Brandon Pickett was able to shine a light on our teenage son, seeing Andrew's gifts, sensitivity, and his hidden yet deep desire to be felt by another and to feel safe. How? He approached Andrew through a brain and body state of connection. This teacher created that environment and growing ease of presence, and this was—and is—relational discipline at its best.

One late Monday afternoon several years ago, as I frantically prepared for my Monday night class, an email appeared in my university inbox. Looking at the address and then the subject line, my heart began to flutter nervously, and a feeling of impending dread filled my body in a matter of seconds. I took a hesitant deep breath, clicked the mouse button, and began to read. "Andrew is sitting with his group and working tremendously hard on his project. He is attentive and appears happy and motivated. I thought you would like to know." And then as I scrolled down a few lines, there was one last sentence that brought tears to my eyes, touching and reopening my heart with a sense of hope that I had not experienced for the past several months. Mr. Pickett ended the email with this statement. *"Please let me know how I may serve you in the days and weeks to come."* Now I understood the subject line: "Andrew in action," which had brought such dread moments earlier. Those few words placed not only a smile on my face but gave me the courage and desire, as Andrew's mom, to keep going and to keep hoping. This ninth-grade Spanish teacher had taken three minutes to share his perspective of a teaching experience that for many would have gone unnoticed. Mr. Pickett was able to embrace another perspective, connecting with Andrew to see the possibilities in this young man who had been recently struggling in a world of tremendous adolescent chaos, and then sharing that connection with me. When I read the email to Andrew a few hours later, he beamed with renewed confidence, and his effort and grades in this class soared during the remainder of the semester. This was the one class where he felt "felt" and safe.

I will never forget this experience as an educator, but mostly as a mom. I watched the gradual and extraordinary shift that a few sincere words created in Andrew's self-confidence and in my own life. A question of service breathed life back into my body as I realized that this experience is discipline on the front end. This is the new lens for discipline when we notice what is going right and well in our students' lives, especially because sometimes those nuggets are not easy to find, share, and secure. The truth is, we work for people we like. We respect the people who respect us.

Discipline and classroom management have ranked near the top of school concerns for decades. Even today, school discipline joins school safety among the top concerns in nearly every poll conducted on the major issues that face our schools. It often tops the list of reasons that teachers decide to leave our profession. We have been constantly writing, publishing, reading, and debating behavior management for the past 60-plus years, yet we still haven't changed the deeply flawed and pervasive idea that discipline and punishment are linked. As I sit beside educators from all over the country, it becomes increasingly clear how our own experiences of being raised, and those of generations before us, have molded and embedded our cognitive belief systems into a stream of thoughts and actions that we deem correct, appropriate, and relevant no matter the current research or changes in our communities and worlds.

I liken this resistance to our innate negative brain bias, which has been a part of our earliest biology because of the survival instinct. The brain's foremost purpose in our lives is to help us survive. Unless we feel safe, we cannot move forward with connecting and developing the relationships we need to regulate, learn, and thrive. Human beings perceive the world with a wary and fearful eye, and we protect and defend ourselves and those we love with a fierce evolutionary instinct that is often rooted in survival, and therefore in fear. Yet this instinct is sometimes more focused on our need to feel powerful and in control for the short term, and we opt to "fix" a deeper problem by enforcing compliance and obedience. When we desire sustainable shifts in discipline, we sometimes forget that the repeated negative behaviors we see are signals communicating emotional, mental, or physiological needs. Often, these needs are bathed in pain. All behavior is communication, and these behaviors can be very challenging for us to unwrap when 30-plus students need us in the same moment.

A child's life space is filled with thousands of moving parts, and we can't always know what those parts are. In an article honoring Teacher Appreciation Week last year, *Indianapolis Star* sportswriter Gregg Doyel wrote, "Teachers have always boggled my mind. They've chosen a career of long hours and low pay, where they will take a lot of guff from kids and parents. They've chosen a career to serve others. They've chosen a career to help raise our children."[1] These words continue to ring through my mind as I write this opening chapter. As educators, we intimately touch the emotional, social, and cognitive worlds of all our students. This is a delicate, multifaceted art, not a science. Anxiety and depression are entering the life spaces of our students at an accelerated pace, and the research below shares the implications of the mental and emotional challenges, and therefore the growing discipline issues our educators are encountering in this time.

In a 2017 study by the Children's Defense Fund, every day in America:
- 589 public school students are corporally punished.
- 2,805 children are arrested.
- 2,857 high school students drop out.
- 12,816 public school students are suspended.[2]

Our school systems have adopted new programs and strategies over the decades. Some of the newer programs include Positive Behavior Interventions and Supports (PBIS), Response to Intervention (RTI), Leader in Me, and Restorative Justice. Yet rarely have these programs changed schools' continued practice of providing a consequence when a child or adolescent violates a school rule. Peruse almost any school-level code of conduct policy and you will find lists of infractions and the punishments associated with them. While framed in "positive language," they remain based on this underlying principle: Do as you are told or we (the school) will need to punish you. If that continues not to work, we will banish you to our "alternative school" or simply force you to drop out or expel you.

Collectively, we are creatures of habit and instinctually follow the traditions and belief systems that have preceded us. It is all too rare when we question why a child or adolescent may be acting out because, honestly, it's much easier to take the problem situation out of the classroom so that we can teach! I know this feeling too well, as I have both instinctively and intentionally removed students who interfered with my ability to teach their 29 other classmates.

I hope to be very clear in these first few paragraphs as I explain that every child has the right to learn, and that other students' externalizing behaviors and negative aggressions can be very stressful not only for the educators, but for the rest of the class.

Connections Over Compliance will address school discipline through the understanding of brain development and the impact of toxic stress, trauma, and adversity on the developing brain and body. As rewiring our perceptions of discipline calls for relational mediated discipline, this book will explore the dire need for preventive brain-aligned strategies and practices that are built into a school's or classroom's procedures, routines, structure, and environments. This new lens for discipline is not about adding another program to the already crowded daily agendas that teachers need to complete with their students. This book will outline, explore, and discuss a framework that calls for educators and parents to make a personal shift in how they perceive the current problems associated with student behavior. We will look underneath the surface behaviors that interfere with our abilities to teach the young people in our classrooms, identifying the core issues that we need to address: making the changes that impact our students in a positive, sustainable, and connective manner.

This framework calls for us to be consciously aware of our own brain states and self-care as we discipline our students. It calls for us to be aware of the sacred space which Dr. Thom Garfat calls "the interpersonal in-between," where we have an opportunity to either connect with one another or to unintentionally escalate one another.[3] This new lens for discipline calls for us to be aware of our students' sensory differences and challenges as we intentionally observe and learn about the environments and experiences from which they travel when entering school. Trauma and adversity are bodily over-whelming, and therefore sensory regulation will be an integral part of this book. I have now learned to ask: "What kind of world has this student inherited?" Experiences shape brains. Our brains are expe-rience-dependent, so adversities and trauma, as well as supportive nurturing experiences, build our students' and our own brains and bodies. We are teaching to these invisible experiences every moment of the day!

This new lens for discipline searches and yearns for sustainable behavioral changes, not just short-term compliance or obedience. If we are to be culturally and relationally responsive, then brain-aligned relational AND preventive discipline is at the forefront of the chal-lenging and ever-changing brain and body states that our students, our families, and especially ourselves carry into our lives, our work, and our homes. Our traditional discipline policies and protocols have been reactive and reflexive, focusing primarily on consequences. We are now beginning to shift this outdated perception by focusing more on the process, which means acknowledging one another's relation-ships and brain states. We are exploring prevention, the front end of discipline, as we redefine conventional discipline and all the punitive and pain-filled baggage that we've been hauling from schools to home and back to schools again for far too long!

The challenge with conscious discipline is that most of us are not conscious when we discipline. We unintentionally become stuck in the vulnerable webs of power struggles and conflict cycles with students, as our in-stinctual survival brain state can override the regulated calm capabilities that our children and adolescents need in times of height-ened stress and chronic adversity. *Traditional discipline works for the kids who don't need it and doesn't touch the kids whose behaviors need discipline— but not punishment.*

When I researched the definition of discipline, I found words such as control, direction, authority, rule, correct, penalize, and punish. Yet the origin on this word is "disciple—one who teaches." How have we become so far removed from that meaning? *Connections Over Compliance* will share the Adverse Childhood Experiences study as well as the Adverse Community Environment study, highlighting how this new research is critically informing the need to change the way we perceive and implement discipline inside our schools. We will also explore the levels of stress experienced by all our children, including the explosion of anxiety disorders, depression, and the increasing rates of self-harm and suicide in our children and adolescents.

The brain-aligned discipline strategies contained in this book are designed for all students who enter our schools and classrooms, which society expects will attend to the emotional, mental, physiological, and social needs and health of our youth. These brain-aligned discipline strategies and practices are essential for all students, and could therefore be activated and implemented on Tier One of the RTI model and embraced in the Multi-Tiered Systems of Support (MTSS) templates and movement that are growing in popularity. MTSS addresses multi-layered systems of care and connection for our students, families, and educators with the inclusion of discipline, social and emotional learning, academics, and community supports and resources.

Connections Over Compliance is a new template highlighting the equitable and exciting operationalized relationship between Applied Educational Neuroscience and MTSS! Many of the practices and strategies are shared in the Resource Section. These practices in all four areas of MTSS are brain-aligned preventive relational discipline templates that are built into our procedures, routines, and transitions. These strategies are more than just another box to check off every day. They call for us to be more intentional in how we approach the practice of teaching—and how we approach our students as individuals."

"All truth passes through three stages: First, it is ridiculed. Second, it is violently opposed. Third, it is accepted as being self-evident.'
ARTHUR SCHOPENHAUER

To begin understanding the differences between punishment and discipline, let's return to our societal, cultural, and educational history. What has sustained the antiquated practices and belief systems of punishment in the face of all the scientific research and evidence to the contrary? We now understand that when brains are developing through infancy and early childhood, they require secure attachments for sensory and motor regulation, and this occurs with a caregiver who is predictable, emotionally available, and consistent. This caregiver can regulate and provide the emotional buffers of the environmental stimuli and internal sensations constantly streaming into the developing brain and body.[4] When an infant doesn't have these early nurturing attachment experiences that are patterned and repetitive, the young brain begins its development with overactive, disorganized emotional areas. This means that, from the beginning, that brain will experience chronic dysregulation and perceive life as threatening and unsafe. This occurs because the survival brain is chronically turned on and continuously flooded with cortisol and adrenaline, which produce emotions of fear and pain, as well as toxic stress levels.[5]

The inability to self-regulate is conditioned and learned, and it can produce an incapability to cope with long-term, everyday life stressors. When the stress is intense, frequent, unpredictable, and overwhelming to the infant and child, its developing brain becomes increasingly bathed in pain. Tragically, those stressors and adversities often originate from the very places and people that should be providing support, attachment, and nurturance. Dr. Bruce Perry states that in this time, our home environments are often some of the most violent places in America.[6]

What cultural, societal, and personal belief systems have anchored many of us into believing that the pain and perils of harsh punishment will create resilient, socially engaged mindsets in children and youth? Dr. Nick Long and Dr. Larry Brendtro ask, "How have we landed below the waterline of reason believing that severe punishment is effective in meeting the increasing defiance and delinquency in our children and adolescents?"[7] A contributing editor for the journal *Reclaiming Children and Youth*, psychologist Martin Brokenleg shares his research and experiences. He has observed that each of us drags behind us a "cultural tail—a thousand-year-long tail that is the culmination of our personal childrearing experiences, our cultures in which we were raised, and the errors in thinking of the generations before us."[8] It takes courage and intention to challenge antiquated and outdated ways of doing and being, and as I write this book, I have observed this collective cultural tail close up and personal.

Last year, I presented the new brain research on trauma and adversity to a school district in Mississippi. The reactions and responses from a few of the educators regarding behaviors and punishment were positioned perfectly for how they have been conditioned and raised with the belief systems they carry into the schools. I kept hearing, "Punish that bad stuff right out of the child!" During and following my presentation, responses included: "I have never thought about why a child behaves this way." "The belt was used on me, and I am just fine." "Well, the Bible tells us to whip our kids into shape, and I follow the Bible." These statements are culturally justifiable through hundreds of years of belief systems that have been passed down from generation to generation. I understand well, and it is with a heavy yet passionate and informed heart and mind that we must continually share the research and knowledge of what we now understand through science, attachment theory, and how trauma and adversity compromise and detrimentally affect the developing brain, stress response systems, behaviors, and well-being of our youth.

When the Europeans invaded North America, they brought a code of conduct, wrapped tightly in obedience and compliance, stating that children must always obey adults. This same code informed the 20th century models of discipline embodied in the authoritarian regimes of Adolph Hitler and Joseph Stalin.[9] We've come a long way since those times of distorted and punitive childrearing, but remnants of the coercion, obedience, and compliance models intimately connected to the societal thinking errors still permeate many of our nation's schools. The United States is one of the only democracies that still permits adults to hit children in school and that allows our court systems to try children as adult criminals with adult sanctions.[10]

In Indiana at this time, a state senate bill that advocates say "would just add three words to Indiana's juvenile waiver statute" is being met with strong opposition led by JauNae Hanger, attorney and president of the Children's Policy and Law Initiative, who has gathered local and national support through researching the dangerous and devastating consequences of trying young adolescents as adults for serious crimes. Senate Bill 279 would allow children as young as 12 to be waived into adult court after being charged with attempted murder.[11]

Many educators and researchers were asked to write letters supporting the resistance by citing the research about the use of such punitive measures with youth experiencing trauma at 12 years of age. Below is my letter to our state policy leaders regarding the cultural punitive tails that we still carry into modern-day society.

Dear Indiana Lawmakers,

The adolescent brain begins entering a stage of extreme vulnerability and fragility around nine to ten years of age. This chaotic development can linger through mid-to-late twenties and is compromised and critically stagnated by high numbers of adverse childhood experiences. This period of erratic brain development, coupled with a significant number of childhood adversities, often produces an adolescent brain that is functioning from a survival brain state, a state of constant fear, anger, turmoil, and violence which is characterized by pain-based behaviors, a response to life events that has been in part neurobiologically created by personal, environmental, and life experiences that produce toxic and distorted levels of brain development and functioning.

Adverse childhood experiences (ACEs) have been identified as a key risk factor associated with a wide range of negative life outcomes, including juvenile delinquency. Research has demonstrated a strong relationship between ACEs, substance use disorders, and severe behavioral problems. When children are exposed to chronic stressful events, their neurodevelopment can be disrupted. As a result, the child's cognitive functioning or ability to cope with negative or disruptive emotions may be greatly impaired. Over time, and often during adolescence, the child may adopt negative coping mechanisms, such as substance use, self-harm, or harm to others. Eventually, these unhealthy coping mechanisms can contribute to disease, disability, and social problems, as well as premature mortality.

Prior research on adverse and traumatic experiences, as well as mental health problems of juvenile justice-involved youth, has revealed higher prevalence rates of adversity and trauma for these youth compared to youth in the general population (Dierkhising et al., 2013). Furthermore, compared to youth in the general population, juvenile justice-involved youth have been found to have a greater likelihood of having experienced multiple forms of trauma (Abram et al., 2004), with one-third reporting exposure to multiple types of trauma each year (Dierkhising et al., 2013). Placement in Child Protective Services and foster care due to parental maltreatment made unique contributions to the risk for delinquency in 99,602 officially delinquent youth, compared to the same number of matched youths in one study (Barrett, Katsiyannis, Zhang, & Zhang, 2013). In the realm of criminology, we know that among offenders, experiencing childhood physical abuse and other forms of maltreatment leads to higher rates of self-reported total offending, violent offending, and property offending, even after controlling for prior delinquent behavior (Teague, Mazerolle, Legosz, & Sanderson, 2008). Experiencing parental divorce has also been well documented to have a strong association with delinquency, with meta-analysis on the topic showing moderate effect sizes (Amato, 2001). Even with the increased social acceptability and increased prevalence of divorce in recent decades, the differences in delinquency between youth exposed to parental divorce and those from intact families has not decreased (Amato, 2001; D'Onofrio et al., 2005).

In conclusion, the emotional age of a youth who has experienced significant adverse childhood experiences with cognitive functioning greatly compromised equates to approximately half the chronological age of that adolescent. To waive to adult court for attempted murder or probable cause with a child identified at 12 or within the early adolescent years is inhumane and grossly contradicts the research of adverse childhood experiences and brain development. ACEs and brain development are deeply affected by environmental, community, and generational experiences and trauma cycles. This bill unacceptably and inaccurately contradicts the brain and psychopathology research purporting how we must approach and identify our youth who have committed these unbearable and pain-driven crimes. These children must be assessed for the emotional and toxic adversities they have experienced with a community outreach that bridges the gaps of what we know through new neuroscience research and how we have traditionally practiced, imparted and recycled the family-to-school-to-prison pipeline with our nation's and state's youth. The Indiana Youth Institute recently published the 2019 data on the mental and emotional challenges of our state's children, and the statistics are sobering and eye opening, with Indiana scoring higher than the national statistics on many if not most of the at-risk indicators from this study/survey for childhood well-being. When we know better, we can do better.

Respectfully,

Dr. Lori Desautels

"There is no such thing as a baby; there is a baby and someone."
DONALD WOODS WINNICOTT

While Michael McKnight and I made this point in the previous book *Eyes Are Never Quiet,* the idea is so central to relational brain-aligned discipline that I need to repeat it here: Secure, trusting bonds with caring adults are critical to human beings during the unfolding of their innate potential. For our children to thrive, they need to be connected and cared for in an ongoing and persistent manner for years.[12]

Relationships provide the oxygen for connection. When these connective relationships and care are impaired or absent from a child's life, the child communicates this mistrust and detachment through behaviors we often misunderstand. The most challenging and difficult children and youth have often inherited a world of chronic adversity. What happens to the parents happens to the child because children are very open and experience the pain and suffering of their caregivers. Maybe the question we begin to ask is this: "What kind of world did our students inherit?" Children and youth in our schools, classrooms, foster care placements, and juvenile facilities will subconsciously take on the suffering and pain to which they were exposed in early development, and therefore when bad things are happening, they will internalize and personalize these toxic experiences—and blame themselves. Young children are developmentally narcissistic and think everything *around* them is *about* them, including the bad things.

Even a cursory look at the state of children and youth in America can give any teacher, parent, or youth worker cause for concern. A 2017 report from the Children's Defense Fund, for example, sheds some light on the current ways that many children are growing up in the richest country on earth.

According to the report, millions of America's children today are still suffering from hunger, homelessness, and hopelessness. More than 13.2 million children are poor—nearly one in five. About 70 percent of them are children of color (this 2017 report projected that by 2020, the amount would be even greater). More than 1.2 million homeless children are enrolled in public schools. About 14.8 million children struggle against hunger in food-insecure households. Despite great progress, 3.9 million children lack the health coverage they need to survive and thrive. Millions of young children need quality early childhood programs during their critical years of early brain development, yet only five percent of eligible infants and toddlers are enrolled in Early Head Start, and only 54 percent of eligible three- and four-year-olds are served by Head Start. Most of public school students in the fourth and eighth grades cannot read at grade level, including more than 75 percent of Black, Hispanic and American Indian/Alaska Native children. Every 47 seconds, a child is abused or neglected, and the number of children in foster care is increasing rapidly in some parts of our country as the opioid crisis spins out of control.[13]

The United States finds itself engulfed in the opioid crisis, which stems from overuse of drugs designed to reduce pain. These include both legal painkillers, like morphine prescribed by doctors for acute or chronic pain, and illegal drugs, such as heroin or illicitly made fentanyl. To put the crisis into numerical terms, during 2016, there were more than 63,600 overdose deaths in the United States, including 42,249 that involved an opioid (66.4 percent). That's an average of 115 opioid overdose deaths each day.[14] We now understand that addiction to any substance is not the core issue. Addiction can be the "mask" for deep, unaddressed emotional pain—pain that has spread throughout the developing brain and body desperately seeking relief and rest.

In November 2016, I traveled to Austin, a town in southern Indiana, where the opioid epidemic had made national news in 2015. This small community recognized that their students, educators, and families were in a perpetual state of crisis and survival. The elementary, middle, and high schools were feeling the effects of a community ravaged by drugs and alcohol. The students' negative behaviors—their lack of engagement and motivation—were showing up day after day during this community crisis.

This past year, I have spent time in Fort Wayne, Indiana at Abbett Elementary. This school opens its doors each day to students who carry in significant adversity and trauma. Principal Frank Kline and the school staff have completely shifted their discipline protocols, but this shift has been a time-consuming process. Following, Frank shares the story of Abbett Elementary.

The Abbett Story
Shared by Principal Frank Kline
Abbett Elementary, Fort Wayne Community Schools

Abbett Elementary, Fort Wayne Community Schools, is in a post-WWII inner-city neighborhood. The school was built in 1949 and dedicated in the fall of 1950. Abbett opened for grades kindergarten through eighth grade at this time.

Abbett today is a Title I school located in the southeast quadrant of Fort Wayne, Indiana. The students attending Abbett all live within a mile of the school, which helps create the neighborhood school environment. The official student population of Abbett Elementary is 497 students for the 2019/2020 school year. Abbett is a minority-majority school, comprised of 43% African American, 40% Hispanic, 10% Multi-Racial, 4% Caucasian, and 3% Asian. The percentage of students that qualify for Free/Reduced Lunch support is 85%, as reported by the Indiana Department of Education.

The neighborhood around Abbett reports 38.9% of its residents living below the poverty line. The median household income in the 46806 zip code is $27,449, which is far below the state median household income.

Abbett resides in a neighborhood that has the third-highest infant mortality rate in the state of Indiana, at 14.3 deaths per 1,000 live births, almost double the state infant mortality rate and almost three times the national infant mortality rate.

The 46806 zip code has a violent crime index of 64.1. The national violent crime index is 22.7. The property crime index for the 46806 zip code is 74, and the national average property crime index is 35.4.

Many Abbett students come to school each day carrying several adversities and experiences that impact their social and emotional well-being. The burdens being shouldered by the students led to a learning environment that was more dependent on children and adults surviving through the day and less aligned with learning.

In May 2018, the faculty of Abbett committed to becoming a trauma-sensitive school. This commitment was a mind shift for the faculty, staff, and administration on how we would view the root causes of student behavior. We could no longer view student behavior as an intentional choice, but rather as a symptom of the adversity our students are experiencing. This commitment to becoming a trauma-sensitive school would require a shift in priorities for our students and, more important, a perceptual shift for the staff. One of our first short-term goals was to provide safe spaces in each classroom and to grow our safe spaces to become a schoolwide safe place for students. Our second goal was to begin teaching our students about their brains, how the different brain states impact our ability to engage in content learning as well as the impact on controlling behavior. Our third goal was to bring consistency to the daily lives of our students. A sampling of the ways we worked toward consistency included: using concise PBIS structures; posting picture schedules in the classrooms; and morning meeting structures. We started our mission of becoming a trauma-sensitive school with the belief that consistency, compassion, and comprehensive learning about how our brains operate would have a direct impact on student well-being at Abbett. We were intentional in scheduling the first 45 minutes of the day to build relationships using the Responsive Classroom format, allowing teachers time to use the SEL lessons, educational neuroscience lessons, and replacing morning work with STEM-based busy boxes.

During the 2018-'19 school year, we had a significant increase in student referrals as we learned the variety of strategies we knew our students needed. We also started our year with a list of over 100 students who we considered students of concern. We began to create a plan to meet each student at their point of need and best utilize the resources we had available. We started by placing many students on CHECK-IN/CHECK-OUT as well as scheduled breaks throughout the school day. We changed our arrival procedures in November 2018 to address behaviors that were occurring before the start of the school day. We also became intentional about creating touch points for our students at the beginning of the day with our new arrival procedure. At least four adults greet all Abbett students as they make their way into the school each morning. Midway through the first semester of the '18-'19 school year, we were assigned a therapeutic counselor. We immediately started forming special groups for our counselor to meet with as well as assigning the more intense student needs some one-on-one time with our counselor.

By January 2019, we began to see success. Our referral count had fallen to match the referral count from the previous year. Each month of the second semester for the '18-'19 school year had a significant drop in referrals from the same month a year earlier. Midway through March 2019, we made another significant schedule change in recess supervision. This change, which now allowed classroom teachers to spend time at recess with their students, significantly reduced office referrals. We followed up with many teachers about a month after the recess change, and one of the consistent responses I received was, "I am spending more time teaching in the afternoon because I am taking care of recess issues as they happen."

At the end of the '18-'19 school year, the administrative team reviewed all the structures we had put into place through the lens of deciding what worked and what did not work in creating a safe place for Abbett students. The goal of this review was to keep the working structures and change or eliminate those structures that did not yield the results of helping students learn to self-regulate and establish a safe learning environment.

Our critical review of the structures we implemented during '18-'19 revealed several successes and areas where we needed additional changes. The arrival changes, changes in recess supervision, providing time for all classroom teachers to work with students on the SEL/neuroscience lessons, and replacing morning work with STEM-based busy boxes have all contributed to calming many of the students. These changes contributed to more students finding success in the school environment.

We also discovered that the scheduled breaks we'd put into place initially helped several of our students complete a successful day at school; however, the breaks transitioned from regulation to reward and eventually entitlement. Many of our students intentionally did not graduate from our CHECK-IN/CHECK-OUT system because they knew they would lose their breaks. We also noticed that many of our students would work hard to get their first green-break but would then return to making poor choices because there was no external motivator for the remainder of the day.

Our CHECK-IN/CHECK-OUT system was initially based on external motivators. Students on the program would initially be rewarded a small treat or trinket for returning their forms or having a green day. When students also fell short of their daily goals, they would experience another type of adversity that would manifest itself in the form of rage, uncontrollable crying, or complete shutdown. These student meltdowns during check-out often happened at the end of what had been a successful school day. These daily episodes undermined the conversation the CHECK-IN/CHECK-OUT coach was trying to have with students about their behavior and how they could make better choices.

Jamie Rice (Abbett Elementary Instructional Coach) and I met with Dr. Lori Desautels after the end of the '18-'19 school year and discussed our successes and areas of improvement. Our discussions centered on our CHECK-IN/CHECK-OUT system and why it was triggering our students. We concluded that the students were more concerned about receiving points instead of understanding their brain states and how to actively self-regulate. Dr. Desautels and Ms. Rice collaborated to create the Brain State Regulation Sheet. This form takes away the point value of behavior. It helps the students look at segments of their day and determine which brain state they were in, especially when they were struggling with the targeted behaviors noted on the Brain State Regulation Sheet.

Abbett did not implement this immediately as a part of the CHECK-IN/CHECK-OUT system, because we wanted to ensure that all the students in our school had adequate knowledge of the various brain states and the impact on behavior. During the first grading period, Abbett teachers actively taught students about their brain states and the relationships between brain state and behavior. These lessons not only prepared students for using the Brain State Regulation Sheet, but the lessons also began an overall cultural change at Abbett and our view of student discipline.

During the fall of 2019, Abbett teachers began instituting a variety of tier-one strategies in their classrooms to help students regulate emotions. Strategies such as Focused Attention Practices before recess, scheduled classroom brain intervals, and the implementation of schoolwide neuroscience language are just a few examples that have contributed to an overall reduction in referrals during the first semester of the 2019-'20 school year.

At the beginning of October 2018, the Abbett leadership team created a students of concern list. Our initial list had over 100 student names; most of the students on the list were behavior concerns. After we created our initial students of concern list, we began aggressively scheduling SST (Student Support Team) meetings to identify the supports each student would need in order to best prepare them for success. Each SST includes the classroom teacher's input about the concern and the interventions they have already implemented. We also looked at all available resources and aligned what was necessary to support each student's needs.

At the beginning of October 2019, our leadership team met again to discuss our students of concern. We discussed all the previous students (currently enrolled) whom we had listed from the previous year as well as new student concerns. When our discussion was complete, we had a list of 14 students. We concluded that our SST process of aggressively aligning the right supports for students, our teaching, the use of neuroscience lessons in the classroom, and our overall changes in arrival and recess procedures have all contributed to the reduction of classroom referrals and students of concern. Our work continues and is a process, but we now feel we are addressing the root pain beneath so many of the pain-based behaviors we are seeing each day.

Toxic Levels of Stress on Our Children—My Life Story

Bang! Bang!
That is when life fell apart
Not only I lose my home
But I lost my dogs too
My world was blackened
I felt I was dying on the inside
And I did not want to see

My taste buds were not there
The gunshots I could not bear
It smelled like smoke and I walked out
And saw the gun casing on the ground
I could not touch my mom because she was on her way to the
    hospital
My world was blackened
After the storm passed by, the sun rise
And that is when my aunt Kimberly rise
To the challenge of taking me in
I did not have a place to call home
My world was blackened
But my aunt Kimberly called me in her home
This made me feel love because I had a place to go home again
ORDER! ORDER! ORDER!
I saw a rainbow
And I came back home
My world was blackened
But no longer it was
I finally was color again
I was back home with my family
I was finally happy
STUDENT FROM ABBETT ELEMENTARY

In children, anger is fear's bodyguard. Because emotionally troubled children and youth have learned to associate adult intervention with adult rejection, our goal as educators is to help our students reappraise and reframe these distorted beliefs and thoughts so that we may gradually create safety, trust, and connection with our students.

Students' toxic levels of stress need to be understood in the context of how the body's stress response system works. Within this system, there are three broad categories of stress—not all of which, of course, are bad—that make up our stress response system: positive stress, tolerable stress, and toxic stress.[16]

Positive stress is a type of stress that helps us learn how to cope with the ups and downs of life and is considered the first level of the stress response system. This type of stress is an important part of childhood development. When we feel threatened, the human body is designed to respond automatically by increasing our heart and respiration rates, increasing our blood pressure, and releasing stress hormones such as cortisol and adrenaline. When a child's stress system becomes activated within an environment of care, the physical and damaging effects of the stress can be buffered, helping the body to find calm and return itself to homeostasis. Over time and with caring adults, co-regulation of a child's stress response results in the healthy development of this stress response.[17]

The next type of stress is **tolerable stress**. This is the second level of the human stress response system in which more severe difficulties or challenges activate the stress response. These can include a host of negative experiences that often feel momentous, such as a death in the family, a car accident, or any kind of emergency. This level of stress can also be supported and buffered by adults in the child's life.[18]

The highest level of the human stress response system is **toxic stress**. This type of stress is triggered when a child is exposed to ongoing elevated levels of adversity, often unpredictable. This can include a wide variety of toxic experiences along a continuum: chronic neglect, physical abuse, ongoing emotional abuse, exposure to violence in the community, social rejection and humiliation, and other negative experiences that increase chronic levels of anxiety occurring without the healthy co-regulation of an adult.[19]

These are the indicators that influence the adverse childhood experiences. Prolonged and persistent mistreatment activates the stress response system and can impact neurological development. Without ongoing adult support, this level of stress impacts all facets of the young person's life and can even reprogram a young person's development into adulthood. These children and adolescents are in pain. They are emotionally and behaviorally in a persistent state of alarm.

When our stress response systems are constantly turned on with little to no time for repair and recovery, our brains and bodies are hijacked by a brain state that produces chronic amounts of cortisol and adrenaline, which can shut off the areas of the brain responsible for learning, emotional regulation, attention, and working memory. Every day, educators across the country are seeing the effects of chronically activated stress response systems, and students are expressing this anxiety, fear, and angst through negative behaviors. The students' behaviors, to the outside world, often look apathetic, shut down, and unmotivated, but their brain's physiology tells a different story. These students are often feeling immobilized, frozen, and shut down from the adversities and trauma they have experienced or are experiencing.

Our nation's school districts, moreover, are observing patterns in children's behaviors, eventually recognizing that these negative behaviors would often escalate on Friday afternoons when students began to anticipate the weekend ahead. These weekends were often filled with unpredictability for the students, as a child might not know where they would sleep, what they would eat, or who would be caring for them. Some high schools have reported greater absences on Mondays, when students were staying home from school to make sure their caregivers came out of the alcohol and drug binges that had taken place over the weekend. These patterns of continuity were becoming unintentionally normalized, just as they have been and continue to be in many other communities around the country.

In all the school districts where we share the application of applied educational neuroscience, we're excited to see staff and students learning about their own neuroanatomy. They are learning together, and no one has to be the expert. We have found that when students and staff learn together about their brain structures and functions, these times of learning become touch points for building relationships. We are sharing tools, practices, and strategies, all of which help the students regulate their emotions and stress response systems with an adult who is staying connected through all conflicts. Although we have a long road to travel, the application of educational neuroscience framework continues to grow and develop through a preventive, connective lens for discipline. Students are learning how their brains have a superpower: neuroplasticity! Put another way, these students are learning that their brains change structurally and functionally with every experience they encounter. To help create circuits of resiliency and well-being, it is critical to reach students at a young age when the brain has much more plasticity and malleability.

In 2006, the first significant and long-term research study concerning the effects of ACEs on adult health outcomes was published by Dr. Vincent Felitti and Dr. Robert Anda.[20] This landmark study documented the frequency of traumatic life experiences in the childhoods of over 17,000 adults enrolled in the Kaiser Permanente heath care system. Defying conventional belief, this in-depth analysis revealed a powerful relationship between our emotional experiences as children and our physical and mental health as adults.

Certainly, these statistics are alarming to all of us, but what do they have to do with teaching and learning? Everything. A student walking into our classrooms with four or more ACEs is at extreme risk for academic and behavioral challenges. Although many educators and communities are aware of the Adverse Childhood Experience studies, I feel it is helpful to review the implications of the initial study and the growing number of ACEs that did not exist when the original study was conducted and shared.

The Adverse Childhood Experiences that Felitti and Anda discovered in their study include the following:

1) Emotional abuse

2) Physical abuse

3) Sexual abuse

4) Physical neglect

5) Emotional neglect

6) Substance abuse in the household

7) Mental illness in the household

8) Mother treated violently

9) Divorce or parental separation

10) A household member in jail

The total number of adverse experiences in a person's life is that person's ACE score, meaning that the highest possible ACE score a person can receive is 10. After documenting the various traumatic life experiences in their study, Felitti and Anda then correlated the person's ACE score with health-risk behaviors and outcomes. They discovered that ACEs were extremely common. Of those who partic-ipated in the study, for instance, 67% had at least 1 ACE, while 12.6% had four or more ACEs.[21] This idea of a composite total ACE score is critical to our understanding of how adversity impacts children and youth. Put simply, the higher the ACE score, the more likely the young person will experience emotional and mental challenges in their lives.

Since the original ACE study was conducted in 2006, other similar studies have been carried out. In 2012, the Institute for Safe Families formed the ACE Task Force to study the prevalence and impact of ACEs in Philadelphia, a large city with a socially and racially diverse population. A total of 1,784 adults completed the Philadelphia Urban ACE Survey. This survey found a higher prevalence of ACEs than were found in previous studies. For example, 33.2% of Philadelphia adults experienced emotional abuse, and 35% experienced physical abuse during their childhood. Approximately 35% of adults grew up in a household with a substance-abusing member; 24.1% lived in a house-hold with someone who was mentally ill; and 12.9% lived in a household with someone who had served time or was sentenced to serve time in prison.

The Philadelphia Urban ACE Survey also examined the stressors that exist in the communities where people live. The study found that 40.5% of Philadelphia adults witnessed violence while growing up, which includes seeing or hearing someone being beaten, stabbed, or shot. More than one-third (34.5%) of adults reported experiencing discrimination based on their race or ethnicity, while almost three in ten adults (27.3%) reported having felt unsafe in their neighbor-hoods or not trusting their neighbors during childhood. Overall, 37% of Philadelphia respondents reported four or more ACEs.[22] Clearly, then, large segments of Philadelphia's population are growing up in the face of tremendous adversity.

Wendy Ellis and Bill Dietz's recent research, which explores the community environments where our children and adolescents grow up, has expanded the concept of adversity to help consider the effects of living in environments where ACEs are all too common. While it seems obvious that our children and youth experience adversity in their individual family situations, Ellis and Dietz argue that adversity can also manifest itself in our actual communities. In their framework, the symptoms of Adverse Community Environments (not be confused with Adverse Childhood Experiences) include the following:

Poverty

Discrimination

Community disruption

Violence

Lack of opportunity or economic mobility and social capital

Poor housing quality

Unaffordable housing[23]

Foster care children, it should be pointed out, are at an extreme risk for poor emotional, social, and physiological health outcomes and have high rates of Adverse Childhood Experiences. A study by Kristin Turney and Christopher Wildeman shows that 61% of children in foster care were removed from their home due to abusive neglect, while 32% of children were removed from their homes due to parental drug abuse. Moreover, 14% of children were removed due to the inability of the caregiver to cope, and 12% of children were removed from their home due to physical abuse.[24]

However, trauma can come in other forms, too. Kenneth V. Hardy, a therapist and a professor at Drexel University, has written extensively on the hidden wounds of racial trauma. His work has deepened and expanded the understanding of trauma to include racial oppression. Hardy has brought attention to a far too often neglected topic of the hidden wounds of racial oppression. In his framework, Hardy identifies five hidden wounds of racial trauma, including:

1) internalized devaluation

2) assaulted sense of self

3) internalized voicelessness

4) the wound of rage

5) the sense of being a nobody.[25]

Many of the new adverse childhood experiences include the over-identification and disproportionate number of students being punished in our schools today! Michael McKnight and I shared in detail the research of Dr. Hardy's work in the wounds of racial trauma in our book *Eyes Are Never Quiet*. But it is worth mentioning that these racial adversities and trauma, along with the vulnerability of our multi-racial population and our LGBTQ population, have also been recently identified and are emotional, social, and physiological health risk factors in this time for students along with the traditional ACEs.[26]

Taken together, then, the research and statistics are clear. Our most troubled children and youth have experienced high levels of stress, adversity, and trauma in their lives. Adversity—in line with the expanded concept mentioned above—can also include natural disasters, accidents, social rejection, and humiliation. For many of our students, educators, and parents, schools are areas filled with adversity, with negative experiences accumulating each year. Schools, in other words, are turned from places of learning into places of pain that often lives beneath the behaviors we face daily in our schools. Without awareness and action, our biographies can turn into our biology.

What all these statistics show is clear: Our children are hurting. What these statistics do not show, however, is that our children are resilient. When one child, family, or community is struck with adversity, it can affect the entire system. Our nation is a collective system that is currently in a survival brain state, with gun violence on our streets and in our schools. This violence, however, has generated a community response unlike any we have seen in recent times through March for Our Lives, a movement led by our nation's youth a couple of years ago.

These young people shared their trauma and stories of loss and hope. As we listen to the speeches of our youth today, we hear similar calls for change. In addition to thoughts and prayers, we hear our youth plead for action. They share how they have learned how to duck from bullets before learning to read. This movement transcends race, gender, politics, and ethnicity. These children and youth are asking for educational justice. They live in the here and now, attending schools where zero tolerance policies, added security, and armed teachers are not working. They are pleading for increased mental health services, restorative justice programs, and work-funded mental health resources and support. They are exhausted from the profiling and criminalizing of their black and brown brothers and sisters. Many of our young people have experienced the intimate loss of a loved one through gun violence. We must begin awakening to the conditions that breed these adversities individually and collectively.

We have a great opportunity to do this in our school systems. Students spend, on average, around 1,000 hours a year in school. These can be places of connection and inspiration where students can thrive with healthy interactions. They can be places of opportunities that shine a light on strengths and passions, and environments that feel safe and secure. We are far from there, but we are hopeful that together we can pave the way for these systemic changes. We have an opening to meet these emotional challenges with understanding, relationships, and hope. This opening is a new lens for discipline, a brain-aligned lens addressing the childhood adversities and the pain-based behaviors that are permeating an educational culture with unconditional awareness like no other time in our history! Have these adversities and traumas become more prevalent? Yes. Have these adversities and traumas always been a part of our social fabric? Yes. I am learning that as we shine a light on the attachment and neuroscience research of the developing brain and body, interfacing this research with childhood adversity and trauma, we cannot afford to ignore it. We are creatures of habit hardwired for survival, but we also now recognize we have the complex and beautiful brain architecture to change our thoughts, feelings, behaviors, and perceptions with every experience we encounter. Our shift comes from viewing discipline not as something that we *do to* another, but rather as something we want to *create within* another.

Following is an ACE survey that, with the help of my co-instructor and graduate assistant, I created for our students at Butler University. I have shared this survey with many educators and school districts across the country as we have updated many of the adversities that are being experienced in 2020. This survey is meant for young adults and our teaching staff, not for children. We hope that a growing number of educators will take their own Adverse Childhood Experience survey to understand how common ACEs are and to help each one of us with the understanding that our developing years are never too far away, but with the knowledge and science of resiliency, our adversities do not have the last word. As we move into the following chapters, I am reminded of these words:

"We tend to view misbehavior as resistance because we know where we want children to go. Children view misbehavior as protection because they know where they have been."

L. TOBIN

Adverse Childhood Experiences (ACE) Survey

This is an anonymous survey; therefore, your scores and details of your answers will not be linked with your name. Please answer the following questions as honestly as possible. At the end of the survey add up all of your "yes" answers; this is your ACE score.

Prior to your 18th birthday …

Did a parent or other adult in the household often or very often … Swear at you, insult you, put you down, or humiliate you; or act in a way that made you afraid that you might be physically hurt?   No __ Yes __

Did a parent or other adult in the household often or very often … Push, grab, slap, or throw something at you; or ever hit you so hard that you had marks or were injured?   No __ Yes __

Did an adult or person at least 5 years older than you ever … Touch or fondle you, or have you touch their body in a sexual way; or attempt or actually have oral, anal, or vaginal intercourse with you?   No __ Yes __

Did you often or very often feel that … No one in your family loved you or thought you were important or special; or that your family didn't look out for each other, feel close to each other, or support each other?   No __ Yes __

Did you often or very often feel that … You didn't have enough to eat, had to wear dirty clothes, and had no one to protect you; or that your parents were too drunk or high to take care of you or take you to the doctor if you needed it?   No __ Yes __

Were your parents ever separated or divorced?   No __ Yes __

Was your mother or stepmother ... Often or very
often pushed, grabbed, slapped, or had something thrown at her; or sometimes, often, or very
often kicked, bitten, hit with a fist, or hit with   No __ Yes __
something hard; or ever repeatedly hit over at
least a few minutes or threatened with a gun or
knife?

Did you live with anyone who was a problem
drinker or alcoholic, or who used street drugs?   No __ Yes __

Was a household member depressed or mentally
ill; or did a household member attempt suicide?   No __ Yes __

Did a household member go to prison?   No __ Yes __

Did you experience the loss or death of someone
you loved?   No __ Yes __

Were you often or very often charged with the
responsibility of daily care and well-being of
younger siblings (meaning that you were taking   No __ Yes __
on the role of caregiver)?

Did you experience a devastating natural
disaster?   No __ Yes __

Did you experience early childhood illnesses
beyond that of the common cold, flu, sore   No __ Yes __
throat, ear infection, etc.?

Were you ever hospitalized as a child (meaning
that you were admitted to a hospital for a period
of several consecutive days)?   No __ Yes __

Did you experience significant anxiety or depression during these early years, to the point of shutting down or feeling hopeless over a long period of time?　　　　　No ___ Yes ___

Were you often treated or judged unfairly based on race or ethnicity?　　　　　No ___ Yes ___

Were you often treated or judged unfairly based on sexual orientation and/or gender identity?　　　　　No ___ Yes ___

Were you often treated or judged unfairly by peers in social contexts, in school and/or out of school?　　　　　No ___ Yes ___

Add up all of your "yes" answers, this is your ACE score:　　　　　_____

CHAPTER 2

Student Behaviors Start with You!

"When we truly care for ourselves, it becomes possible to care more profoundly for other people. The more alert and sensitive we are to our own needs, the more loving and generous we can be toward others."

EDA LESHAN

Behavior management is not about students. Behavior management is about the adults. If we are to shift our perceptions of discipline, I feel we need to move away from the words "behavior management," as we are never called to manage another person. Why begin exploring this new perception of discipline with educator and parent brain state? This is important because it's the initial shift in re-envisioning discipline, and it begins with looking under the hood at our own brain state, which consists of personal beliefs, perceptions, and an accumulation of experiences that have generated how we view and implement discipline in this moment. A dysregulated adult cannot regulate a child.

An educator who listens deeply, stays connected through the chaos, and perceives a crisis as an opportunity is the person at the heart of brain-aligned relational discipline. The research originating from the developmental social neurosciences is clear. Secure attachments with a caregiver promote healthy brain development and the ability to emotionally regulate through the child's and adolescent's developing years. Dr. Allen Schore explains the development in this way: "The quality of early attachment is known to affect social relationships later in life. Therefore, it is conceivable that the level of opiate activity in a mother and her infant may not only affect behaviors during infancy but may also affect the development of an individual's style of engaging and seeking out supportive relationships later in life."[1]

We can no longer discuss and explore discipline and behavior management without considering the brain state of the adult and the relational temperature between student and educator. As Dr. Bruce Perry states, "The key to the success of any educational experience is the capacity to 'get to the cortex.' Yet, each year, nearly one-third of all children attending U.S. public schools will have significantly impaired cortical functioning and behavioral challenges due to abuse, neglect, domestic violence, poverty, and other adversities."[2] Understanding the effects of trauma and adversity on a child's brain and how these effects alter the ability to learn and behave is essential to improving our public education system, which is currently facing a significant increase with the mental and emotional health needs of our students. These emotional and mental challenges often show up as negative behaviors. Children who have experienced significant adversity and trauma will be in a persistent state of alarm and will often be unable to focus and concentrate when they walk into our classrooms and schools. We now are beginning to understand that when students are in this survival brain state, everything they perceive as unsafe and unfamiliar becomes a threat! In this survival state, relational brain-aligned discipline must start with the educator's brain state.

Being aware and adjusting my tone of voice, posture, and facial expression can either soothe or unintentionally escalate a child's or adolescent's activated stress response systems. Because of this, students will pay more attention to a teacher's nonverbal cues. How I care for my brain state and ability to regulate my own emotions is critical in implementing a relational brain-aligned and preventive discipline framework. Educator brain state and co-regulation are at the heart of relational discipline. We begin to build sustainable relationships, mutual respect, and trust through emotional attunement described as a dyadic comforting conversation between educator and student. The truth is that we work harder for people we like, and when students feel respected and trust us, we are helping to shape brain architecture that produces their reasoning, regulation, problem-solving, and attentional skills. When children remain in alarm states, cognitive learning is impaired.

The following graphic created by our colleague Dr. Shelia Dennis shares the pathway to resiliency through the application of these relational practices. It illustrates how teacher brain state can drive this shift in our thinking and belief systems, creating a new lens through which we can perceive—and embrace—relational discipline!

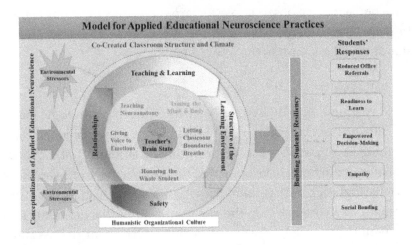

Brain-aligned relational discipline embraces the knowledge and understanding that discipline is an expression of a compassionate presence, warm demanding, and guidance without coercion. Discipline is not something we do to students; it is something we want to develop within them. The foundation for this new perception of school discipline is grounded in the social neurosciences speaking to attachment, co-regulation, educator brain state, and the strengthening of touch points, which are relationship and connection moments in our children's and adolescents' lives. Students spend over 13,000 hours in school; educators during this time have an opportunity to create a culture and climate conducive to the biosocial needs of human growth and development.

We traditionally and historically have implemented punishment and coercion techniques into our discipline practices, hoping that a bit of power, control, discomfort, or pain will change the students' behaviors. This is far from what occurs, as the most recent research shares. When we are disciplining children and adolescents who carry in pain-based behaviors, traditional discipline can inadvertently escalate negative behaviors in both teacher and student, as survival brains cannot process rewards, consequences, or reason.

Our understanding continues to deepen in the knowledge that all behavior is communication. I have learned that the discipline of a student begins with my own state of mind, and that the chronic negative behaviors we observe so often are the results of brains bathed in pain. The students who need the most connection and understanding will ask for it in the most unloving ways.

June

A year ago, my course release at the University brought me to our fifth-grade classroom in the Indianapolis Public Schools. I was teaching two mornings a week, introducing students to their neuroanatomy and brain development. From my perspective, I was using novelty and high-engagement activities, absolutely enjoying every moment as a co-teacher in the classroom—until this moment. This moment began on a Wednesday morning with our entire class gathered in groups and tables of four. Walking the room, checking in with each group as they worked on the activity, I heard a thunderous crash followed by loud yelling as I jerked back around in alarm. One of the class's quietest, most introverted boys was lying on the floor next to his crumpled glasses. I ran over to him, crouched beside him, and looked up to see June (not her real name), a young adolescent girl twice the size of this boy, standing over both of us with her fist in the air. In that moment, as my heart continued to pound loudly, my ears rang, and the saliva left my mouth, I started screaming questions at her. "What did you do? What just happened?! Why did you do this?" "Fuck you," she screamed back at me. I raised my voice again and told her to leave the classroom, trembling and pointing to the door. I did not take a deep breath. I did not regulate my own nervous system. I unintentionally escalated her anger and most likely her fear ... all over again. I was completely dysregulated and shaking! We all felt high emotions as the classroom became increasingly chaotic. I had very little to no reasoning ability in that moment, as my prefrontal cortex had gone offline. I'd forgotten about pain-based behavior and everything that I'd been teaching and presenting for the past few years.

Emotions are contagious. We all see and experience this when we unintentionally enter a power struggle or conflict with a student. Behavior management isn't about the student; it's about *me*. If I'm feeling rough and dysregulated, I become the mirror and reflection for those students who become increasingly irritated, defiant, oppositional, or shut down. Many of our most emotionally challenging students are walking into our classrooms and schools carrying in so much pain. That pain is often misunderstood and seen as intentional disrespect, indifference, or deviant behavior. Much pain must be met with much love, and this begins with us. We must care and attend to our own brain states and emotional barometers if we're to meet our students where they are in their brain development. When a student walks into class feeling distrustful and unsafe, we must meet them with connection, creating an environment where they are seen, felt, and heard.

This can be so challenging, as we can unknowingly interpret students' actions and words through our own emotional filters that our history of beliefs and past experience may have distorted. The awareness of how our own private logic is filled with experiences, relationships, pain, biases, and embedded belief systems is a critical part of the brain-aligned relational discipline process with our students. Self-reflection on the part of the educator is the cornerstone for relational discipline that begins creating new pathways for resiliency.

Educator Brain States

As I think about the opening quote of this chapter, I have never been more aware of how not only our own self-care affects our emotional, physical, and mental health, but also how the adversities and trauma of our children and others can create a secondary firestorm inside our own nervous systems as we re-experience the life adversities we thought we'd overcome. Secondary traumatic stress coupled with emotional fatigue profoundly affects our experiences of everyday life and relationships. When we are constantly attuning to negative emotion, co-regulating students who are agitated, buffering the pain-based behaviors that trigger children and adolescents, *and* resetting boundaries with challenging behaviors and emotions from others, we often carry these worries into our perceptions, thoughts, and daily life experiences.

As Franciscan priest Richard Rohr states, "Our own pain can either transform us or we transmit it. Nobody benefits when we mirror the behaviors of children and adolescents in pain."[3]

All of this creates an emotional contagion of sorts, which is capable of slowly diminishing our sense of agency and purpose inside our own lives. We forget, moreover, that this emotional contagion is a part of our social survival, as our brains are social organs sensing and detecting the range of emotions and sensations we intuit from others in all moments. We are neurobiologically wired for attachment and relationships, and we are constantly reading the nonverbal and verbal communication cues of others as we evaluate what feels safe, familiar, threatening, distressing, hopeless, or exhausting.

Time and time again, I have experienced this process as an educator and a mother. I have felt my own emotions escalate when I unintentionally entered a conflict with a child or adolescent who had triggered me, activating my survival protective and defensive instincts so that my thinking and reasoning were shut down. This is exactly what happened to me on that Wednesday morning a year ago with our fifth-grade students. I was furious, sparked, and began asking questions and using words in the very moment of the chaos, which was only activating June's stress response and elevating my own! Words are not effective or even heard when spoken from this survival state of mind, and on those days of unintentional conflict, I left school feeling emotionally spent and somewhat hopeless. What we have learned through the years is that there is no easy way to "fix" our students. The behaviors triggered by toxic stress and trauma are not remediated quickly. Young people that bring high levels of stress, adversity, and trauma often take three steps backward for every two steps forward. Staying connected and regulated through a conflict is at the core of educator well-being and brain-aligned relational discipline.

For the past few years, we've sat beside educators in a variety of schools from around the country. "Exhaustion peppered with hopelessness," is an apt description for the emotional state of those who work with our students. At the risk of repeating myself, it seems impossible to teach a student the mandated academic standards when the student's brain is wired for survival, which means that the students are prepared to protect, defend, flee, and fight the minute they walk into the school.

Teaching is an organic process, and schools are living systems. When we say that our most troubled children and adolescents create "discipline" issues in our schools, it's an acknowledgment that young people in pain often act out their pain in our schools. When we attempt to control these children and adolescents, what we get instead is an escalation of their inappropriate behaviors. This can quickly spiral out of control, and the culture of the school—the health of that living system—becomes negatively affected. In these environments, troubled students are punished at excessive rates and are often expelled to nowhere.

Stress is contagious. Toxic levels of it, when carried into our schools by students who have experienced high levels of adversity in their lives, can dramatically affect the entire culture and emotional climate of a school. Decades ago, Nicholas Long, the founder of the Life Space Crisis Intervention Institute and leader in the field of mental health and special education for more than 50 years, made the connection between a troubled child's behavior and adults' reactions towards that behavior. According to Long, "Kids in stress create in us their feelings, and if we are not trained to this process, we (the adult) will mirror their behaviors."[4] Long also argues that when a student is stressed, those emotions will also reflect in the adult. If the adult is neither trained nor prepared to accept their own counter-aggressive feelings, the adult will act on them, in effect mirroring the student's behavior. He offers several reasons that adults become counter-aggressive with the young people they serve. These can include, for example, the adult being caught in the student's conflict cycle, or the adult's reaction to being in a bad mood. Other reasons are the adult's perception of having their value system or beliefs violated by a student, or even the adult's feeling of rejection and hopelessness.[5]

Teachers, administrators, and all adults working with traumatized children and youth must become intentional and reflective in their actions if they are to succeed in helping to heal our most wounded students. To do so, we must be extremely cautious not to treat children and youth in pain with pain-based discipline techniques. As Bessel van der Kolk warns, "Faced with a range of challenging behaviors, caregivers have a tendency to deal with their frustration by retaliating in ways that often uncannily repeat the children's early trauma."[6] It is critically important for adults working with traumatized students to remember that the motivation for change in our most troubled children and youth depends on the adult's ability to communicate respectfully in times of crisis and extreme stress.

Professor William Morse of the University of Michigan shared this with teachers in training: "The day you forget that under some life circumstances, you could have ended up like your most troubled student is the day you should quit. You will have lost your ability to respond with empathy."[7]

What can we do to elevate our own sense of purpose, connection, and well-being? This question is personal and needs to be answered by each of us. Although this book cannot provide a recipe for well-being, this chapter offers some self-reflective and mindful practices that will allow educators to increase their effectiveness working in high-stress environments with students who carry deep pain into classrooms and schools.

June Continued...

Last year on that Wednesday morning when June shoved her classmate onto the floor, I was unprepared emotionally to co-regulate with her. Co-regulation is modeling the behaviors we want to see from our students, and I will discuss this at length in the following chapters. What I needed to do before I gave consequences or even attempted to discipline was to breathe deeply for a few seconds or a minute and then shift my facial expression, posture, and tone of voice as I approached her, suggesting we both get some air and walk.

I did not.

From personal and professional experiences, I have learned that force, anger, and sarcasm only deepen the wounds when we communicate with children and adolescents who have experienced significant adversity. Until we meet a child with understanding and authenticity, we will rarely experience or see an intrinsic desire to learn or feel her excitement from a fresh discovery. Author and teacher Parker Palmer states: "Teaching tugs at the heart, opens the heart, even breaks the heart—and the more one loves teaching, the more heartbreaking it can be. The courage to teach is the courage to keep one's heart open for the questions, the mystery, and in those very moments when the heart feels full to capacity."[8]

When we inadvertently take the "soul" out of education, we are left with a skeletal caricature that distorts and diminishes the significance of the beating hearts inside our classrooms. Education is much more than content acquisition and test scores. It is the vehicle that drives us to question, creates curiosity, and can bring us to an *understanding* about ourselves and the world around us. When we discover meaning and relevance in our own lives, we can fill the emptiness and voids in our students' lives, and this is relational discipline.

Brea Thomas, a former graduate student and secondary educator, shares these words of soulful teaching as she learns about herself each day through time spent with her students:

> There is meaning in a hug—and hugs can be verbal, not just physical. This is what I've learned in my few years as a high school English teacher. This notion guides me as I maneuver through this hypersensitive time period in schools when even sideways hugs or complimentary pats on the back are scrutinized. Though there might be tremendous, and even necessary, restrictions on human caring, I like to challenge myself to address this idea of how to show students that we, the teachers, really care, and that they, the students, truly matter to us.
>
> It sounds cheesy to us, perhaps, to say that "we care" or that "someone matters," because we're living in times of

cynicism and distrust. I reflected on this dilemma last August as I began the year with multiple intelligence surveys and interpersonal activities to "get to know" my students.

How can I tell them, I brainstormed, without sounding cheesy, that their smiles and frowns matter; their puzzled and inquisitive brows matter; their sighs and chuckles and complaints matter to me, and guide my daily teaching? Indeed, every caring teacher will consent to the fact that the verbals and nonverbals of her/his students get packed away and shuffled home, along with grading and lesson plans, to be analyzed and strategically reworked for the next day.

So, after issuing a three-page syllabus to my 11th Grade AP/IB Language students on Day 2 of last school year, following introductory exercises and "get to know yous" (as all teachers in our department are advised to do), I noticed that my students were flipping their noses and contorting their faces into the "I don't care—she must not care, either" look. So, I decided to write them a poem that would let them know how much I cared.

Night Letter to My Students

I jolt from slumber, and begin the day's ascent
A sprinter on the track,
A bloom reaching for the sun,
only to stand in my pjs
an ordinary teacher
enveloped by mini mountains of papers and books.
If I were eighteen, I might be pondering
the colors of my nail polish, and the true meaning of the text
message that my friend just sent me,
and the cruelty of a snooze button that won't last for eternity.
But as it is, I am simply awake,
a teacher in pjs, thought-full
still sensing your distress from the day before
and the furrowing of your brows

and the immensity of the accelerated tasks before us.
The apple cinnamon candles lull me forward
from slumber to coffee, from oatmeal to lunch-packing
and I rampage the kitchen to soothe the morning hunger
mountains in my belly.
iTunes have followed me out and down the porch steps
and humming them, I start the engine thinking
It's a Beautiful Day as morning's potential curls her lips
into a smile.
The smell of my mums
waves good luck as I'm off to our garden
of classics and classes and clases de classicus ...
and there's something about the streetlights
torching against the darkness that makes me emboldened
to continue goading you to torch brightly, effervescently
but perhaps you aren't even listening
perhaps the droll or daunting of the day, of so many dreams
has you checked-out or singing a different tune—
specs of chalk dust, flecks of markers and pen ink
and she wants us to have binders?
But this is all that I want to do—
Tell you that in all of this ... apples and dust, classics and
classes ...
and binders
There is meaning, I promise.
EDUCATOR BREA THOMAS

After reading this poem to my students, I noticed that some of them opened up—not, I believe, as a result of any poetic devices or exquisite linguistics, but because I opened up to them and made my caring transparent and personal. The rest of that initial week of school, I heard fewer moans and groans about books and early lessons, and I even received a few statements of appreciation from them.

So, what did I learn from this 15-minute homework exercise for myself, and the 15 minutes that it took to share this simplistic poem with my students? I learned that caring for another is not a manufactured process or action. It is organic; it is a way of living and breathing each day, hoping for positive results from selfless efforts. This is serving; this is teaching.

I share this poem and words from Brea because her self-reflection with her students is not only healthy for resetting her own sense of calm and regulated brain state, but this is also an example of relational discipline on the front end—preventive relational discipline. Brea took a risk and shared a part of herself. She modeled the behaviors she wanted to see from her students. This is an example of self-care and modeling the conversations that these adolescents had rarely experienced in their developing years. I will share more of these self-reflective strategies at the end of this chapter to emphasize that relational discipline is not something that we *do to* students, but something we want to *create within* them, and this occurs when we sit by their side reflecting on our own adversities, traumas, and resiliency.

June and the Journey

Leaving our fifth-grade class on that Wednesday late morning, I felt defeated and somewhat incapable of continuing with my pre-sentations to educator audiences on emotional contagion and pain-based behaviors. Pulling into my driveway, I mindlessly jumped out of the car and began walking. I walked and walked, quite possibly trying to regulate my own nervous system, thinking about what went wrong! I saw June's eyes in my mind. I remembered the shouting. I remembered a blank empty stare. I remembered seeing through those dark, pain-filled eyes. Taking a deep breath, I sat on a large rock by our neighborhood's creek, remembering that empathy and kindness are learned in the human brain just like reading or math, but they must be taught with opportunities and experiences that provide repetition and practice. As I thought back on the last few hours with the students and June, I knew that June hadn't been consistently exposed to the experiences and skills of kindness and empathy within her foster home environments over the past several years. Her 12 years had been filled with toxic levels of stress and with people and experiences that did not feel safe or trusting. Few adults in her young life had been consistently kind, emotionally available and present.

June was suspended after that Wednesday morning, and I was unable to connect with her until the following week. I knew that her suspension wouldn't change any of her behaviors, that this type of punishment would most likely reinforce what she was already experiencing, and that she already knew this sad personal "truth" at a gut level: "Adults are not to be trusted." Returning the following week, I came into the classroom and asked June if she would take a walk with me. She accepted my invitation, and we left the room and began silently walking to the school's courtyard.

When I felt we had established a rhythm, a calm cadence as we moved through the courtyard, I began to share. "June, I made a huge mistake last week when I saw you so angry. I was more scared than angry, and I didn't know what to do! I yelled at you, and now I realize that I upset you more. I am so sorry, June, and I'm wondering if we could talk about a plan for what we can do together when we both feel our brains becoming hot and triggered."

We continued this conversation as we walked. I asked for her suggestions and ideas about what she could do at those times when she began to feel edgy and rough, and I wrote some of her ideas on a scrap of paper. She instantly related to "edgy and rough," words that describe sensations rather than feelings. I was sharing with her the languages of adversity, and I began to discuss the coping strategies that could be a part of her language of resiliency. I knew that by talking with her when our brains were feeling calm and by asking for her voice and choices, I was also building a relationship and subtly giving her experiences and ideas to ponder. It wasn't a solution or a fix, but I was helping to create an environment that would begin to feel much safer and offering her opportunities to notice when she began feeling edgy and rough. We were taking small steps on an untraveled path, but we both had some hope as we continued to test the choppy, unpredictable waters in the following days and weeks.

When we know better, we do better.

I wish I could write a happier ending about my experiences with June, but I cannot. Several weeks after this incident, June unexpectedly moved into another foster home and left the school. I didn't have an opportunity to say goodbye, and as I write these words, I'm left with a lump in my throat and feelings of concern, uncertainty, and hope.

We educators are much like our students in that we also need a safe place to do our work. We, too, need connection from those around us! When we feel felt, heard, and safe, our sense of purpose and agency improves and flourishes. A regulated and calm staff and school has a much better relational opportunity with students than a school that feels fragmented, censored, threatened, or filled with stress.

Dr. Dan Siegel, author, motivational speaker, and psychiatrist, explains an important relational skill inherent in all people called *emotional contagion*. We all seem to automatically sense another person's internal state of mind. This interconnectedness is based on the neurological connections from mirror neurons that activate when we experience actions or words from one another. When I watch a sad movie, I cry even though what I'm seeing isn't a part of my personal experience. We yawn when we observe yawning in others. These examples are the results of activated mirror neurons. In *Mindsight*, his most recent book, Dan Siegel explains: "The internal states of others—from joy and play to sadness and fear—directly affect our own state of mind. This contagion can even make us interpret unrelated events with an uncertain bias—so for example, after we've been around someone who is depressed, we interpret someone else's seriousness as sadness ... Our awareness of another person's state of mind depends on how well we know our own—we notice the belly fill with laughter at a party or with sadness at the funeral home. This is the main reason that people who are more aware of their bodies have been found to be more empathetic."[9]

In conclusion, when we are aware and open to our own feelings and emotions, the primary pathway for how well we resonate with others and sense their states of mind and accompanying feelings is wide open.

I once read that the vital difference between a good teacher and a superior teacher is the one who self-reflects. After reading the notions and research from Dr. Siegel, I feel this statement could lead to compelling positive changes in *how* we relate and therefore reach out to all students, but especially those who dare us to teach and trust them. Do we reflect and think about how we perceive the world? Do we transfer our own emotions subconsciously or consciously onto those who walk into our classrooms each day? I think these questions are worth thinking about as we examine and explore compassionate relational educator and student well-being inside our schools.

In my own life, I must listen deeply when I ask my students, family, or friends: *What can I do? How can I help you? What do you need?* Only when listening deeply am I able to observe and then understand the meaning of a response beyond the uttered words, inappropriate gestures, or angry behaviors. Forfeiting deep listening, I fall back to the ways of correction or coercion, rapidly searching for solutions and quick fixes. It is difficult to listen and then rest with the discomfort of not knowing. Sharing some of this discomfort with our students seeds an authentic trust and mutual respect.

Educator Resilience Strategies and Interventions

In this section, I will share strategies and practices that have the potential to calm and regulate our own nervous systems and dysregulated brain states as we interface with our colleagues and students each day. When I'm caring for myself even in the smallest of ways, my students and those around me benefit greatly because I can begin to approach them from a place of calm, relatable connection. In the Resource Section of this book, my co-instructor and graduate assistant Courtney Boyle created an eBook of regulation strategies for all educators to use when we have only a minute or two to regain our calm before addressing an escalating disagreement or power struggle. These regulatory strategies have been sectioned into three categories that align with brain function, including regulation, connection, and cortical strategies. We thank our graduate students at Butler University (cohort 4) for creating this list, and we hope you will all find it very helpful in attuning to your own self-care and well-being.

Language of Adversity and Resilience

This past year, I asked my graduate students, many of whom are educators, to reflect upon their languages of adversity and resiliency. Our languages of adversity are the repetitive words, sentences, or even nonverbal reactions that we habitually activate when we are feeling rough and upset. What are the words you constantly hear or repeat in your own life when experiences and people disappoint you, or when you disappoint or are angry with yourself? This is our language of adversity! There are patterns, repetitions, and often behaviors that we activate when feeling sad, lonely, anxious, frustrated, sharp, edgy, angry, or enraged. And when we hear the patterns from these words, we are indirectly asking for or needing experiences or activities that will provide a sense of relief and ease. Maybe our language is telling us we need more connection, touch, pressure, clarity, movement, some space or time, warmth, or coolness. Maybe we need to be heard with warm eye contact. Maybe we need alone time and some quiet. All behavior is communication! Recognizing and writing out or noting our own languages of adversity can be calming and comforting.

Following is a chart that one of my graduate students created after our Tuesday night class when the educators shared and explored their own languages of adversity and resilience, adding how they meet their students with these languages when emotional challenges are present. This exercise in recognizing our own languages of adversity and resilience is a powerful strategy in self-reflection and healing the pain and hurt that is often picked up during moments of conflict with children and youth, who are carrying their own pain and adversity.

Examples of Adversity and Resilience Languages

As a school leader or administrator, it is critical to model "connection" with your staff. Educator well-being is intimately tied to the workplace environment, and those in a leadership position have a powerful opportunity to deepen relationships with staff and educators. The following statements are examples of touch points—words to promote safe and secure attachments—which create compassionate leadership in so many ways. This is where brain-aligned relational discipline begins. When we as a staff become emotionally attuned and attentive to one another, our students will experience this emotional contagion as well. Imagine if we shared these statements with our students when we are feeling calm and regulated!

Language of Adversity Internal/External Verbal/Nonverbal	Language of Resilience Internal/External Verbal/Nonverbal	How Do You Meet the Student in Regulation?
I am quiet and reserved when I am upset.	When I speak through it, talk about it with those I trust, and process it, I can overcome it.	Talking with students when they are regulated is critical. Learn and know the signs of how their body, heart, and mind are presenting when they are feeling dysregulated. I am learning how each child calms down differently.
My neck becomes red and blotchy, and I am shorter with my words.	Connections and relationships with others. Allowing myself time to recharge when needed. I talk it out, sometimes with myself.	Opportunity to be present, listen, and work with at-risk students. With this opportunity, we can model effective strategies, work with students to create essential agreements, or at least components that they could accept, but only when they are calm.
I am quick to blame. "You're not listening!"	I can name what is going on with me. I can verbalize what is happening in my brain for my students.	I also need to establish students' own routine to follow when they are also feeling the stress and the adversity in the classroom.

Language of Adversity Internal/External Verbal/Nonverbal	Language of Resilience Internal/External Verbal/Nonverbal	How Do You Meet the Student in Regulation?
"I'm overwhelmed," "I'll figure this out," "I just need a minute," or I will just fall silent.	Taking time for myself. Getting on the treadmill helps with stress release.	Find out what works well when they are experiencing stress.
"You don't run the show here."	I invite my class to take deep breaths with me.	When they say, "I don't care," they may be really saying, "Nothing matters; whatever you say just adds to the troubles."
"It is what it is." I isolate myself.	Serenity Prayer	"I am in your corner."
I can't stop thinking about whatever it is that I'm stressed about.	I voice my feelings; modeling behavior which transfers to them and allows the classroom to be a safe place to display and work through feelings.	Front loading information; their best is my only expectation. Working through the really tough stuff together before expecting them to conquer it alone.
"You can't, you're not good enough to ..."	"I got this." "We got this." Modeling positive self-talk.	Touch points of connection with other adults who can regulate a student throughout the day.
My body tenses up and pulls in ... tight, tense, and contracted.	Is it a "true" stressor or perceived? Use tools from cognitive behavioral therapy. Yoga and setting big goals to help me feel successful.	Model behavior—get down on their level—meeting them in the brain state they are in. Be with them in their frustration.
Tension, anxiety, jabs to my self-worth.	Being gentle with myself and others. Gentleness is not permissiveness.	"I look into my children's eyes a little longer and hold tight to their hug a little longer when they are dysregulated."
Frustrated, exhausted.	Respond; before being dismissive, share.	Amygdala Reset Area, yoga, self-awareness.

CONNECTIONS OVER COMPLIANCE

Language of Adversity Internal/External Verbal/Nonverbal	Language of Resilience Internal/External Verbal/Nonverbal	How Do You Meet the Student in Regulation?
Anxiety and anger go hand in hand. Triggers are feeling left out, misunderstood, and dismissed. Knowing these is helpful.	Reach out; find help. We don't realize how much pain we may be in. Talk about behavior, talk about mental health, talk about behavior and the brain.	Observe, notice, go easy and slow. Consistency, caring, connection, and follow through.
Shut down, don't talk, not interacting.	Time and space. Solace in humor. Use more touch points with others so that I can talk about it.	Talking to students away from class about issues they face when they come to school. Create a plan with academic/emotional support.
"Are you kidding me?" "Here we go again!" "I don't have time for this!"	Breathe, don't let the new moment be confused with experience. Ask myself WHO AM I BEING and is this in alignment? What's missing; trust, partnership, and play. "You've got this!"	Staying curious about what makes a student "tick." Maintain calm, steady movements and tone. Partnering with a parent and demonstrating that I'm not giving up on the student.
Talking fast, pacing, then silence.	I'm more prepared for the adversity now. I can breathe, meditate, or color and use art in different ways.	We have to move to the tune and rhythm of the student, instead of moving to our own.
Short, shallow breaths, and I start to babble.	Learning about professional boundaries and saying no; stretch and breathe.	Give them space. Let them speak. Talk in calm, low voice. Sit beside them. Drawing a picture of your feelings and sensations.
"I just need a break." "I'm tired."	Holding weekends sacred. Sleep. Set boundaries, say no.	Classroom mantra, "We can do hard things," works well if someone says, "This is too hard." Spacing out work so it's manageable, and checking in more frequently with feedback that is neutral.
TIRED. TIRED. TIRED. TIRED.	Put less pressure on myself. 90-Second Rule. "I'm glad that feeling of anger is temporary!"	15-minute mindful sessions (magic carpet ride), yoga poses, coloring, breathing.

Language of Adversity Internal/External Verbal/Nonverbal	Language of Resilience Internal/External Verbal/Nonverbal	How Do You Meet the Student in Regulation?
Increased heart rate and ringing in ears. "Where are we going?" I look at glass half empty!	Understand that there are things in life I cannot plan or prepare for. Stay in the moment rather than worry.	Scheduled breaks in Amygdala Reset Room. In-class whole group movement and breathing. Take a step further to see data related to tracking focused attention practices and hopefully fewer nurse visits/calls to office.
Dissociation, internal expressions.	Deep breathing, what was my part? What are my triggers, how do I release them? Look to trusted friends, and professionals.	Adult/student interaction; looking at stillness to regulate vs. activity. Balance app on phone. Helper for younger grades.

Resilience Touch Points: Statements for Deepening Relationships With Staff and Students

- I respect you and trust you for who you are. There is nothing you could do to change that!

- I may have been asking of you what you are not comfortable sharing or doing. Please help me to understand.

- I will give you the space you need. That is important to me.

- I too feel rough on some days and have probably taken my own frustrations out on you. I am sorry. I am going to be very aware of my own feelings just as I have asked of you.

- It must feel confusing and overwhelming when there is so much asked of you.

- I am so sorry.

- What do you need?

- How can I help you?

- What can we do to make this better?

Remember to Breathe

Deep breaths and movement calm our stress response systems, lowering our heart rates, blood pressure, and respiration. Deep breathing on a regular basis is critical to positive emotion, clarity of thought, and emotional regulation. When we use breathing or focused attention practices to quiet the emotional center of our brains, we activate neural circuits in the brain that strengthen the flow of oxygen and glucose through the prefrontal cortex. Each day, make it a practice to breathe intentionally.

1. Two-minute stress release: Before falling asleep, first thing in the morning, or whenever you need it, take two minutes to breathe deeply. Place one hand on your chest and the other on your forehead. As you inhale, feel the pressure of your hands on your skin, and then exhale out a worry or concern that has recently taken up space in your brain. Each time you inhale and exhale, try to extend the exhale by two or three seconds. Reflecting on your two minutes, ask yourself: Can I personally change this worrisome experience or thought? How much of it is in my control? How much of it is out of my control?

2. The deep-dive breath: This is a kundalini yoga breath practice and visualization. Inhale for four counts, hold for four, and exhale slowly for four counts. You can increase the holding of breath by a few seconds once you find the rhythm of the exercise. As you rhythmically find this breath, each time you inhale imagine diving deeper into a pool of blue water. As you complete your last breath and exhale, imagine yourself floating to the surface, renewed and weightless.

3. Energizing breath: This one, also from kundalini yoga, may seem a little odd, but give it a try. Pant like a dog with your mouth open and your tongue out for 30 seconds, while trying to take three energizing pant-breaths per second. Then continue for another 30 seconds with your mouth closed as you take short belly breaths through your nose with one hand on the belly. After a full minute, switch to the deep-dive breathing above. This is an excellent technique to use before you walk into school. There are many health benefits to this yoga breath.[10]

4. Calming sound: The right sound can be very powerful for engaging a calm response. For example, I listen almost daily to a recording of Tibetan bowls and chimes to clear my mind. You can find this—or nature or water sounds, if you prefer—on YouTube. Any sound that you associate with a calm state of mind will work.

5. Space for reflection: In your office, classroom, or at home, create an area that's just right for your personal relaxation. Consider details such as furniture, pillows, lighting, pictures, a gratitude journal, music, art, and snacks. Make sure that you regularly relax in this special space for at least a few minutes. In your classroom, you might just have a plant or some flowers, some hand lotion, or your gratitude journal. Take a minute or two in this space for a few deep breaths, a sip of water, or writing down a thought or feeling. One benefit of creating this space is to model an intentional calming practice for your students.

6. Peer support: Partner with a colleague to share and reflect on a challenging day, hour, or week. Be present with your partner for 7 to 10 minutes two or three times a week, or as often as you both agree. In these few minutes together, practice validating what you're hearing from each other—listen to learn, not to respond. Ask one another a very important question and listen deeply to the answer: "What's most important to you in this situation?" As you listen, you begin to co-regulate, calming each other's stress response systems. In *Beyond Engagement*, Brady Wilson writes that when we feel attention being paid to us, our bodies produce more of the neurohormone oxytocin, which produces a sense of trust and bonding.[11]

I am closing this chapter with a letter that I've written from the heart. Every educator needs to acknowledge that they have embarked on a hero's journey, whether it's their first year in the classroom or their third decade of shaping students' lives. I want to honor the discovery that they make—or could be making—every day: although they are here to teach, they are also here to learn. It's an ongoing process that takes them from confusion to clarity, from vulnerability to empowerment, from the mystery of who their students are to the revelation of who they are as teachers. This process will repeat many times, and each time through, they need to recognize that they aren't just going in circles. They are ascending in an upward spiral!

This is my letter of love and hope to all of them—to all of you!

To My Pre-Service Educators and to All New and Seasoned Educators

I am writing this letter from grace, my own mistakes, life experiences, and the contrast that 30 years in education has taught me. As I write these words, our world is undergoing a very tumultuous, frightening, and unknown time with the coronavirus sweeping across our globe, creating a pandemic of disease, great fear, and unpredictability. We have only just begun to understand the ramifications of this virus, as schools have closed, businesses and communities are shutting down, retreating into an unknown landscape as millions of families and communities have more questions and fear than answers and hope.

Although the research has continuously shared the growing challenges of the mental and emotional health needs of our nation's youth, we are now layering this new viral adversity inside the fragility of the emotional and mental health challenges facing so many children, adolescents, educators, and families in this time!

I once thought that becoming a teacher meant that my expertise in the chosen or general subject matter would be assessed and revered no matter the time period, grade level, or educational institution. I once was taught that it took one effective teacher to change a school climate. I once thought that becoming a teacher meant that I would need to be the expert not only in the academic arena, but an expert in behaviors, discipline, and fixing what I deemed broken.

I was nervous about not being able to control my class, losing the power struggle especially on the days I was observed by administration. I once thought that when a student lashed out at me, I was ineffective, and they needed harsher consequences. I once thought my preparation in higher education prepared me for all the obstacles I would face in the classroom. I once thought that, faced with challenging days, I was the only one feeling it or experiencing it, so I needed to put on a strong face and armor up!

What I have learned, am learning, and want to share are these notions.

I am teaching a spirit pulsating with its own signature—my student. My agenda, beliefs, worries, and challenges are mine and not my student's. I am learning to respond to the sensations and feelings of my students without labeling, fixing, or adjusting in any way during the moment of intense conflict. I have found myself so conditioned to lecture, threaten, or demand respect through words that I have left my own brain and body state out of the relational equation. I am learning that relationships matter more than any technique, strategy, or practice I invoke. I am learning that discipline is meeting the student in their agenda and paying attention to mine! I am learning that I have held beliefs, values, and assumptions that I have not examined and have unintentionally projected those onto my students.

It is no surprise we have fallen into a myth of what teaching is or should be because so many of us have neglected our own inner landscape. Psychologist and author Dr. Shefali Tsabary shares these words about parenting, and I feel they are so appropriate for teachers. "How can we feel the beat of their hearts and the spirit within when we have unintentionally lost our inner compass? Our children (students) pay a heavy price when we lack consciousness. Over-indulged, over-medicated, and over-labeled, many of our students (children and adolescents) are unhappy, and despite our best intentions, we often unintentionally bind them to the emotional inheritance we received from our parents, unconsciously holding them to the legacy of all ancestors past. The nature of unconsciousness is such that until it's metabolized, it will seep through generation after generation. Only through awareness can the cycles of pain end in our families and in our schools."[12]

I have learned to pay attention to my thoughts, feelings, sensations, doubts, and fears. I have learned to try and calm my own heart and mind during chaos and conflict. I have learned that emotions are deeply contagious and that my perceptions can leak into every student I sit beside. I am learning that teaching, like parenting, is not a science but a complex relational art form that is constantly moving, changing, and allowing us to see conflicts as powerful moments of growth for both teacher and student. I am learning that no matter the age of a human being, our perceived self-images are limitless, and it is often our expectations and childhood experiences that hold us captive to these inaccurate inner visions of ourselves!

In this time of teaching and learning, am I allowing myself the grace to learn more about myself with every encounter with a student?

In this time, can I challenge and *be* with my own fears and doubts, knowing that every relationship with a student is sacred and teaching me more about myself?

＊ All children are born with a pure and loving essence, and this new lens for discipline calls us to attune and attend to their *being* and not just their doing.

＊ I want to thank myself for showing up every day with an open heart and mind, as I thank my students for being a part of this classroom.

＊ I want to thank my students every day for teaching me no matter how difficult the lesson.

＊ I am learning that when I begin to trust the essence of every student, they begin to see their inner worlds as worthy and good, no matter what happens on the outside.

＊ I am learning to acknowledge the smallest of smiles, gestures, showing up in class, walking in the door each day as a miraculous gift that I will hold in my mind and heart, knowing that the teaching and learning process is an evolutionary journey!

Conclusion

Research in the social neurosciences has demonstrated how emotions and learning are intimately connected and processed in the brain. The story of the educator is about emotions and cognition. The message from social and affective neuroscience is clear: No longer can we focus solely on the individual student's academic level to analyze effective strategies for classroom instruction, discipline, and behaviors. Teachers and students interact and learn from one another in ways that cannot be understood by examining only the cold cognitive aspects of academic skills. When we look inward and explore the adversities, obstacles, passions, and life processes of our own lives, we model this reflective practice for our students and their pain-filled experiences. It is in this space of self-reflection that we might subtly alter how we present ourselves inside our classrooms, allowing us to return to the joy of teaching. This is operationalized relational discipline.

In the Resource Section of this book, you'll find the print version of an eBook of brain-aligned strategies for educators created by educators. Our graduate students in the applied educational neuroscience cohort created this book of approximately one-minute practices and strategies to implement on the spot and in the moment. I hope that you will not only enjoy these regulation strategies, but that you will share some of these with students, modeling the practices that calm all brains for learning, teaching, and leadership. I would encourage you to build three or four of these regulation practices into a routine that you can implement in moments when you begin to feel agitated, rough, and moving toward a dysregulated state.

I love these words from Dr. Mona Delahooke: "Our emotional tone is the 'raw material' that allows us to help children with behavioral challenges. This raw material that we each embrace is transmitted through our body language. When we feel safe, we have soft eyes, a prosodic voice, and a relaxed posture."[13]

I'd like to finish with this thought: Where you place your eyes and mind is what you will see and experience.

CHAPTER 3

The Masks of Pain and the Power of Regulation

"When you finally learn a person's behavior has more to do with their own internal struggle than it ever did with you ... you learn grace."
ALLISON AARS

I open this chapter with a very important thought to keep in mind when beginning this journey through a brain-aligned pathway for relational discipline: *There is no definitive code or specific fix for behavior management.*

Trauma-responsive schools are places that have collectively shifted their perceptions of discipline; and at the core of this shift, co-regulation and the educator's brain and body state are the critical change agents. Co-regulation is a relational dyadic exchange that exudes feelings of safety and belonging. Co-regulation requires the adult to maintain a calm brain during the conflict. It's essential as we begin to drain off the negative emotion from the child by intentionally using our regulated tone of voice, our gentle facial expression, and our open posture as nonverbal invitations for the young person to calm their own nervous system. We must constantly remember that emotions are always contagious.

Trauma-responsive schools and districts must begin to understand that most negative behaviors can be signals of distress, and that many of our most challenging behaviors represent the body's response to stress. In the words of psychologist Dr. Mona Delahooke, "When we see a behavior that is problematic or confusing, the first question we should ask isn't 'How do we get rid of it?' but rather, 'What is this telling us about the child?'"[1] To be truly trauma-responsive schools, we must implement discipline protocols that focus on the well-being of our educators, along with relational brain-aligned practices that are preventive, occurring within our procedures, rituals, and routines with staff and students. These schools are moving away from traditional discipline and behavior management models with the understanding that, while these traditional programs might bring short-term compliance and obedience, they aren't diving into the primary pain of student and educator brain states. The traditional model asks, "What is wrong with this student?" However, the trauma-responsive model asks, "What's happening here, and how does this student interpret it?"

Troubled children and youth often come to our classrooms carrying pain-based behaviors, mistrust, and a brain that is swimming in toxic levels of stress. When stress is present, our perceptions are deeply affected. Disruptive behaviors are often symptoms or signals of a student's distorted perceptions, thoughts, and feelings arising from great fear masked by anger. *Brain-aligned discipline can help our students reconstruct their inner map, integrating a sense of trust and confidence in their future.*

Physician and author Dr. Bessel Van Der Kolk shares that our most intimate sense of self is created in our minute-by-minute interactions with our caregivers, and that feelings of trust and safety do not occur overnight.[2] These exchanges incrementally build security. Many of our children and adolescents walk into our schools not trusting adults and perceiving most environments to be unsafe and threatening. Why? Because these youth may have experienced relationships, environments, and events that have been chronically unpredictable, and because the adults that they need to trust and rely on for protection and comfort haven't been emotionally available and consistent because of their own unmet emotional, mental, and social needs.

Children are always acting out their attachment dynamics! If we want to discipline our children and adolescents from a place of connection and trust, then we must invite them to be disciples, as described in Chapter 1. A disciple is not someone who's afraid of you, but rather someone who wants to follow you, cares for you, desires to walk beside you, and is consistently present.

B.F. Skinner observed that discipline has become synonymous with punishment, when in fact discipline is the opposite of punishment! When we isolate, timeout, and threaten to withdraw our presence from children and youth who carry in significant trauma and adversity, our students learn that the relationship is conditional, and the cycle of mistrust begins again. Many of our most troubled students are relationship resistant, a resistance that has been learned over time when children have had their biological instinct to attach thwarted again and again. As educators, we too bring in a history of developmental experiences that may be filled with trauma and adversity, triggering our own feelings of powerlessness, loss, and fear. What happens when an educator without self-reflection and awareness is confronted with the behavior from a disconnected and disruptive student? The authors of *Conflict in the Classroom* explain, "When a teacher and a disconnected student exchange words during a conflict, a surplus of hot and hollow words and talk occurs. Disconnected students can zap the very core of a teacher's energy and are a major contributor to professional stress."[3]

I love the analogy of a cell phone: When the phone is charged, it connects you with others, yet this charge won't last without frequent visits to a power source. Co-regulation calls us to recharge through self-reflection, and to be self-aware by implementing the power source of connection within our own brain and body state. Our children and youth create feelings and sensations within us, as human brain states are contagious. If you want to know how a child is feeling, tap into your own emotions and sensations. When we feel charged and replenished, we develop the capacity to listen deeply and validate our students, peeling back the layers of their disruptive or shut-down behavior to recognize their underlying need. How? The following questions, shared from the authors of *Conflict in the Classroom*, can be helpful as we shift from the perceptions of contagious anger to the perceptions of curiosity and wonder. Maybe the students who cause a teacher the most discomfort are the teacher's most reliable source of insight, awareness, and change.[4]

1. Why is this student upsetting me?
2. Why is it so easy for this student to push my emotional buttons?
3. Why do I anger so quickly?
4. Does my value system interfere in this situation?
5. What are the hidden strengths I am not seeing and supporting from this student?[5]

Don't ask why the behavior.
Ask, why the pain?
He's Violent, you say.
Perhaps. But imagine what it takes for a child to strike an adult—his only
source of survival. Imagine the depth of terror behind this bravado—
Imagine the depth of hurt.

L. TOBIN

Trauma-responsive, brain-aligned schools understand that every child's greatest innate resource is his or her ability to emotionally regulate, but this is a skill that is learned much like math or reading. This skill needs patterned, repetitive experiences and opportunities to grow and develop. Research shows that securely attached infants and children develop the ability to emotionally regulate, while children who lack physical and emotional attunement are vulnerable to shutting down and turning off the direct feedback from their bodies, the seat of pleasure, purpose, and direction.[6] Understanding how adversities affect the developing brain and body can gently rewire our own perceptions of discipline.

What is regulation? Although there are many definitions, I am defining regulation as one's ability to tolerate stress, and to experience stress within an individual's window of tolerance. When a child can begin to tolerate bits and pieces of stressful situations, we are gradually increasing his or her capacity to create a pause instead of going directly to an explosive reaction. Negative behaviors grab our attention, and we often don't receive any type of a distress signal before that behavior is activated! In our own rising anger, we forget that there could be accumulated thoughts, feelings, and perceptions justifying these behaviors to the student. Most behaviors are predictable if we begin to look at the patterns of triggering situations, prompts, conditions, and people.

Traditional punishment with emotionally challenged children and youth often escalates power struggles and activates conflict cycles, generating an increased stress response in the brain and body. Punishment is traditionally implemented as an attempt to force compliance. Many current school discipline procedures are forms of punishment that work best with the students who need them the least. With our most difficult students, the current discipline models don't change their behavior, often escalating the challenges and problems by unintentionally reactivating those students' stress response systems.

Discipline, unlike punishment, is proactive and begins before there are problems or challenges. It means seeing conflict as an opportunity to problem solve. Discipline provides guidance, focuses on prevention, enhances communication, models respect, and embraces natural consequences. It teaches fairness, responsibility, life skills, and problem solving. Why change the way that we've always disciplined/punished? As stated in the opening chapter, this model is not working! If you disagree, take a hard, long look at your own discipline data. What patterns and gaps do you see? Gaps are actually a good starting point, as they can help us identify the work that needs to be done when we are creating the disciplinary and relational shifts that begin to rewire our own perceptions along this new pathway of brain-aligned relational discipline.

We in the educational community have been constantly writing, publishing, reading, and debating behavior management for the past 30 plus years, and we still have not changed the deeply flawed and pervasive idea that discipline and punishment are linked. Referring back to the Children's Defense Fund findings[7] mentioned in Chapter 1, regarding the alarming daily numbers for corporal punishment, arrests, dropouts, and suspensions in U.S. public schools, it's clear that many thousands of children are suffering because of institutional practices that fail to address their actual needs. Trauma and adversity change the nervous system, the developing brain, and almost every physiological system in our bodies. Punishing children and adolescents for how they express their pain is cruelly misinformed!

Although this sounds bleak and hopeless, research shares the good news of how resiliency can have the last word.

Our brains act like muscles, but they are organs that require social experiences. They are experience-dependent and require us to seek social connections and attachment through touch, pressure, comfort, warm eye contact, soft melodic prosody, and rhythm. These sensory attachment experiences are often nonverbal communications with an emotionally available, consistent, and present caregiver throughout infancy and early childhood, and are the building blocks for creating secure attachments in early and later in life by providing repetitive opportunities for the developing skills of self and emotional regulation. Dr. Allan Schore describes brain development in this way: "The research indicates that the mother functions in the short term as a regulator of the child's homeostatic alterations and in the long term influences the child's capacity to cope adaptively with the social-emotional environment. Although the mother initially provides an external regulating mechanism for the infant's immature neurobiological processes, by the end of the first postnatal year, the infant begins to develop the self-regulating behaviors through the dyadic emotional relationship with the caregiver."[8]

In accord with these conceptualizations, a National Institute of Child and Human Development study on the mother-child relationship and affect dysregulation concluded, "Self-regulation in infancy is best conceptualized as a quality of the infant-caregiver relationship, rather than a characteristic of the infant alone."[9] The authors cited a large body of data that "emphasize the importance of the child's relationship with the primary caregiver as central to understanding the developmental processes leading from early affective arousal and attention control to later functioning. Children's inability to control negative affect in early interactions with their caregivers may forecast continuing difficulties with affective regulation across multiple contexts."[10] When the child's developing sensory systems are continuously met with unpredictable chronic adversity, this also leads to the dysregulation of the stress hormones which can cause inflammation in the developing brain that may actually shrink the size of the brain's developing hippocampus, an area responsible for learning, emotion, and memory, while intimately affecting our immune, hormonal, and perceptual systems, and later our behavior and cognition.[11] When children and youth carry to school four or more adversities, they are 32.6 times more likely to experience academic and behavioral challenges.[12] In a recent presentation from Dr. Nadine Burke Harris, we learned that only three percent of children with no adverse childhood experiences show learning and behavior problems while children with four or more adversities has grown to 51%![13]

The brain develops from the bottom up. The brain stem, the seat of our autonomic functions, is the only part that is fully developed at birth. The rest of the developing brain is waiting for experiences to assist in its growth and maturation, and because the brain stem is also the area that initiates our stress response systems, this area must be regulated and integrated for children and adolescents to feel safe and calm. Dr. Bruce Perry shares, "People with developmental trauma can start to feel so threatened that they rapidly move into a fight-flight alarm state, and the higher parts of the brain shut down. First the stress chemicals shut down their frontal cortex (thinking brain). Now they physically cannot think. Next the emotional brain (limbic brain) shuts down. They have attachment trauma, so people feel threatened and unsafe, prohibiting reward from emotional or relational interaction. The only part of the brain left functioning is the most primitive: the brain stem, and this area is known as Grand Central Station as it is where we begin to feel a sense of safety or danger, activating our heart rates, respiration, and blood pressure."[14]

All behaviors are communicating and signaling unmet needs, and most of our chronic behavioral challenges are regulation challenges, which are also physiological challenges. The brain stem and lower brain regions are alarming the brain and body to threats 24 hours a day, even when there are none. Brains in this survival state do not attend to consequences, rewards, promises, logic, control, long term goals, or even stickers! Why? Because adversity and chronic stress take the logical thinking part of the brain offline. Our ability to create a pause, emotionally regulate, plan ahead, problem solve, and think through choices is not accessible to a brain drowning in cortisol and adrenaline. Children who walk into our schools rough and dys-regulated are not capable of accessing the executive functions located in the cortex—functions that they need for doing school or doing life!

If we want a child to access the cortical/thinking part of the brain, the brain stem and the brain's limbic functions need to be regulated and integrated. This development begins in the early years when an emotionally present caregiver is mitigating and regulating the en-vironmental stimuli that bombard our brains each moment of each day. Infants and children require predictable and consistent envi-ronments with emotionally available caregivers, and if the attachment processes are disrupted by early chronic stress, we can see behaviors that look disrespectful, oppositional, shut down, apathetic and often aggressive. These pain-based behaviors will not go away with tradi-tional punishment, but will begin to lessen and shift when we meet students' needs with brain development practices.

The challenge for all of us making this perceptual shift will be to understand that regulating an anxious and angry brain is vastly different from rewarding negative behavior. These two processes can appear the same, but when we look beneath the hood of behaviors, we see that regulation ad-dresses and activates the regions of the brain that are showing up in the behaviors. Dr. Bruce Perry refers to this practice as specificity. To change neural circuits in the brain, we need to activate those brain regions. Dr. Perry likens this practice to learning how to play the piano. We can't learn this instrument by reading a book or watching a video. We must put our fingers on the keys, and this is exactly what we need to do when calming the irritated, anxious, or shut-down brain of a student. We meet this student in their fight-flight or immobilized response, modeling the interventions and tools of so-matosensory processing using breath, rhythm, movement, or other sensations that comfort and relax the survival brain state.[15] Many of our students may walk into our schools with a much lower emo-tional/developmental age than their chronological age because of their accumulated adversities, which can be frustrating for educators with 30-plus students who have an overwhelming variety of social and emotional needs.

I previously shared that discipline, unlike punishment, is proactive and begins before there are problems. Through this new lens, we begin seeing conflict as an opportunity to problem solve. In the following pages, I will discuss specific practices that assist in the stress response capabilities we have. In a brain-aligned model of discipline, we must teach the behaviors we want to see, laying the groundwork for preventive systems and brain-aligned practices and strategies. These strategies and practices are built into our procedures, routines, and rituals throughout the day. According to Perry, "The more developmentally delayed children are, the more desperately they need social interactions and repetitive regulatory experiences that meet them in their brain's development."[16]

PREVENTIVE BRAIN-ALIGNED DISCIPLINE STRATEGIES

Preventive brain-aligned discipline systems are taught as procedures and routines. They are collaborative and filled with choice. Their purpose is to create a sustainable behavioral change, not just compliance or obedience for a short period of time. As we begin to explore our rituals, procedures, routines, and transitions in the classrooms, below are a few conditions and beliefs that I feel are essential to explore and discuss.

1. Although it is important to acknowledge the emotional and mental challenges of our students, we need to acknowledge the students' strengths, interests, and passions as we meet them in emotional brain development.

2. Under stress, emotionally challenged students will behave in ways that can often reflect an emotional age that is half their chronological age. In a survival brain state, we are more apt to fight, run, yell, threaten, and show up with behaviors that look disrespectful, disruptive, and sometimes volatile.

3. Emotional contagion can occur so quickly with students in conflict. We must be prepared in our own brain and body states when these conflicts arise. Before we go directly to discussing consequences, speaking words that will be hard to take back, or verbally reacting in any way, co-regulation requires us to drain off the child's negative emotion with our own calm state. A one-moment soothing and gentle nonverbal exchange can calm an anxious brain.

4. We should expect and accept some normal amount of hostility, irritation, and resistance when we begin the process of replacing the student's pain-based reactions with behaviors that are aligned to what he or she needs. We may be very good at stopping the behaviors we cannot tolerate, but replacing and learning new behaviors is a process and can be an endurance event. It takes a regulated adult providing patterned repetitive experiences to begin activating these sustainable behavioral changes. I am always exploring and discussing how every educator brings his or her developmental history into the building and classroom each day. When I am feeling rough, I need to acknowledge how these dys-regulated sensations and feelings within me could impact the feelings and behaviors of my most vulnerable students.

Where do we begin as we look at regulatory practices built into our procedures, morning meetings, bell work, and routines creating an environment of predictability which promotes safety and trust?

A. We teach students about their neuroanatomy, so they can understand what happens in their brains when they become stressed, angry, or anxious. When we begin to understand how our brain's structure and function affect how we feel, behave, and think, we begin to feel relieved and empowered. We are very intentional about using the language of science with our staff and students. The science is empowering and repeatedly addresses activated stress states. We explain how trauma and adversity are not disorders, dysfunctions, or disturbances, but are instead a reordering of neural networks in the brain's structures.

B. During morning meetings or whole-class time, we spend a few minutes discussing and exploring the prefrontal cortex, the amygdala, and neuroplasticity with students. We identify and create lists of our emotional triggers and coping strategies, and we teach students to use their breath, movement, or any sensation that feels calming and comforting in times of heightened negative emotion. Students can create a personal routine of regulatory strategies that is theirs to implement when they begin to feel anxious, irritated, angry, or simply rough. We help our students create this routine ahead of time and model how to use these regulatory strategies. At the end of this chapter, you'll find a chart of strategies that address safety and connection. Students and educators can add to this list and share with one another.

Body Reflection

We are learning more each day that the best way we can care for our children and students is to care for ourselves. We begin with noticing and naming the sensations we experience in our bodies as trauma and adversity become lodged and embodied in areas where we feel tight, tense, knotted up, numb, empty, brittle, etc. Therapist Bonnie Badenoch shares that we encode 11 million bits of information per second implicitly, while we store only 6 to 50 bits of information consciously.[17] These 11 million bits of unconsciously embodied experiences are living within us, and we struggle without conscious awareness to integrate a felt sense of experiences. Fortunately, our own bodies can be our greatest teachers, so when we're able to share and name these sensations, they begin to lessen. A *body reflection* begins with a body scan during which we allow ourselves to notice how we are experiencing these sensations. We have traditionally talked about self-reflection and self-awareness through the written word or conversation, but in times of heightened adversity, it becomes more important to delve deeper into where these experiences are held and buried.

We can identify and draw household objects to help us visualize and reflect on our inner sensations of experiences. For example, a bar of soap might show that we feel refreshed, a knotted rope might show tension and tightness, or an empty container might show how depleted we feel. Creating a simple or even playful representation of these ideas can help us better understand how we are experiencing these moments of great anxiety or discomfort. This is a wonderful routine that we can also do a few times each day as a check-in with our children and youth.

C.   Have we checked in with the student to see if they can identify one or two adults in the building whom they trust and to whom they would like to reach out when they begin to feel dysregulated and emotional? Can this adult provide a space or place where the student can reset their brain state, regrouping and calming their stress response systems? Are we teaching these strategies as procedures ahead of a time when a student needs to regulate away from the class? This adult connection can be part of the routine of strategies that I previously addressed. These regulatory strategies, like traditional procedures, are taught in a neutral time and are a part of our brain-aligned procedures and routines. Students will need opportunities for repetition in implementing these regulatory strategies, as this is a process and their current habits of reactive and reflexive responses won't change overnight. These regulatory practices are healthy for all students!

D.   Could your school create an area where both teachers and students can go when they need to reset their emotional state? This area could be stocked with paper, markers, crayons, water, soft music and lighting, a jump rope, a stationary bike, lavender scented cotton balls, and jars for affirmations or worries, along with a rocking chair, weighted blanket, neck massager, or other body/sensory interventions. Students will need to be taught ahead of time how to use these Amygdala Reset Areas, with an understanding of their purpose, the duration of time spent there, and the brain's ability to refocus on preparing to return to classwork.

These Amygdala First Aid Stations and Amygdala Reset Areas are modeled and implemented in celebratory moments and not just regulatory times, because if we are not intentional in how we roll these into our procedures, they may become punitive and equate to time-out areas. (You can learn more about Amygdala Reset Stations in the Resource Section.)

As previously stated (and worth repeating), the most challenging perceptual shift for the adults as we embark upon this new brain-aligned discipline journey will be understanding the differences between regulation and rewarding negative behaviors. Children who have not adequately experienced kindness, empathy, and emotional regulation may not have the neuronal circuits in their brain's architecture for these social and emotional skills. These developing functions and skills need actual experiences to shape new circuits for new brain functions, which will eventually produce sustainable behavioral changes and not just behaviors originating from compliance or conformity.

Our first step is exploring the sensory, emotional, and attachment needs of this child or adolescent. Behaviors of children and adolescents are observable but aren't always explained or understood from our perspective! Dr. Mona Delahooke describes it this way: "Behavior is the observable response to our internal and external experiences. Teaching works so very well when the student is neurodevelopmentally ready to be taught, but the foundation for helping children and youth is created through the experiences of love, safety, trust, and connection in relationships."[18]

In the world of traditional education, we create behavior plans, functional behavioral analyses, behavior charts, and point and level systems based on the outward signals of disruptions and defiance, which usually involve talking, reasoning, consequences and logic. These behavioral plans and programs do not work with our roughest students, because those students aren't functioning in areas of the brain where we problem solve, pause, regulate, and reason. Most chronic negative behaviors originate from lower brain regions, which are survival states. In these survival states, we feel and sense everything around us, scanning every inch of our environments for predator-like threats, unfamiliarity, and anything that feels unsafe or threatening to our bodies and brains. These are reflexive and reactive responses, and in this survival state, we need sensory repairing interventions. Please remember that our behaviors are always adaptations to our environments and our physiological states, so just as the brain develops from bottom up and inside out, we must shift our behavioral approaches to meet the student in their current developmental brain state.

I have developed a tool that allows us to peel back the layers of a repetitious negative behavior so that we can explore what this behavior is communicating to us. The student's physiological state is communicating the signal or behavior, so we address sensory challenges, where the behavior is mostly occurring, what experiences feel threatening, what experiences feel safe, and what tasks or academic assignments feel overwhelming to the student's stress response system.

A SECRET

What?

This tool is designed for students who are struggling with regulation issues due to an over- or under-responsive sensory system which may have been compromised and impaired by adversities and trauma in the developing years. The acronym **A SECRET** was originally created for parents by Dr. Lucy Jane Miller, founder and clinical director of the STAR Center and the research director of the Sensory Processing Disorder Foundation. This template can serve as a road map for both educators and parents as we move to the core issues underlying the behavior challenges. According to Dr. Miller, "A SECRET provides a simplified way to remember problem-solving fundamentals in everyday life."[19] I have adapted and modified this tool for students who are struggling emotionally and socially in our classrooms and schools. These are the students who need us to meet them in brain development through exploring their sensory and emotional systems, relationships, cultures, tasks, and environments. This tool and application are intended for a collaborative gathering of educators and students exploring and preparing for moments of dysregulation before they occur.

(The acronym A SECRET is not a secret! It stands for Attention, Sensory, Emotions, Culture, Relationships, Environment/Experiences, and Tasks.)

Why?

Traditional discipline is reactionary. We react immediately when a problem is presented, a reflexive approach that hasn't been beneficial with our most dysregulated and anxious children and youth. When implementing this **A SECRET** tool, we act as a pre-op team. That's a useful medical analogy, because prior to surgeries and medical interventions, physicians and staff gather to make sure that all required personnel, instrumentation, directions, and plans are present and in order. **A SECRET** acts in much the same way. We congregate to be preventive and consistent in our brain-aligned strategies to meet the child or adolescent in regulatory and connective practices.

To use this tool, we need to deeply understand that trauma and adversities are held in our bodies, not just in our thoughts and feelings. Trauma affects our physiological and unconscious need for safety, which can manifest in an increased sensitivity to normal sensory input, reprogramming a young person's stress response systems to become sensitized to the world around them, and affecting their relationships, tasks, attention, emotions, feelings, and thoughts. Our perceptual, hormonal, endocrine, and stress response systems can be impacted by these past experiences—as well as experiences that are chronic and continuous. Not only does the body prepare to go into a fight-flight response, but when feeling terrorized or immobile, our bodies and brains can shut down, moving us into a protective dissociated response where we can become under-responsive to the sensory world around us.

Almost all behavior arises out of a stress response state and shapes the brain state of the child or adolescent. We begin to see patterns and repetitions of responses that can inform and teach us each student's needs. The brain stem, which is at the heart of the autonomic system, regulates the automatic responses to a person's inner world and outer world through heart rate, respiration, blood pressure, sleep rhythms, etc. In a state of dysregulation, our responses become primitive as we read facial expressions, postures, and most importantly, tone of voices within a very threatening context.

How?

A **SECRET** is a template, providing a multitude of ways that we can adjust, modify, and accommodate each student's needs to ensure feelings of safety and connection. As you begin using this tool, keep a small notebook of experiences, environments, persons, and times throughout the day that can trigger and unintentionally dysregulate behavior. Next is a list of questions to assist in understanding sensory preferences, experiences, and persons or relationships that will be helpful to access during challenging moments when behaviors go awry. Following the initial template are additional questions to think about when addressing under-responsive and/or dissociative behaviors, along with a survey designed to elicit student input. This tool represents discipline that is relational, preventive, and brain-aligned. Much like grade-level teams, RTI teams, and academic departments, we gather to explore the below areas of disruptions and needs, and to plan for academic practices and student success by creating a roadmap that will assist us in collaborative problem solving ahead of the emotional challenges.

Redirecting attention is a very beneficial practice for calming the child before they reach the point of no return. By creating a collaborative list of what we notice, we can dampen down the agitated behaviors, which is a critical starting point for replacing them with the behaviors we want to see. We begin to be intentional about creating experiences that align with the people, activities, interests, and things that the child or adolescent enjoys and deems comforting or soothing.

A SECRET: Guiding Questions

A = Attention

- What experiences, things, people, or processes hold this student's attention?
- What types of attention feel good to them?
- What do they enjoy?
- What experiences, interests, and activities do they discuss often?

S = Sensory

What sensory needs is the behavior communicating? Below are a few examples of sensory agitations that might be interfering with behaviors and learning. These troubling sensations that we often observe as "patterns." When we are aware of these patterns, we can substitute troubling sensations with repairing sensations to calm the stress response systems so that we can access the areas in the brain needed for learning and regulation. These are just a few examples—and you can probably think of many more to add.

Troubling Sensations	Repairing Sensations
Yelling, loud noises, abrupt movements, harsh tones	Headphones, quiet area, more predictable transitions
Crowds, too many people	Space, a buddy, create chunks of time in large spaces
Sitting still	Movement
Hot, angry, sweaty	Ice pack, portable fan, a walk outside
Jumpy, irritated	Rhythm, weighted pad, an errand, stationary bike, lifting heavy objects or weights

E = Emotions

In this section, we look deeply for the emotions that might be masked, patterned, or repetitive. We know that anger is sometimes the bodyguard of fear, and that beneath disruptive, aggressive, or volatile outbursts, there is fear and anxiety. Below are the core feelings followed by ways to connect or regulate with the student. Many of these connection strategies we call "touch points."

What are the dominant emotions beneath the behavior, and what can we provide?

Anger/Irritated

Validate: Validation, a calming and brain-aligned discipline strategy, is part of the co-regulation process that models for the student an adult who is listening to learn and creating empathic resonance. Examples of validation are: "You must feel so angry." "I cannot imagine how frustrating this must feel." I will share more examples in the upcoming chapter as we discuss how to strengthen relationships through moment-to-moment connections.

Notice Me: By noticing new shoes, a new haircut, a smile, tears, some shared music, or any other personal detail, we're saying to the student, "I see you and I am right here." Noticing is not praising or encouraging. It's a way to create two seconds of being present with the students.

More Space, Less Talking: Many times when we begin to feel angry or irritated, we just need to be left alone with a little space and some time. This is true for any of us. We need to find some emotional and physical distance from the event or circumstance that elevated our emotions. Giving consequences, nagging, lecturing, or using words in the heat of the moment only escalates everyone and does not change behaviors. I so wish that I had known this truth years ago as a mom and an educator.

Sad: As appropriate to the situation (because it's critical for educators to respect personal boundaries), we might respond with or encourage touch, connection, warmth, pressure, or offers of service. Some examples are: "What do you need?" "How can I help?" "What can we do to make this better?"

Edgy: We can address edginess with encouraging deep breaths or movement, or Focused Attention Practices that use breath, taste, visualization, or sound. (Focused Attention Practices are included in the Resource Section in this book.)

Worried: We can address worry by validating the student's concerns. We can encourage them to create art through drawing, coloring, molding with clay, doodling, or sketching. We might also offer the options of journaling, writing a letter to someone they trust, or visiting a trusted adult in the building who is available to connect with them during moments of emotional distress.

Anxious: Students can benefit from exploring their anxieties through journaling, as described above. They can also be introduced to Focused Attention Practice or EFT practices.

According to my colleague Dr. Amy Gaesser, Emotional Freedom Technique (EFT), also known as Tapping, is "an emerging research-based intervention that has been found to be an effective stress and anxiety management tool for students and school personnel. This is an acupoint stimulation that has been linked to regulation of activity in the brain's limbic system, which is our brain's emotional center and is connected to our stress response systems."[20] Dr. Gaesser adds, "This technique is in its infancy within the school settings, but the studies are promising, and with proper training, school personnel report that it is most beneficial to use EFT for two to four weeks to be become comfortable with the techniques, to feel competent, and we encourage educators to use this anxiety-reducing technique on themselves for added confidence and support."[21] EFT is another way to use movement, breath, and a reframing of negative emotions that is preventive and can become a class ritual or procedure each day or a few times a day. We will share resources for this in the Resource Section of the book.

C = Culture

Where and when is the behavior occurring? The timing and place of a specific behavior often shows up in patterns throughout a day or week. When we are intentional about looking beneath the behavior and addressing the root of this signal, we can often create interventions or practices that lessen the emotional pain that plays out in specific actions, words, or repetitive patterns. The below questions will help us to determine what we can shift in the environment to address these emotional challenges.

- Was the behavior activated or triggered in the cafeteria, hallway, recess, bathroom, classroom, or school bus?
- What does the student need? (A different space, less noise, improved smells, etc.)
- Does student need a different adult or a different relationship with the adult currently in charge?
- Does the student need different arrangements of classrooms, time, or space?

R = Relationships

Relationships create healthy brain development and nervous systems that are calm and regulated. When an adult is emotionally available, consistent, and present, this interpersonal invention can damp down the stress response systems that have been accessing the higher cortical areas of the brain. This gives the student space to think, problem solve, emotionally regulate, pause, pay attention, and hold memories.

Who does the student trust? Who does the student need? If that adult is unavailable in the moments of distress, I suggest a phone call or text, drawing a picture, writing a letter, and preparing to send it.

E = Environment/Experiences

What is happening in the environment to activate the growing stress? This question applies to both the student's internal and external environment. Dr. Stephen Porges, neuroscientist, author, and creator of the Polyvagal Theory, coined the term **neuroception**, referring to how each individual scans for and detects, often without conscious awareness, cues of safety or danger in their surroundings and how each of us senses our world internally. Dr. Porges describes neuroception as a neural process that enables humans and other mammals to engage in social behaviors by distinguishing safe from dangerous contexts. Neuroception is proposed as a plausible mechanism mediating both the expression and the disruption of positive social behavior, emotion regulation, and visceral homeostasis.[22] We can use the following set of questions to help us determine a student's neuroceptive state.

1. Is the child or adolescent experiencing a lack of structure, routine, predictability, or rituals?
2. Do we need to provide more predictable practices in the mornings or afternoons, or during transition times?
3. Who does the student need? Are there adults or other students who provide a sense of calm and ease for this student?
4. What experiences could we provide to calm and regulate this child or adolescent?
5. What does the student need in the environment? A different place to work? Co-regulation? A routine of three regulation practices built into the time of day or specific moment when we notice a pattern of repetitive disruptions or distress?

T = Task

Tasks can be thought of as the required academic work in school, and many students act out, flee, or shut down when the work feels too difficult, too complicated, too tedious, and too overwhelming. We know that children and youth will always choose to look misbehaved before they look stupid in front of their peers. When we are experiencing chronic adversity and our stress response systems are activated, the brain's prefrontal cortex goes offline, and we are unable to pay attention, problem solve, use our memory reliably, and plan for goals. What can we do? Below are a few questions that are helpful to ask as a team, individually, or with parents and preferably the students in a time when everyone who is collaborating feels calm and regulated.

1. What work feels overwhelming?
2. Is it difficult to get started?
3. Is it difficult staying focused? Is to too easy to be distracted?
4. What can we do with these challenging tasks?

We can begin by breaking the task into smaller chunks to create feelings of success by giving shorter assignments, offering frequent feedback, and initiating regular check-ins. We can gradually present the student with more challenging tasks once he or she has mastered a challenging section of an assignment or completed two problems in a reasonable amount of time. We can also rearrange the timing of an assignment with constant feedback and validation.

A significant aspect of this strategy is the inclusion of student feedback and input as part of the preventive brain-aligned discipline protocol. Below is a list of possible questions for garnering helpful information from the student's perspective, feelings, and thoughts.

1. What activities and learning do you like the most?
2. What are two topics you would love to learn about?
3. What would be the perfect classroom, lunchroom, hallway, and recess yard? What would those areas look, smell, feel, and sound like? Design your own special school areas with all the colors, sounds, tastes, and activities that you'd love to have there.
4. What upsets you the most when you are at school?
5. What makes you the happiest at school?
6. Who are the people you trust and like to hang out with at school?
7. Who are the people that upset you at school?

8. Name two activities or things that happen in school that make you angry. How would you change those?
9. What makes you feel peaceful and calm at school? Why?
10. What are three activities, events, or conditions in the classroom or school that you'd like to see changed this year?
11. What are your favorite foods?
12. What smells or food make you feel grumpy?
13. What are three activities or strategies that you could do to help you to feel calm and comfortable?

Below is an example of this template that was filled out after observing a third-grade student who was struggling with anger, frustration, and a sense of unfairness as he felt he should have earned more points on his behavior chart. This eight-year-old boy was sent to a time-out area because he ripped up his behavior chart and knocked over a desk and chair. He yelled at the teachers and then threw himself on the floor. The following chart was created during a Pre-Op meeting, which is a time of collaboration to preventively plan a new intervention, practice, or strategy based on the relational, sensory, cultural, experiential, and task needs of the student.

I feel this example will be helpful as you work together looking below the surface of a student's signal or behavior. To help you in your own practice, I've included a blank version of this template in the Resource Section of the book.

A SECRET – Protocol

This protocol can be used while thinking of a specific student and situation, or after observing a scenario.

1. Reflecting on the situation/scenario of focus, use the guiding questions to fill in the first column of the chart. What did you see? What did you notice?
2. In the second column, use the guiding questions to create alternative accommodations/supports. What could we do in the future? What proactive strategies or practices can we put into place?

A SECRET – Example Chart

OBSERVATIONS/REFLECTIONS	PRE-OP
A = Attention: What caused the disruption? · He wanted to return to class and kept asking, "Can I go back?" · Saw behavior point sheet and a felt sense of unfairness.	**A = Attention** · We need to validate instead of telling, and begin to use waiting time. · Use a fidget or sensory tool to shift focus. · Provide more physical space.

S = Sensory
· He was very tired and explained he had to wake up at 2 AM and "go to work."
· Did not want to be sitting.
	S = Sensory: What can we do?
	· Different seating options:
	  ◦ Large exercise ball – movement
	  ◦ Bean bag – provides noise in the silence, low to the ground to encourage a feeling of being grounded
	· Softer lighting options
	· More open space

E = Emotions · Anger · Irritation · Wants someone to "notice me"	**E = Emotions** · Validation · Active Constructive Responding: asking for details from his perspective about the unfairness of the situation
C = Culture · In the time-out area, there was a feeling of oppression. · Dark, closed in, small · Resembles an interrogation	**C = Culture** · Change in arrangement of seating · Choices of seating · Fewer adults in the room when being questioned one-on-one

R = Relationships
· We did not notice any secure sustainable relationships in the building that were seen or that the student shared.
	R = Relationships
	· Finding touch points
	  ◦ Is there anyone here at school you would like to spend some time with?
	  ◦ Who do you need?
	  ◦ If it is not someone at school, can we write them a letter? Email? Text? Call them on the phone?

OBSERVATIONS/REFLECTIONS

E = Environment/Experiences
Closed-in space
During the escalation and immediately following, there was not an opportunity for this student to co-regulate with a trusted adult. There was not an opportunity to watch the nonverbal gentleness from an adult who was able to model the behaviors in times of distress.

T = Tasks
• Behavior point sheet – overwhelming, goal seems out of reach

PRE-OP

E = Environment/Experiences
Open space
New experiences: Help him create a pause with a visual reminder (object, rubber band, or providing a sensory list of choices or a signal he could implement ahead of time when he begins to feel irritation and frustration).

T = Tasks
• Create more opportunities for success on the task.
• Implement a brain reflection sheet so the discussion moves away from behavior to brain state. See Below!

I want to share a few sample strategies of sensory, connection, and cortical practices that are included in the Resource Section of this book. I've found these brain-aligned strategies extremely helpful in calming the nervous system, invoking feelings of safety, and strengthening students' connections with their teacher and classmates. My hope is that you will also find some of these practices helpful as a part of your procedures and routines—and that students will develop their personal routines by choosing which practices can best help them move to the cortex where learning happens! I liken this chart to a buffet table with a variety of foods to choose from. This variety can provide students with some autonomy as they sample and explore the regulatory practices that feel good to them.

The 7/11 Breath	Inhale for 7 seconds and exhale for 11.
Sensation Word Drawing	This is a great way of using imagery and art to activate the right hemisphere while integrating both hemispheres for cognition. Students choose a sensation word and draw an image of this word using size, shape and color, and possibly where they feel it on their bodies (tired, numb, tense, full, fuzzy, soft, open, flowing, teary, edgy, tight, etc.).

Monster Drawing	With a partner, silently create a silly monster in one minute! Take turns adding to each other's drawing with shapes, lines and colors for one minute.
Newsletter/Website/ Social Media	Create a classroom newsletter, website, or a social media account for sharing with parents to recognize the familial tribe of connection these students and this teacher have to-gether! This could also be done in other communities such as a bus, a specials class, or an after-school group.

Create Brain Maps	What would our map of safety look like? What about our map of experiences that feel scary or fearful?
E-Story	Create an electronic story of personal and school life. In this E-Story, students have the opportunity to let you know who they are through their dreams, goals, and stories. These E-Stories will change much like a time capsule, which is great for reflection, feedback, and relationship building! They will also encourage personal narratives, research, and a free form of creative writing and reading ... literacy made fun!

You can find these and many more brain-aligned strategies in the Resource Section.

At times, so much of what I learned in education classes seem so irrelevant.
Huddled on the floor before me is a terrified ten-year-old—ten years of joys,
discoveries and fears, now in a state of total dysfunction.
I hold her to keep her from falling apart. I know how to teach her math,
and someday I will.
But can I teach her to believe that her life will be better?
L. TOBIN

CONNECTIONS OVER COMPLIANCE

DAILY BRAIN REFLECTION/FEEDBACK REPORT

NAME _____ DATE _____

TARGETED CHALLENGE	Morning Mtg 8:30 – 8:50	Subject Time	Subject Time	BREAK	Subject Time	Subject Time	Subject Time	Subject Time	Subject Time	BREAK	Subject Time	Subject Time	Subject Time
	1	**2**	**3**	**4**	**5**	**6**	**7**	**8**	**9**	**10**	**11**	**12**	**13**
Completing Work	Green Red Blue	Green Red Blue	Green Red Blue	Green Red Blue	Green Red Blue	Green Red Blue	Green Red Blue	Green Red Blue	Green Red Blue	Green Red Blue	Green Red Blue	Green Red Blue	Green Red Blue

TARGETED CHALLENGE	Morning Mtg 8:30 – 8:50	Subject Time	Subject Time	BREAK	Subject Time	Subject Time	Subject Time	Subject Time	Subject Time	BREAK	Subject Time	Subject Time	Subject Time
	1	**2**	**3**	**4**	**5**	**6**	**7**	**8**	**9**	**10**	**11**	**12**	**13**
Kind feet, hands, words (no aggression with others)	Green Red Blue	Green Red Blue	Green Red Blue	Green Red Blue	Green Red Blue	Green Red Blue	Green Red Blue	Green Red Blue	Green Red Blue	Green Red Blue	Green Red Blue	Green Red Blue	Green Red Blue

Green **CORTEX** **Peaceful, Calm** *HIGHER-ORDER THINKING*	Red **LIMBIC SYSTEM** **Angry, Irritated, Sad** *EMOTIONS*	Blue **BRAIN STEM** **Shut down** *SURVIVAL*
Safe and Calm Safe and Calm 	Angry or Irritated 	Shut Down
Ready to Talk 	Worried or Sad 	Numb or Frozen
Problem Solver 	Ready to Yell, Fight, or Run FIGHT or FLIGHT 	Disengaged

CHAPTER 4
Touch Points Are Maps to Connections

"We live within and beyond our own skin at the same time."
BONNIE BADENOCH

Touch points are discipline through *a new lens*—relational brain-aligned discipline. In this chapter, I will be expanding upon many of those points of connection with newly created practices and strategies that are as much about the adults in the workplace as they are about the students. A regulated and "felt" staff ensures a regulated and connected student body. What I have learned is that the leadership in our buildings must be involved in implementing these points of connection if our goal is ensuring that students create sustainable behavioral shifts toward social, emotional, and cognitive well-being!

One Tuesday before the COVID-19 pandemic closed our schools, it was both a sad and inspiring day in our fifth-grade classroom. That Tuesday I learned from our students and Ms. Spitole. I learned more than any lab experience, textbook, clinical study, or conference could ever teach me. At 10 a.m., I begrudgingly walked into IPS 55, the Butler Lab School, because honestly, I just wanted to be home! It was gray, drizzling, and bone-chilling cold. It was Butler University's spring break and I was not spring breaking! Entering my classroom, the students and Ms. Spitole were gathered on the floor in a morning meeting, so I quietly sat and waited until the end of the activity. The brain lesson for the day was a follow-up to a prior discussion about the similarities between gardens and our brains. I was ready to further this conversation by delving into these questions: What type of seeds are you planting? Are they seeds of anger or seeds of gratitude? Are the seeds filled with worry or calm?

As we began to share about the seeds we'd planted and how our brain states are greatly affected by our thoughts, feelings, and experiences, the floodgates opened as multiple students began sharing their pain, losses, worries, hopes, and memories. Hands were just flying into the air as each student shared a story while their classmates listened deeply. I was stunned at the respect and deep listening that each student was providing their classmates. One young girl, with wide eyes, black-rimmed glasses, and a frantic yet eager desire to be heard and seen, raised her hand, waving it wildly in the air for the fourth or fifth time. It was as if each time she spoke, her worries and fears lessened a bit, and these shared narratives were calming her in front of us all.

Then she spoke these words: *"Not too long ago, I was so sad and angry that I thought a lot about killing myself, and when I finally told my family, they sent me to a therapist. I still see this therapist, and when she talks to me once a week, I don't trust her. She sits across from me and writes notes on a pad and gives me a calming tool to play with in my hands. It is not calming as I squeeze it harder! Sometimes, I don't trust my own mom, and I am not sure why. But I just don't trust her ... but I do trust my friends and they hear me, and they just know how to make me feel better. They listen to me!"*

After 20 minutes of being washed in this deep well of truth sharing, there was a huge part of me that wanted to encourage well-being, fix these students' problems, and frantically cheer them on. Yet I silently reminded myself to keep listening and validating as Ms. Spitole and I continually exchanged eye-to-eye communication, checking in with one another. There was nothing I could say that would have been half as powerful as the deep listening taking place throughout the entire sea of 27 students. It was a vivid demonstration of what I've studied and shared with so many educators and my students: "The more healthy relationships a child has, the more likely he will be to recover from trauma and thrive. Relationships are the agents of change, and the most powerful therapy is human love."[1] Therapy can be lifesaving, hopeful, and healing, but it is certainly not the panacea for all well-being. Often, a once-a-week scheduled therapy appointment doesn't meet the student where she is developmentally, and this most often occurs within environments that are natural spaces where the child or adolescent "does life!"

That Tuesday I learned that children can co-regulate the adults in their lives, and the leadership embracing a compassionate presence doesn't always originate from the adult. Walking to my car, there was a spring in my step that hadn't been there when I walked into the classroom a few hours earlier! Co-regulation is a touch point. It is an opportunity to be silently *present* with another. Words and conversation can frequently stifle the opportunities to connect, heal, and transform perceptions, because no matter what our age or background, we all sense and feel our worlds before we think.

The balancing act of creating healthy, evolving relationships is that these connections with others are intimately impacted by our own states of mind and the self-awareness we carry into all conversations and connections with others. Reflecting upon that Tuesday's cathartic experience, I sensed how Bridget Spitole's presence in this fifth-grade classroom creates a culture of safety and trust. She beautifully integrates and accepts her own inner emotional state that feels authentic and safe for her students to uphold and embrace. This compassionate presence that educators can create is not a steadfast science, but rather an art that shares its own fragility and vulnerability through all spoken moments and silent interchanges.

Educational settings such as a classroom offer an extremely diverse environment where 30-plus minds and hearts can begin to weave a climate of felt safety, trust, and connection. But this is a process, and on many days that classroom can feel like a minefield where a comment, tone of voice, look, sarcastic remark, gesture, or posture can ignite an explosion of chaotic contagion. We are overwhelmed with in-the-moment issues!

I recently heard the term, "initiative fatigue," which I think this is an accurate definition for how so many of us feel when it comes to attending one more presentation, one more workshop, and listening to one more so-called expert telling us to do one more thing in our classrooms! To add to this frustration, we have traditionally learned to hold and view discipline inside a world associated with punishment. This is no small feat, as many of our schools are seeing an unprecedented escalation of pain-based behaviors and mental health challenges. We do recognize and see the behavioral challenges before us, and we know in our minds and guts that these challenges our kids are carrying into our classrooms and schools require so much more help than we currently know how to give. At times, we feel overwhelmed, helpless, and hopeless, which can create added stress in our own lives. Yet where do we begin? Where is the relief?

What I am learning every day is that our traditional value systems leave the significance of connections out of the discipline/punishment conversation. Many of our traditional belief systems in the United States are deeply rooted in choices and consequences. "If you did something wrong, you need to be isolated so that you will experience some fear and pain and make a better choice the next time!"

After all, it is all about choices ...

A brain that understands cause and effect is a brain that does well with traditional behavior management programs. But our children and youth who are carrying in pain-based behavior have a brain that is wired for fight, flight, and shutdown, and this brain has a desperate need for connection! Strong connections, which we call touch points, assist in the development of emotional regulation. Rebecca Lewis Pankritz shared these notions in a recent blog: "Refreshingly, Behaviorism is no longer the end-all, be-all to why children and adults act like we do, nor is it the singular road map to change it. Behaviorism is not to be totally abandoned, but it is to be understood as only a surface-level approach that truly lies in the thinking brain and not the survival brain."[2]

What we now know is that kids who spend a lot of time in their survival brain require a connection through their relational brain, and this where co-regulation helps them to get back into their thinking brain. Once a student reclaims their thinking brain, all sorts of amazing things can happen! Healing and learning begin to manifest along with behavioral shifts that are sustainable.

A teacher's single, unintentional, misplaced reaction or response to a situation or behavior can weaken or shrivel a child's spirit; whereas validation and acknowledgment can encourage and grow a child's or adolescent's developing brain and body state. In other words, why escalate a student by reactivating their stress response systems when, as teachers, we have this powerful opportunity to co-regulate a child's growing agitation and anxiety? The good news is that our brains and bodies are continuously trying to return to a homeostatic state where we can experience a calm, relaxed alertness in most moments. As I have shared, a student walking into our classrooms and schools with an elevated ACE (adverse childhood experience) score and without sufficient emotional buffers—such as predictable, emotionally available, nurturing, and supportive relationships—is often a student carrying in pain-based behaviors that can present as offensive, defiant, and oppositional or as a shut-down state filled with quiet shame and hopelessness. These students dare us to connect with them, because they often don't trust adults. That distrust is rooted in their developing years, when the adults that should have attuned to their needs and cared for their developing brains and bodies were unable to do so and, perhaps unintentionally, added to their existing pain by creating additional adversity. This kind of developmental disruption can alter and compromise not only our biology but also our developing perceptual systems.

Each one of us carries a perceptual map of how we see our world. As previously shared, neuroscientist Dr. Stephen Porges, the creator of the Polyvagal Theory, has created the term **neuroception**, which refers to the subconscious processes of how everyone interprets his or her environment.[3] Neuroception is one of the most effective ways for educators to understand and support children and adolescents with emotional and behavioral challenges. Each of us, through our unique neuroception, has created a subconscious map of our own world, and within those maps we have denoted what environments, relationships, and experiences feel safe or dangerous to us. These maps are based on our lived experiences. If those experiences have been filled with pain, then our perceptions of the world are often filled with fear, isolation, and distrust. Secure attachment is the carrier of all brain development, and these foundational attachments are the context of nervous system development. When these secure attachments fail to develop during the early months and years of life, our sensory and motor systems are greatly affected, compromising our sense of safety and connection. For these reasons, many of our children and youth look to schools and educators for these points of connection, which we are calling touch points. Our challenge is that many of our students ask for relational experiences in the most unloving ways.

Rewiring our perceptions of relational discipline calls us to look within ourselves during these challenging moments of connecting with a troubled child. Difficult as this may be, it's helpful to tune into who we are, through our self-awareness and self-reflections, and separate our own needs, beliefs, and agendas from what our students need from us. Can we meet each of them "where they are," respecting the moments, experiences, and environments that have sculpted and contributed to those behaviors or signals that can derail us and the classroom in just a few chaotic minutes? As Dr. Gabor Maté has shared so often, "We all have brains prepared to be wired for happiness, but when this happiness is threatened at a deep level by traumas in our past that were never resolved, we resort to survival behaviors, trying hard to regulate our worlds in hopes of restoring the happiness and regulation we are craving!"[4]

Relational brain-aligned discipline calls us to explore the profound benefits of "family privilege," which is explained by Dr. John Seita in his book *Kids Who Outwit Adults*, co-authored with Dr. Larry Brendtro. Family privilege is invisible and healing. It is the safety and connective tissue that holds families together during times of discord, tragedy, celebrations, and acceptance. The authors share this description: "'Family privilege' is an invisible package of assets and pathways that provide us with a sense of belonging, safety, unconditional love, and spiritual values. It is a form of human capital that compounds its benefits over time, and it is never a given, as those of us with family privilege take it for granted. Family privilege is like oxygen—we don't notice its absence unless we are suffocating."[5] We have the fortunate opportunity to create family privilege for all students in our classrooms and schools. Ironically, this occurs when our discipline protocols emphasize the obligation to include the intentionality and strengthening of relationships. Traditionally, schools are better at pulling weeds than at planting flowers.[6] In many of our schools, disrespectful, oppositional, and defiant students are pulled out only to return the next hour, day, or week indirectly begging for connection through a lens that alters perceptions of trusted adults. *Relationship-resistant* children and youth challenge adults in authority because, more times than not, they were abandoned by those who were supposed to love and care for them. The research shares that by fourth grade, students who have experienced continual behavioral challenges with staff and other students begin to adopt a "bad kid" identity and slowly gravitate to any group where they feel social acceptance and family privilege.[7] We know all too well that the streets are calling for these kids as much as we are, and the brain and body are constantly looking for attachment and connection because love is the most powerful need of children and youth.[8] School and community violence are often carried out by disconnected youth and children who carry pain-based behaviors into schools and are trying like hell to mitigate this deep emotional pain on their own. Developmental experiences build brains, and when children grow up in environments where the adults are not consistently emotionally available and predictable in helping to soften the incoming stimuli from their internal and external worlds, the brain and body stress activation patterns become disrupted, compromising their ability to emotionally regulate, create healthy relationships, and feel emotionally and socially safe. Attachment is the carrier of all development, and angry, defiant youth often have a history of painful experiences with the adults in their lives.

We are not excusing these negative, volatile, or shut-down behaviors, but we need to understand not only the neurobiology of trauma and adversity, but also how our schools have traditionally created climates that unintentionally add secondary pain on top of primary pain. Most importantly, we need to understand how this has occurred—and is still occurring—through traditional discipline protocols. Dr. Seita and Dr. Brendtro share these notions. "Negative school climates occur when educators view students and their families as adversaries rather than valued partners. Students see the school as rule bound with discipline administered unfairly by adults who don't really care about them."[9] In these schools, the emphasis is on punishment and arbitrary consequences and is not preventive. The gap between staff, students, and families can feel overwhelming to the point of hopelessness, manifesting in chronic resistance and divisiveness. Negative school cultures aren't always about those communities in deprived, oppressed neighborhoods. Schools existing in communities of privilege and wealth may be suffering from *relational wealth* and are seedbeds for further alienation.

Why are touch points so critical to the way we need to discipline all students, but particularly our most troubled students? Below is an excerpt from a young man, a high school student who shares his distrust of adults.

"I am so over consequences! They actually relieve me of the f**** boring work and prison-like classroom that makes me nauseous every day! There is nothing anyone can do to me that would be any more shocking and devastating than what has already happened. Adults try to punish me into obedience, the obedience that feels right to them! Loss of privileges, threats, yelling, suspensions, and expulsions only reinforced my distrust for these people who could never be trusted!"

Touch points are connections where we feel seen, heard, and present with one another. Touch points are not lectures, or moments of redirection, but they are experiences that hold a nonjudgmental space of respect and a willingness to learn deeply about one another. In *Eyes Are Never Quiet,* my most recent book written with friend and colleague Michael McKnight, we dedicated a brief chapter to exploring the implementation of touch points and how we can employ them inside our classrooms and schools.

Following is a story shared by a school administrator and a former graduate student from our Butler University certification in Applied Educational Neuroscience/Brain and Adversity. Dr. Silverman has spent her professional life creating points of connection with children and adolescents who carry pain into our schools and classrooms. This is a tough read and the language is rough, but I feel it conveys the power of resiliency through the endurance event of connecting to our youth who distrust adults. Dr. John Seita shares, "In every culture, humans are hardwired to do unto others as they do unto us. This is not the Golden Rule but rather the tit-for-tat rule, and viewing these human encounters through a lens of distrust throws us into a survival mode where our goal is to protect and defend."[10]

Who Would Have Thought?

The Resilience of a Principal and a School Shooter

April 2018 is when I learned I can't do it all, or so I thought. I truly thought I was invincible. I am Dr. S, or as some call me so lovingly Ms. Dr. S. This student, who after a year I have come to love and understand, calls me Dr. S, but our story doesn't start so easily. I know him by his real name, but many know him as SuicideHenryK, his Instagram handle.

The shit I think can be confusing sometimes. Hell, I even confuse myself with my own thoughts.

SuicideHenryK arrived at my school after being arrested the day he planned to shoot up his school.

So yeah, I was going to shoot up my school. But before you stop reading, just take a minute to hear me out.

He had been detained and then sent to us, a residential facility in Indianapolis. The residential side was prepared to treat him and provide the much-needed therapy. He was brought to me, Dr. S, the Director of Education. I was warned.

People like me don't do this kind of shit because they want to. People usually assume that we're just some fucked up kids that have the thirst to kill, but that's really not true. I'm going to share with you a tiny part of my life that influenced those thoughts and almost made me do what I had planned to do.

I read the file, but then I met him. He was introverted and quiet. I didn't care. I didn't want to know his story. I didn't want to teach him. I did not want to know him. He wanted to blow up a school. I hated him before I ever met him. Let me explain.

It all started the summer of 2017. Some shit happened and I moved in with my grandfather, who I thought was a pretty cool dude, until about a month later when he started abusing me. Yeah, sucks pretty fucking bad. Not only that, but I was being bullied at school and some other shit was going on. So, around Christmas of 2017, a thought popped into my head. This thought was the thought to shoot up my school.

I have always loved the challenge of my job. Working with troubled youth and pushing them through their adversities to their strengths has always been my magic. I see the silver linings and the cup half full. I believe my purpose is to believe in the children that many have given up on already. I have a special passion that cannot be explained. I love to see my kids each day. It fills my heart. I have worked with children from the Department of Child Services and from the probation department. I have been called every name in the book. With that said, I have reached many of them. We grow together and I see the lights come back and shine in their eyes. I see children trying to be adults at a young age learn to enjoy childhood again. Trust develops and I remain their champion as long as possible.

After about a week, my grandpa kicked me out of his apartment, forcing me to move in with my great grandmother. While there, I had continued my plan to shoot up my school.

But I had never met a school shooter. I never met anyone who wanted to take away innocent lives like this young man dreamed of doing. I was horrified and couldn't get past it.

Before I continue, I just wanted to say my great grandma was a huge gun collector. I mean she had a little bit of everything from black powder guns to military rifles. My favorite gun was this World War Two military rifle that had a sick bayonet. It was a pretty cool gun, and it was what I was going to use, along with a revolver and some pipe bombs that I actually learned to make from a movie called Zero Day. This brings me to my next point, parents: NEVER LET YOUR KIDS WATCH A MOVIE THAT DOES NOT LOOK NORMAL!!

I shared with his therapist that I would do my job, but the minimum required and not to expect my typical loving Dr. S, as I wanted nothing to do with this boy beyond that. I wasn't willing to add the extra Dr. S magic, the extra time needed to connect and build relationships that our kids need so desperately. Why do the extra with a child who wanted to go into a school and kill others? I couldn't wrap my head around it. My wall was up, and my feelings were in a dark place where I couldn't let this youth inside. I simply had watched the news and heard the stories. I was a Dean of Students when Columbine happened—the first of the school shootings. The beginning of how we looked at school safety. I was interviewed the next day along with the other Dean at Manual High School. This was so long ago, but the haunts are real and now I was expected to work with one of THEM.

I think it's safe to say that I was pretty fucked up in the head. Well, more shit happened, and my great grandma passed away. So here I am, sitting on my couch, thinking what the hell I'm supposed to next. Next thing I know people are coming in and moving stuff out. It was happening. My plan was being sabotaged.

I just was disturbed and unable to understand the uneasiness I had inside. I went home that night and called my dad. I asked for advice. My dad, my hero, was speechless at first. He listened as I explained that I may be at a point in my career where I may be ready to give up. Maybe I finally found a kid who didn't give me any reason to hope. He told me that I would be ok and that I didn't give up on kids. He told me to find my courage and my strength because this child needed just one person to make a difference. I didn't sleep that night. I have lost hours of sleep over this youth that I have commonly referred to as "school shooter" or "my favorite kiddo."

So I moved back in with my mother and, while sitting in my room one day, started thinking and I realized how fucked up my thinking had been.

Over the next few months, I watched. Henry, the school shooter, sat quietly in class and did not cause any problems. He didn't cause problems either in class or on the unit. He was easy, silent, and in a strange way a bit fascinating. He has this very deep voice and lanky body with blond curly hair. One would never imagine he would be so broken. I didn't understand. Teachers liked him. He didn't cause any problems. What I quickly learned is that my team didn't know him. So I decided to begin to say hello and get to know him. What a nice kid Henry was and not at all the stereotype of a school shooter— except he liked the color black and was quiet and easily could be skipped over.

So, I picked up my phone and called one of my best friends. When she picked up, I said nothing more than "don't go to school tomorrow" and hung up. Of course, she called the police and I got arrested, went to juvenile for a good month and a half and ended up here. A year later, I'm sitting here, typing what you're reading right now. It's been a long and tough ride, but I persevered through it for the people around me because some of them I care about.

I have this reputation at my job of being able to connect with the kids. Most of them respect me and like me most of the time. I was determined to get to know Suicide Henry. I started saying hello, asking him how school was and striking up conversation. I was building our drum room, and ironically he carries drumsticks EVERY-WHERE. This was an easy commonality. As I got to know Henry, I realized that he was truly an amazing kid. It wasn't until after that February court hearing that I learned he had considered running away. Between February and his April court date we had built a trust, and I asked him to promise me he would not consider jumping. He first said he wouldn't promise, but then when I asked him if he promised not to put me through the pain of losing someone I care so much about, he promised that he would return to our building safely. He agreed to promise on these terms. I was full of joy when I saw him the next day at school. I think he had given up on people following through and caring about him. The important thing about working with trauma is never lying—never ever lying.

Don't think I'm going to get all cute and emotional, but that right there is a true statement. I'm mostly changing for my mom, who is one of my biggest advocates.

So why the anger? What are the triggers? I learned that Henry had been bullied from some oddities as a result of Tourette's. There had also been inappropriate sexual behaviors from grandfather, finding mom during a suicide attempt, being moved around as a result of DCS placements along with the challenge of being in middle school. It has not been easy. Henry has had to play the role of a parent. During his time with us, he has hit walls. He doesn't like to be touched. He likes distance from others and his personal space. He has given up on childhood and follow-through from adults.

Another one of my biggest advocates is the principal at the school here, Dr. S, and let me tell you, not very many people get to see a school shooter and a principal hanging out or writing a paper together. When I first arrived here, apparently, she was totally pissed off at me. I mean, I can see why, because who would want a school shooter at their school? I wouldn't.

I have had to be the good guy and the bad guy. Because of this, it has been important that I am also the honest one. I made it crystal clear that getting him back to school was going to be the challenge of my career. Legally, he cannot be expelled for more than a year. However, it was going to be a challenge because the school board, school community, and staff are going to feel uneasy. I have kept everything honest, because once a trust is broken it cannot be returned. I am also working on teaching Henry that there are people who care. I told him I was going to pat him on the shoulder when I see him but warn him first. Today it is not a big deal. If I give him a side hug or a pat on the back, it is normal. One of my treasured pictures is one we took together, and he SMILED!

Anyways, now we're writing a paper together and yeah, here I am. This brings me to my next point, people can change, even if they are really fucked up in the head. I mean, look at me, I've changed a freakin' lot!

✦

I share this story because, as extreme as it is, writing this collaborative paper with his principal gave Henry the opportunity to feel a sense of purpose, partnership, and trust with an adult who reached out to him without judgment. Learned trust is the most powerful belief we can hold about ourselves, others, and the world we live within. Writing a shared paper gave Henry a sense of autonomy, and the process of writing this paper with Dr. S began to create new circuitry in his brain that helped him feel safe as he began to feel a part of something!

We now understand that childhood adversities do not have the last word. Dr. Bruce Perry, neuroscientist, author, and leading expert on trauma and brain development, shares, "These powerful regulating effects of healthy relational interactions—mediated by various key neural networks in the brain—are at the core of relationally-based protective mechanisms that help us survive and thrive following trauma and loss. Children with few positive relational interactions have a much more difficult time turning down the trauma-induced activation of the stress response systems."[11]

Touch points are foundational to the new lens of discipline as they address deep trust, a process, safety, and collaboration. We're willing to work for the people we like and respect. We give children who have experienced chronic unpredictability the power to create from these life experiences. Alfred Adler called these meaning-making associations the "private logic" of a child, which defines the personal perceptions and beliefs that strongly influence goals and behavior. Sometimes the only way we can make sense out of a child's or adolescent's behavior is to understand the goal of that behavior, and this is tied to the meaning and associations that our children create in forming their identities.[12]

Adler suggests that the following four areas begin to define a child's private logic and therefore their developing identity from critical life events. A child's or adolescent's private logic may feel maladaptive to us, but it serves a purpose by providing protection when their developing identity feels threatened, giving them a framework for shifting to a survival brain state. Understanding these four constructs helps us to appreciate the coping strategies a student has adopted. With knowledge and understanding, hope and trust follow.

I am ...

Other people ...

The world is ...

Therefore ...[13]

"Fool me once, shame on you. Fool me twice, shame on me." This is the unspoken mantra of manipulative kids who walk through life with emotional pain and often a distrust of adults. Children and youth who have experienced abandonment, brutality, or an accumulation of marginalized conditions have learned to read adult emotions perfectly so they can please or avoid dangerous and unpredictable adults.[14]

"Our students would make the best TSA agents at the airport," shared principal Frank Kline as he described the survival and manipulative energies of many of his elementary students!

Our schools are currently seeing a dramatic increase in students of all ages carrying in anxiety, adversity, and trauma from a variety of ACEs.[15] Social and emotional learning programs are critical for addressing these emotional and mental challenges, but now we must rethink our discipline procedures and policies. We need to understand that traditional discipline works best with the children who need it the least, and works least with the children who need it the most. Ideally, discipline is not something we do to students—it should be a quality we want to develop within them. Co-regulation is at the heart of attachment, and deepening relationships with one another and with our students is at the center of this new lens for discipline.

For students with ACEs, traditional punishments can unintentionally retraumatize and reactivate their stress response systems. Recent research in school discipline is grounded in the neuroscience of attachment, which emphasizes the significance of relationships.[16] Those relationships begin with an adult in a regulated, calm brain state. It takes a calm brain to calm another brain—this co-regulation is something that students with significant adverse childhood experiences may have missed with an emotionally available and present caregiver. Their school can now be an environment where they feel safe and connected even when they make poor choices.

This doesn't mean giving students a pass for misbehavior. There are still consequences for poor choices, but regulating the feelings and sensations that a student experiences is the initial step, one that is critical for a sustainable change in behavior. Staying connected through the conflict is so exhausting but critical! Brain-aligned consequences need to be meaningful, not arbitrary. These consequences require safety and a delivery from an adult that we describe as a warm demander. What is a warm demander? Becoming a warm demander begins with establishing a caring relationship that conveys to students how you truly believe in them. As a warm demander, "how you say it" matters, but who you are and what students believe about your intentions matter more. When students know that you believe in them, that if necessary you'll sit beside them to help them figure things out, they will interpret even tough-sounding comments as declarations of a compassionate presence. As one student commented, "She's mean out of the kindness of her heart."[17]

This quote, pulled from interviews with 200 students in high-poverty middle schools in Philadelphia, highlights the second part of being a warm demander. Warm demanders care enough to unequivocally insist on mutual respect, which includes a significant level of empathic resonance that says to a student, "I see you and feel your hurts, joys, and angst." A warm demander holds the expectations for a student at a level that is a bit challenging, but is appropriate through a neurobiological lens. We meet students where they are, and as they leave their comfort zone of emotional and cognitive learning, we provide continual feedback and support each step of the way. Scaffolding content and emotional and social tasks will begin to create small islands of success for students who need the patterned repetitive experiences and moments of opportunities to build the newly formed neuronal pathways for learning and social and emotional well-being.

A warm demander understands that emotions are contagious, and when a teacher can model a calm presence through their tone, facial expression, and posture, students are less likely to react defensively. When we listen to what is beneath the behavior, focusing on the student's feelings, this type of validation says to the child that we see them and that we are trying to understand. When we take deep breaths, get a drink of water, and create space for reflection for a minute or two, we are modeling the regulation skills we want to see from students.

As a warm demander, we believe improvement will occur because we understand that the brain changes structurally and functionally with patterned repetitive experiences, and that the power of providing small increments or doses of attachment opportunities provides significant benefits to the developing brain. We begin to understand that, much like practicing the skills to improve an academic or performance task, relational tasks are critical for developing environments of safety and connection. When confronted with chronic behavioral issues, it is so valuable to collect day-to-day data helping to understand layers beneath the troubling signals we call "behaviors." We are often so busy each day that we don't see the smallest steps of improvement as they begin to change the landscape. It's similar to the old saying about not being able to see the forest through the trees! Therefore, the tool called A SECRET, which I shared in Chapter 3, is so useful as we begin to detect the student's troubling sensory and environmental issues and challenges before acting. Maybe we begin to approach these challenges holding a reflective state of mind as we consider the following questions.

- What factors might influence this behavior or brain state?
- When does this behavior occur?
- Does this behavior occur during certain times of the day or days of the week?
- How can we use this data to increase points of connection during these times?

When we take a few minutes each day to observe and wonder rather than create and determine a response from our own logic and perspective, we step away from our impulse to blame students for their behavior and open ourselves to the possibilities of what they're actually trying to communicate.

To begin, observe—but on an intuitive level. No checklists, no notes,
no histories—just watch him. Watch him watching his world.
Go silently behind his eyes to see his world. When you see what he feels, you
will have learned all that you need to know ... Then begin!

L. TOBIN

In the midst of teaching and disciplining, when I am called to co-regulate with a student, I begin with the awareness of my own sensations and feelings. It entails a willingness to regulate my brain before I act on my own triggers and impulsive reactions. Personally, I try committing to three quick routines that feel doable to calm me in a short period of time: taking three deep breaths, texting a friend or pulling an affirmation from a prepared jar[18], and stretching and moving for a minute.

When we're feeling irritated and angry, it's much better to wait for a few minutes before we discipline, and this is also excellent modeling for students. They read our nonverbal communication, so paying attention to our facial expression and posture in addition to our tone of voice is critical when teaching the behaviors that we want to see.

Focusing on the student's sensations and the feelings that lie beneath the behavior will help us understand the root causes and patterns of a behavior we might discover (in both the student and ourselves!) when there is rising irritation and anger. I may take a minute or two to redirect, and I use the time by suggesting that the student go and get a drink of water or take a couple of deep breaths to calm down with me before we talk about the challenge.

As we begin to delve into the strategies and practices of sharing touch points with our students, I am reminded of how these connections are the foundation of preventive discipline that happens on the front end. Please explore the graph on the following page as we shift our perceptions of brain-aligned relational and preventive discipline:

Brain Aligned Preventive Discipline – Proactive not Reactive

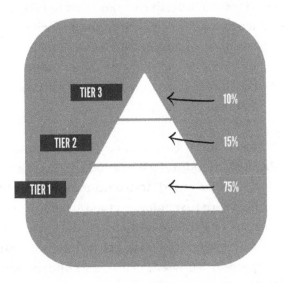

Tier 1 - Preventive Brain-Aligned Discipline happens through our procedures, routines, transitions, morning and afternoon rituals, and through sensory regulation and touch points with our students.

Tier 2 - Some of our students will need regulation and touch point interventions a little more often and with more intensity. Here is where we teach our students how to use the routines of regulation before there is a conflict or irritation.

Tier 3 - "Accommodations Through an ACEs' Lens" happens in this top tier as we are intentional about co-regulation with our students using sensory strategies, validation, "2 by 10," noticing, movement, rhythm, breath, and making sure there are adults and a space in our buildings where students can go if they need to co-regulate away from the classroom.

Touch Point Practices and Strategies

1. Creating a friend-in-need system could be helpful so that each student has a buddy or even an on-site adult ally for when they begin to feel agitated. For the friend-in-need system, teachers ask students to select one or two peers or adults at the school who they trust and with whom they'd feel comfortable if they need to take a break and be in another environment or talk through those challenging moments. This is preventive discipline and a way for students to have options when they begin to feel negative. These calming strategies are taught ahead of time and become a part of our procedures and classroom agreements or guidelines.

2. Validation is powerful way to calm an agitated and angry student. It's calming to be understood and felt by another. The best framework for validation is a practice called **Active Constructive Responding**. Shelly Gable, professor of psychology at the University of California at Santa Barbara has researched and shown that how you actively share, celebrate, or respond to an event or experience with another provides a safe space to feel seen, heard, and understood.[19] Active Constructive Responding means stepping into the experiences with another and responding with questions, details, and interest. It is a form of questioning best practiced when the adult and child are regulated and have found a calm moment. One person asks a range of questions that focus on details when another individual shares something about an experience, event, idea, or relationship. Basically, we are reliving the experience with the child or adolescent—or even our colleague. This form of questioning is a "touch point" (discussed in Chapter 2) as we intentionally step inside another's experience to help them feel felt, seen, and heard. We use Active Constructive Responding to create a sense of presence, safety, and trust which provides space for improved emotional, social, and cognitive well-being.

Here are some examples of questions that may be used to build this skill:

- Where were you when you saw this or heard this?
- Who was with you?
- What were you doing right before this happened?
- What were you doing when this happened?
- How did this feel?
- How will this change things for you now?

Colors, smells, sounds, people, tastes, environments, and any other detail that you can request will increase the quality of a dyadic and dynamic relationship in which we sit beside one another feeling felt, seen, and heard!

While validation opens the door for teacher and student to discuss choices and consequences and to create a plan of action for the next time there's a conflict, I can't emphasize strongly enough the importance of co-regulation for this and so many other practices to be truly effective. My colleague Michael McKnight shares, "It is critical that a teacher's brain should resemble a thermostat rather than a thermometer when it comes to disciplining a student." What does this mean? Like a thermostat, the teacher needs to maintain a steady temperature throughout a moment of conflict, holding the goal of creating conversation and a plan of action with a student who understands their choices and the consequences of those actions. The teacher needs to model the behaviors they want to see, while also modeling self-care and respect during the discipline process.

The "2x10 strategy," developed by psychologist Raymond Wlodkowski, is a powerful brain-aligned strategy to implement with our most challenging students. For two minutes, ten days in a row, teachers engage in a personal conversation with a student about anything the student is interested in, as long as the conversation is G-rated. Wlodkowski found an 85 percent improvement in that one student's behavior. In addition, he found that the behavior of all the other students in the class improved.[20] We have extended the "2x10" strategy to a "1x30" and a "30 x 60," meaning that once we"ve taken two minutes for ten days in a row to begin establishing a relationship with a student or staff member, we continue for shorter amounts of time. One minute for 30 days and then 30 seconds for a couple of months continues to strengthen connection over a longer period of time with frequent check-ins that could be as simple as a greeting, a text, or a question inside a brief conversation.

1. At the district, school, department, grade, or classroom level, we can create these accommodations for our students who walk in ready to fight, flee, or shut down.[21] A change of seating arrangements can sometimes help a student feel safe and focused. This placement or seat may need to be in the back of the classroom or against a wall so that the student can feel the support of seeing everything around and in front of them.

2. This next step takes some work. Educators start by identifying students who are coping with ACEs—chronic discipline issues are usually indicators of which students need a sense of connection and help with self-regulation. For each of these students, identify one or two adults in the school[22] with whom the student feels comfortable and safe. This kind of mentor relationship is a touch point in times of anxiety or dysregulation, and a powerful accommodation that provides a sense of safety for self-regulation and secure connection.

3. Meeting with this mentor every week provides an opportunity for a check-in, during which students can share and discuss their challenges and successes.[23] Discussions might cover points like these:

· **Strengths to Help Me with My Goals:** Students can use a morning meeting time or a bell work time at the beginning of class to list their strengths, which may need a touch point from a trusted adult or classmate to assist in reappraising the student's focus and weaving it into the positive side of an experience. Below are a few examples:
  · I love to learn. I'm seen as a leader and good friend by others.
  · I have a great imagination.
  · I notice everything.
  · I am good at sensing others and nonverbal communication.

- **Interests and Areas of Expertise:** Students list their areas of expertise, passions, and strengths. This exercise can best be completed with a friend or an adult who can brainstorm ideas with the students.
  - I love art.
  - I am interested in animals, especially cats.
  - I have a pet-sitting service.
  - I am good at soccer.

- **Triggers (People or Experiences That Irritate, Anger or Upset Me):** What are some experiences, events, sights, sounds, smells, relationships, or people that cause students to feel anxiety or other negative emotions? With an adult or classmate, the student begins to create a personalized list of regulatory strategies that feel calming in moments of growing, anger, anxiety, or frustration.

4. With a classmate, begin to create and set up a personalized routine of self-regulation accommodations before there are conflicts and behavioral challenges. For example, start with a list of quick breaks—getting a sip of water, taking a walk, taking three deep breaths, drawing or using a favorite art form, moving to a quiet area, or journaling—and have the student choose two or three items from the list that they will employ in times of dysregulation and growing frustration. It is key that these steps be taught and discussed ahead of time so that when the student does get upset, they don't have to make a tough decision about what to do; they have only two or three choices, which they selected for themselves in a moment of calm.

Brain-Aligned Bell and Morning Work

Rituals are so important to all of us as they create predictable and structured experiences that feel safe and familiar. Rituals help the brain regulate because we know what to expect and how it will make us feel. For an extensive (but far from complete!) list of Brain-Aligned Strategies, see the Resource Section of this book. Students and educators are free to pull from, modify, or add their own activities for implementing regulatory practices with those whom we trust. These strategies and practices provide the rituals and predictable experiences to prepare the brain for learning, regulation, and paying attention with increased engagement.

Preventive Discipline: We Are Ready to Take Your Order!

Meeting students and staff in brain state is critical for our emotional, mental, and physiological well-being! This chart shares touch points that will be helpful in connecting with students, regulating and calming their nervous system, and enabling them to learn, reason, create, and make choices that will serve them well. This is also a critical strategy for building and strengthening connections and relationships in our classrooms and schools.

Below are examples of new touch points, activities, and strategies. A few may be familiar to you as bell work or morning meeting practices that you've already integrated into your morning or afternoon rituals. Each of these activities is implemented in collaboration with the whole class or in small groups where students begin to communicate with one another, and these rituals are brain-aligned preventive discipline Tier One practices. Every one of these strategies is as much for administrators as they are for staff. When our administrators are intentional about prioritizing connections with the adults in the building, they're modeling for our students, who most certainly notice these interactions! As I mentioned earlier, a regulated and "felt" staff ensures a regulated and connected student body.

Welcome to the Day! May I Take Your Order? I have shared this touch point many times, but this past year, we have added menus. As an administrator or teacher, I begin with two or three individuals at a time (students and staff) and hand them a menu, explaining, "I want to work for you today, and I would like to know what you'd like to order. We may be out of some of the items, but please choose a couple of entrees off the menu, and I will try my best!" We build this point of connection by preparing our staff and students ahead of time so they know that they can eventually reach out to all students and staff, taking everyone's order. Below are a few of the examples that you could create for your staff and student menus. Be creative and think outside the box as you build touch points of connection. The truth is that we do our best work for the people we like, whether they are students or colleagues. Small moments of connection with a caring adult can have tremendous benefits for our children who carry in pain from relational loss, abandonment, and varying forms of adversity. In the words of Dr. Bruce Perry, "We expect 'therapy'—healing—to take place in the child via episodic, shallow relational interactions with highly educated but poorly nurturing strangers. We undervalue the powerful therapeutic impact of a caring teacher, coach, neighbor, and a host of other potential co-therapists."[24]

Following are just a few examples of many that we can begin creating for touch points.

Take What You Need

DINER

APPETIZERS
BITE-SIZED SUPPORT

PLEASE HUSH PUPPIES

Some alone time in the Amygdala Reset Area or noise cancelling headphones with calming music of your choice.

"APP" - ETIZER SAMPLER PLATTER

_____ minutes on your favorite iPad app.

BACK ON TRACK SNACK

Break for a snack of your choice before getting back to the task.

MAIN COURSE
FILLING PORTIONS OF SELF-CARE

GRILLED SQUEEZE SANDWICH

Sensory pressure from a weighted blanket or vest, or a hug from your teacher.

JALAPENO ERRAND POPPERS

Pop down the hall to run an errand for your teacher.

WRITER WINGS WITH DOODLE DIP

Time and space to write or doodle about any thoughts/feelings.

DESSERTS
SWEET RELIEF

DOUBLE PEER SCOOP

Time to talk and reset with a peer.

MILKSHAKE IT OUT

Get up and move, shake, wiggle, stretch, or dance.

FROZEN FREE TIME

Free time of preferred activity for _____ minutes.

Check

CHECK NO. 4774-1

To know & tell me when you see me trying!

To notice when I am feeling frustrated

give me a break!

let me go to the bathroom one more time!

TAX

TOTAL

Thank You — Call Again

Who Is Your Wise Self?

Guided visualizations invite our imagination to begin changing the neural structures in our brains. When we implement guided imagery, we activate the right hemisphere of the brain, which is responsible for one of many mental processes.[25] In her book *Childhood Disrupted*, journalist Donna Jackson Nakazawa shares a powerful healing and connection technique called "Wise Self," which we are implementing in our classrooms and schools.

Who is your Wise Self that gives soothing comfort and acceptance to the younger version of you or the person you are right now? Is this a person? What do they look like? Is this an animal? What do you imagine your Wise Self doing to calm you and bring you joy? What words of comfort does your Wise Self share? Our fifth-grade class spent a couple of weeks working on this touch point as we designed, discussed, and listed comforting words that our Wise Self might share with us, especially during a difficult time! Below are some of the images that our students created as they imagined and drew their Wise Selves. Each week we visited our wise selves to see if we needed to add any comforting words and phrases, or if our Wise Self needed to share comforting and soothing words with another person. This practice could be a week-long, semester-long, or all-year activity. Feel free to modify, add to, or create a Wise Self moment each day with staff and students.

New Classroom Roles and Responsibilities

We see students survive every day. We ourselves survive every day, whether it's a class, test, conflict, relationship, some kind of adversity, or any other challenge that leads to feelings of isolation and unpredictability. Many students that we see daily bring a degree of their stress into our classrooms. Thankfully, many of them also have supports in their lives that allow them to manage this stress in a productive manner.

However, many of our most struggling students do not have the supports, touch points, and consistent emotional availability of a caring adult. They live in a state of chronic toxic stress, which changes the brain, literally placing it in a survival mode. In this state, the brain loses a sense of direction and purpose, and it seems nearly impossible to problem solve when adversity takes over and the stress feels overwhelming. We walk into our classrooms feeling disconnected from one another, the learning, and our purpose.[26] When we feel shame, anger, sadness, or any negative emotion over an extended period, our brains begin creating neural pathways that ignite habits of feeling in response to the thoughts that call forth these emotions. This self-centered focus on survival greatly inhibits learning. Stressed brains resist new information.

I am redefining the following "classroom professions" as touch points. They can change as needed and are presented as guidelines and ideas for exploring and adapting at all grade levels. These class responsibilities and roles are vitally important in secondary education as well, as we are providing opportunities for our students to experience co-leadership roles rather than being passive recipients of rules, lectures, and dispensed knowledge. Many of these will be familiar to the readers, but I have added new roles and classroom professions that give students and staff a felt sense of purpose and mastery. If I am a school administrator, these roles would be shared by staff as well as students.

1. Giver

This student's responsibility is to give encouragement, affirmation, and acts of kindness throughout the day. The giver may use

Post-its, create signs, deliver spoken messages, or communicate hopefulness by any means.

2. Storyteller

Storytelling could take many forms, such as seeking books to share, or integrating vocabulary or content words into a story. Younger students might create a story with pictures. Older students could work with journal stories, writing, sharing, and turning them into screenplays, or submitting them for publication. Your storyteller may develop an iMovie or blog for the class. They could create a class story with classmate's names and school projects, or weave any content into this context for learning standards or subject matter. The brain adheres to stories!

3. Noticer

This job is to notice what is going well and right. It is the antithesis to tattling or snitching.

4. Kindness Keeper

This student would record all of the kind acts performed throughout the day or week. The kindness keeper reflects on these kindnesses and shares with the class periodically.

5. Resource Manager

The resource manager suggests ideas, resources, or ways to solve a problem or locate information, either academically or behaviorally.

6. Collaborator

This is one role that could be assigned for acting outside the classroom. Maybe another teacher, staff member, or student in the school needs an emotional, social, or cognitive boost. At department and all-staff meetings, the collaborator would share ideas that promote student-to-teacher or student-to-student relationships, or bridging in- and out-group biases that happen when we only perceive differences.

7. Architect

The architect is the designer, builder, or creator. How could you highlight this role in your classroom or school?

8. Artist

The artist could have many responsibilities with visual arts, music selections, and any creative endeavor the class would like to design or share.

9. Neuroscientist

This role shares a topic each week about the brain and how it relates to content, a standard, stress, and brain neuroplasticity. There are so many applications for this new role!

10. Graduate Assistant

This role co-teaches, co-plans, or co-writes assessments with the teacher or administrator, taking on responsibilities that a co-teacher would have in a classroom.

Enjoy these new roles while collecting the perceptual data through surveys, observations, and feedback from one another as the roles change and modify, providing us with new insights about one another's interests, passions, and strengths that we never noticed before. Building community, collaboration, and points of connection happen all day and every day when we integrate these touch points into our procedures, routines, and rituals!

My Brain / My Garden

What type of thought seeds are you planting? Are they seeds of anger? Are they seeds of kindness? These are the questions that introduce this instructional practice of collaboration and learning from one another. Let's plant a garden in our classroom as we tend to the garden of our minds and explore what happens! What will we grow? How will we tend to the plants, and what do we do about the weeds? For the past year, students of all ages have enjoyed this group activity as we explore the garden analogy. It has sprouted discussions about brain architecture, neuroplasticity, connection, and the seeds that we plant to create regulation and emotional well-being.

We began this activity a year ago with middle school students, and the staff joined in. This spring, in our fifth-grade classroom, we observed our own minds and discussed what types of thoughts and feelings we've planted and what we could do if the weeds of continual negative thoughts and feelings were overwhelming the garden. We began with these discussion points, brainstormed together, and began collecting our thoughts and ideas in our brain journals. This is what we came up with:

- Our gardens need water, sunlight, and good, rich soil.

- What is the soil of your mind/garden like? What type of environment and experiences feel nourishing and good to you?

- Our gardens may need some shade and a protective enclosure.

- Who or what experiences watered your mind/garden this week? What types of experiences or persons fill you up and bring you hope and encouragement? Are you getting enough water?

- Who and what experiences are your sunlight? Who can see the best and brightest in you when you or others cannot? Are you getting enough sunlight?

- Sometimes we need a little shade and quiet. Are you getting the shade, the quiet, and reflections you need?

- What places help you to feel safe? What people?

- What sounds feel good to your brain? What types of rooms or outdoor areas?

- Who protects you? What do you do to self-protect? Do you need to repair the fence or enclosure that is your protection?

- How can school and your classmates help your garden to grow and flourish?

- What are the weeds in the garden of your brain? Are you pulling them out by the root? Why is this important?

This spring, as we began observing the seeds that we are always planting in our minds and hearts, we also intended to plant a garden of lavender to watch how our attention and care can nourish the actual plants as they grow. Even as we would have tended our lavender plants, we would have charted and tracked our own brain states to build awareness of the water, sunlight, nutrients, and shade that we always need to flourish. We would have watched our gardens change and grow over the remaining weeks of the school year, and our attention to them would have been a touch point to share with each other. Sadly, because our schools closed so abruptly due to the COVID-19 pandemic, we were unable to invite our students into this living metaphor of co-regulation and well-being. We hope that their learning in Ms. Spitole's classroom from August through March has given them a greater understanding of their brain states and a sense of how much control they truly have over their own well-being. I hope to visit many of these students next school year to check in with how they worked through their brain states—their living gardens—during these days of COVID-19.

In the Resource Section of this book, you will find additional templates, strategies, and practices to enhance your morning meeting rituals and end-of-the-day routines that create points of connection for staff and students.

"Bring students into your calm. Don't let them bring you into their storm."
CAROLINE COMBS

CHAPTER 5

Brain-Aligned Preventive Discipline: Putting it All Together!

"When a child hits a child, we call it aggression.
When a child hits an adult, we call it hostility.
When an adult hits an adult, we call it assault.
When an adult hits a child, we call it punishment."

HAIM G. GINOTT

"School corporal punishment is currently legal in 19 states, and over 160,000 children in these states are subject to corporal punishment in schools each year. Given that the use of school corporal punishment is heavily concentrated in Southern states, and that the federal government has not included corporal punishment in its recent initiatives about improving school discipline, public knowledge of this issue is limited."[1]

"Corporal punishment is defined as the use of physical force with the intention of causing a child to experience pain so as to correct their misbehavior; it is synonymous with physical punishment, but we will use the term 'corporal punishment' in this report because it is the term used by school districts in the U.S."[2]

As you delve into this chapter, my hope is that you now have a greater understanding and knowledge regarding brain development, the effects of adversity and attachment, and the attachment research contradicting the traditional discipline protocols so often applied our most challenging students. We can no longer ignore the science or our discipline data. As I write these words, we are in the midst of a viral pandemic (COVID-19) that is unknown, unpredictable, and leaves us all—educators, children, youth, and families—swimming in the dark, deep waters of fear without the resources and support to assist in adequately reducing and mitigating many of these fears.

Dr. Jack Shonkoff from Harvard University's Center on the Developing Child just issued these words to our communities:

> "The COVID-19 pandemic has the capacity to affect every person in the world—and how each individual responds can potentially affect everyone else. The stresses of caregiving (for children as well as for adults at greater risk) are rising for everyone. For the millions of parents who were already struggling with low-wage work, lack of affordable childcare, and meeting their family's basic needs from paycheck to paycheck, the stresses are increasing exponentially. When unstable housing, food insecurity, social isolation, limited access to medical care, the burdens of racism, and fears related to immigration status are added, the toxic overload of adversities can also lead to increasing rates of substance abuse, family violence, and untreated mental health problems. We cannot lose sight of the massive consequences of these threats to the health and development of our most vulnerable children and their families—now and for years to come. In this time, responsive social interaction is critical and strengthens resiliency, but social distancing is required. The question is not whether we will get through the ordeal that lies ahead—because we will. The important questions are how well we can work together to protect all young children and their families and how much we will learn from this unprecedented challenge and make necessary changes for the future. Please remain connected, stay safe, and share your creative ideas so we can all learn from them.

JACK P. SHONKOFF, M.D.,
Director Center on the Developing Child at Harvard University[3]

In this time and in the near future, our schools and districts will encounter heightened behavioral challenges from students of all ages. This chapter views the chronic behavioral concerns that schools face, examined through the lens of a new discipline protocol. In other words, we are putting it all together in this chapter regarding Pre-K through higher education. As we see anxiety and felt "adversities" growing among all age groups, we must recognize that the behavioral challenges look vastly different between three- and four-year-olds and young adults. These behaviors can manifest as aggressive, defiant, anxious, hyperactive, or shut-down, depending on the individual's age and underlying needs.

Anger is the bodyguard of fear. An overall sense of worry, along with the unpredictable and layered adverse experiences we are now facing in all schools, districts, and communities, are leaving their footprints in the escalation of oppositional, defiant, destructive, shut-down, and withdrawn behaviors. During and after the current pandemic, we will see emotional dysregulation increase in our children and youth. Understanding the "why" of these behaviors is the initial step and one that we will need to keep in the forefront of our minds when facing a child or youth who is coming from a survival brain state. The first step is making schools and districts aware of the contrasting differences between coercive regulation (the traditional model of discipline) and co-regulation (the grounding principle of brain-aligned preventive relational discipline).

Co-Regulation vs. Coercive Regulation

On the following pages is a succinct chart that, step by step, explores the clear differences between co-regulation and coercive regulation, a comparison between these two models for addressing discipline that we hope to integrate into many schools and districts. If we are truly to become trauma responsive, we need to embrace a very different perception of what discipline is and the opportunities we must build while strengthening connections during this process of teaching and learning!

Co-Regulation (Brain-Aligned Preventive Relational Discipline)	Coercive Regulation (Traditional Model of Discipline)
Step 1. Awareness of My Own Feelings · I am aware and paying attention to my feelings and sensation. · I am willing to regulate my own brain before disciplining a student. · I will clearly commit to three quick, easily doable regulatory routines to calm me in a short period of time. · I pay attention to my nonverbal communication. · I will notice how I sense my body when I feel angry, hopeless, anxious, or irritated.	**No Awareness of My Own Feelings and Sensations** · I focus on the child's or adolescent's behavior with little awareness of how I am feeling or sensing this experience. · I need a quick fix. · I need the student to feel the discomfort of their choices. · I need to feel in control, and I use many words in an angry tone to acquire the control and power I feel I have lost.
Step 2. Focus on Child's Sensations and Feelings · I notice the rising irritation, angst, and anger of the student. · I recognize that I may have a minute or less to redirect, reappraise, distract, or suggest the taught procedures for calming the brain, reminding the student they have choices and options.	**Focus on Child's Behavior** · I focus only on what went wrong and the surface behavior that presents as disrespect, opposition, defiance, or growing aggression; or as withdrawn, shut-down, and internalizing behaviors. (These internalizing behaviors can look and feel disrespectful to adults.)
Step 3. Soothing: Assertive Tone · I am aware of my own tone. · I check in to see if my prosody aligns with how I am feeling. · I am aware that my tone of voice speaks louder than my words and can be a tool to calm and regulate draining off the child's or adolescent's growing negativity and dysregulation.	**Loud: Aggressive Tone** · I am using a loud, authoritative voice to stop the behavior that I feel is inappropriate. · My tone escalates each time I confront the student, feeding the growing conflict and power struggle to attain the power and control I feel I am losing.

Co-Regulation (Brain-Aligned Preventive Relational Discipline)	Coercive Regulation (Traditional Model of Discipline)
:p 4. Absorbing and Draining Off Child's Hostility	**Retaliating to Child's Hostility**
sense that the student may need time, pace, movement, touch, warmth, coolness, or a rhythmic activity.	• I sense growing, debilitating, or negative serve-and-return, tit-for-tat hostility.
model for the student how to become calm before we implement conversation and words.	• Our power struggle escalates both educator and student with little reasoning, problem solving, emotional regulation, or intentional time in between the yelling, nagging, and growing discord.
	• Retaliation becomes a battle of the wills.
ep 5. Meeting Child's Support Needs	**Ignoring Child's Needs**
provide and model a routine of regulation strategies aligning with the child's or adolescent's primary needs.	• I shout the consequences for stopping the behavior in the heat of the moment, with the possible use of isolation or loss of a privilege (recess, lunch detention)
can also model my own regulatory strategies (such as a deep breath, five jumping jacks, a drink of water or taking my own pulse) to model the behaviors I want to see from the student.	• There is no plan of action for creating a new reentry following the consequences, or a new routine for starting over or beginning a new day or period of time.
	• I leave the student to recycle the angry thoughts, feelings, and sensations in hopes of some immediate compliance and obedience.
ep 6. Thermostat	**Thermometer**
My brain state needs to resemble a thermostat that is holding a steady temperature and staying connected through the conflict with a goal of creating a preventive, pre-taught routine for the student when the next emotional challenge arises.	• My brain state rises and falls with my student's brain state.
	• I find myself unintentionally caught up in the conflict cycle of yelling, nagging, and threatening.
As a thermostat, I am teaching the behaviors I want to see and modeling self-care and respect during the discipline process.	• I begin to feel the toxic wear and tear of this hostile exchange within myself and within my students.

The following chart shares the "adult" mind shift and perceptual focus that we need to consider and align with when confronted with pain-based behaviors. This alignment is central to the new lens for discipline as we prioritize relationships and the regulation of the nervous system, creating the sustainable changes in the emotional, social, and cognitive outcomes of both teacher and student.

I've created a ladder of brain-aligned discipline with the help of many colleagues who are implementing this framework as they address the discipline struggles and challenges they are facing. This ladder works from the bottom up, just as a home is constructed and built from a strong foundation. I will expand upon each section, exploring how we begin to create environments, relationships, and spaces that feel safe and connected. This ladder of brain-aligned discipline builds upon each section, and just like the brain's development, it is not meant to be a smooth linear journey. There may be days and weeks when we visit and work in one section, or take on two at a time, or revisit sections that may need modifications and adjustments to align with the developmental needs of each student, staff member, or the class as a whole. This ladder of brain-aligned relational discipline applies to all work environments, building upon the prevention of conflicts and power struggles as we collectively lay the groundwork on the front end.

Here is a visual image of this discipline ladder that briefly describes each section from the base or the bottom up. Notice the plus and minus sign at the top of the ladder on each side; much like a battery, we need both charges to activate and run smoothly.

Brain-Aligned Classroom Discipline and Leadership

"+"   **"—"**

"+"	"—"
Reinforcement/Self and Educator Assessments and RTI/MTSS Plans. Check-ins. Adjustments. Adapt new plans, incentivize desired behaviors.	**Large Backup Systems.** Office is involved. Before reintegration, hold restorative practices. RTI/MTSS snapshot is reworked & implemented. Emphasis on relationship/regulation. Brain-aligned reintegration plan with strengths, challenges, triggers, and 3 alternative changes for re-entry that are collaborative/acceptable for all.
Omission Process for Group Behaviors. Incentives. Noticing what is going well. Together, identify troublesome in-class behavior. Work together to eliminate through gradual process. Reduce the number of times behavior occurs. Preparation focused on process. Begin with an attainable benchmark and number.	**Medium Backup Systems.** *Big gap in meeting this need.* Fundamental to discipline shift. Leadership/relationships required. Who can build relationships with our most emotionally challenged students? Co-regulation is critical. What area is available for co-regulation? Dual Brain Sheet.
Omission Process for Individual Behaviors and Negative Brain States. How do I choose one behavior that I want to see less? Students track and record their behavior with teacher feedback. Emotional, social, academic challenges!	**Small Backup Systems.** Routines and a sanction taught, practiced, & modeled. Amygdala Reset Area where students move to regulate. Areas are neutral; do not equate to "time out" areas. Use Amygdala Area to model when you are feeling anxious/overwhelmed. "What do you need when you return to work? How can I help?"
Simple Incentive Systems. How do I structure the first hour or morning? What is our class challenge? Brain Intervals and time to connect after work! Not rewarding. Creating "time" for rejuvenation and service.	**Complex Incentive Systems.** Individualized. Tied to RTI snapshot for individualized systems; chunking assignments, frequent check-ins & feedback. Individualized plans for working through a process of emotional/cognitive growth. Identify strengths/challenges & 2-3 steps needed to begin process of movement.
Positive Connections/Regulation of Brain State. Resiliency touch points. Intentional signals. Warm eye contact. Greeting students. What is your title? Take your order. Noticing Sheets and 2x10	**Limit Setting (Never Go Public).** Emotional contagion; anger is fear's bodyguard. When we call out a student who is triggered, we unintentionally escalate the nervous system. Use your body, not your words: signals, post-its.

CLASSROOM STRUCTURE AND ROUTINES: FOUNDATION OF DISCIPLINE
Teacher Brain State/Well-Being, Routine & Procedure, Teaching Neuroanatomy, Creating Environment of Relaxed Alertness

CLASSROOM STRUCTURE AND ROUTINES: FOUNDATION OF DISCIPLINE

Routine and Procedures, Teaching Neuroanatomy, and Creating Environments of Relaxed Alertness

In this foundation section, we address and emphasize how educator brain and body states create the emotional climate in the classroom, school, or home. Those students, parents, and staff members who enter this space experience safety and connection, whether it's an individual room, building, or area where students and staff are learning, teaching, parenting, or leading. The foundation of this ladder pays significant attention to the routines and procedures in the home, classroom, and school. When mutually agreed upon routines, guidelines, and procedures are in place, this is the launch-pad of preventive relational and brain-aligned discipline. It is here that we explore the aesthetics of the space, of how we greet and meet one another when the doors open and close. Children and youth desire predictable environments, which is why routines of regulation or priming the brain for learning are critical at the base of this ladder. The previous chapters addressed the touch points and brain-aligned practices and strategies that we can implement to build engagement and calm the nervous system before we initiate any learning. As there will be students who need a few more regulatory strategies, time, and space to begin or end the day, these routines and procedures are taught ahead of time just like traditional procedures.

As a class, family, or staff, we are led to understand and respect the individual differences that each of us may require for the focus and connection we need to experience a sense of calm and relaxed alertness. In this section, we'll review: touch points; routines of regulation such as focused attention practices, morning meetings incorporating movement and art, drumming; and ways to build engagement and create a network of relationships from the very start of a day or class period. Prior chapters and the Resource Section of this book provide many practices, strategies, and examples that we can integrate here. Focused attention practices are built into our procedures and become a part of how we begin, end, or implement when we need a go-to strategy during a stressful moment throughout the school day.

Focused attention practices are brain exercises for quieting the thousands of thoughts that distract and frustrate us each day. When the mind is quiet and focused, we are able to be present with a specific sound, sight, or taste. Research repeatedly shows that quieting our minds ignites our parasympathetic nervous system, reducing heart rate and blood pressure while enhancing our coping strategies to effectively handle the day-to-day challenges that keep coming. Our thinking improves and our emotions begin to regulate so that we can approach challenging experiences with variable options. We teach our students about their neuroanatomy as they begin to understand the "why" of these practices. We always give students a choice when we lead these practices, and after each time, we ask them to reflect on how it felt to them. Our enthusiasm and willingness to integrate these into our procedures will be a key factor in how successfully focused attention practices will be embraced. Below are a few examples, but we will share more practices in the Resource Section of this book.

New Focused Attention Practices: Preventive Discipline Through Procedures

- **Lather Up!** Lathering up your hands with soap and with soapy fingers and palms, give yourself a 30-second hand massage, followed by the ten-finger dance. Take each soapy finger and wriggle it and make it dance rinsing under the water one finger at a time!

- **Sparkler Breath!** As you inhale deeply, raise your arms up above your head pretending you have a sparkler in each hand. As you hold your breath for a few seconds, wave your sparkler around, and then as you exhale, make the sound of a sparkler extinguishing in a pretend bucket of water by breathing out between your teeth with your mouth closed. Do this two or three times. Try to slow your exhale way down as you lower the sparklers into the water.

- **Rock and Roll!** Roll a smooth rock, pencil, or pen along your palm from the tips of your fingers to the base of your hands in rhythm with your breath. Try this for one minute.

- **My Superpower!** Hold a superpower balance or pose for 30 seconds, and breathe deeply in that frozen pose. You could do a core pose, a wall sit, or a balancing-toes pose as you stretch your arms up in the air on the tips of your toes. Try to hold this pose for 30 seconds while breathing deeply.

- **Dr. Seuss and Rhythm!** Elementary students love to clap, drum, or do any kind of body percussion to the rhyming books of Dr. Seuss. Do this as a class or family!

- **The "So What?" Breath!** For three deep breaths, inhale while silently saying "so," and exhale while silently saying "what." Variations could be inhaling "so" and exhaling "hum," or breathing in only the sound of your breath and exhaling a peaceful word of your choosing.

- **I've Got This!** Take your pulse when upset, follow up with three deep breaths, and take your pulse again. Breathe deeply four more times with a two-second longer exhale—and watch your heart rate drop!

- **Rooftop Breathing!** Breathe in while counting to four, hold for a count of seven with your tongue on the roof of your mouth, and breathe out for eight. Repeat this pattern two to three times.

- **The Shape of Calm!** Draw a shape on a piece of paper. As you breathe slowly in and out, continue tracing that shape without lifting your pencil or pen until you begin feeling calmer and more relaxed.

- **Slow It Down!** How many long, slow breaths are you taking in 30 seconds? The lower the number, the more powerful the breath. Try four breaths in 30 seconds and then eight breaths in 60 seconds. See if you can reduce your count of breaths by one or two.

- **Ice Cube Sensation!** Place an ice cube in your mouth for one minute, and feel the sensation in different areas as it begins to melt. What did you notice? How did it feel?

- **Rhythm and Art!** With music in the background, begin to draw to the rhythm of your breath and the beat of the music. It may be easier to try breathing or drawing to the beat of the music before combining the two.

- **Hug Yourself!** With one hand under the opposite arm and the other hand on the opposite shoulder, breathe deeply and squeeze gently, giving your upper body the steady pressure with each deep inhale, and then release the squeeze on the exhale. Switch sides and repeat.

- **Forehead and Chest Breath!** Place one hand on your forehead and the other hand on your chest. Take three deep breaths. Switch hands and repeat.

- **Breathing in Color!** Choose your favorite color. Closing your eyes (or leaving them open if you prefer), breathe in and visualize every inhale as a swirling ribbon of color. On the exhale, feel the breeze of a worry begin to leave you. Imagine that swirling color as it moves up to your head and down to the soles of your feet.

Positive Connections: Regulation of Brain State

In this section of the discipline ladder, we become intentional about identifying a few critical moments in which we can create a variety of possible touch points with our students. I shared several of these practices in Chapter 4, but in addition to those strategies, practices, and activities that are also a part of our routines and procedures, touch points don't always have to originate with an adult. Think of how we could focus our students on becoming touch points for one another, sitting side by side as a source of support and connection. Another soothing touch point might be notebooks or journals.

My husband was cleaning out our garage a few months ago and found a box of our oldest son's memorabilia from elementary school, middle school, and young adulthood. Opening a worn leather childhood journal with a rusty and broken lock, we began to sift through the tattered pages. What we found was fascinating! At age ten, Andrew began every journal entry with, "Dear Journal, How are you?" "Dear Journal, Sorry I didn't write to you yesterday!" "Dear Journal, I have missed you!" Then we noticed his entries changed in middle school. The greeting from Andrew read, "Hey! What's up?" "What's crackin'?"

We then began to read entries after high school graduation as his greeting had transitioned into a statement of feeling or simply sharing what was happening in his life. I sat down in our kitchen and thought of the pure unconditional connection this little brown journal had provided for Andrew. This journal was a touch point for Andrew during his darkest and most difficult times, and he relied on it for sharing what he could not with friends or family. Journals have been around for so long and we know their purpose, but in this time, I feel that part of our discipline procedures for staff and students should be offering a small amount of time each day for writing, drawing, or creating art forms to empty out the toxic thoughts and feelings that a child or youth needs to express as a way of experiencing some relief and connection.

Sharing is always a choice, and as I have communicated with administrators, this is a touch point for staff to empty their feelings and thoughts before a meeting, Professional Learning Committee (PLC), or beginning a day of teaching or leadership. Below is a list of strategies shared in this chapter and previous chapters that can also be found in the Resource Section of this book.

- Intentional Signals: Create a funny hand signal to share with a student for redirection. (Chapter 5)

- Warm Eye Contact: We read the eyes of another for regulation, and there is emotional contagion present when a calm glance is read by another set of eyes. (Chapter 4)

- Greeting Students: Warm eye contact, open body posture, and a compassionate greeting set the tone of the day. (Chapter 5)

- Take Your Order: What do you need from me today? (Chapter 4)

- 2 x 10 Strategies: We spend two minutes with a child for ten days in a row, tapping into casual conversation about their interests, passions, and happenings. (Chapter 4)

- Active Constructive Responding: When a child shares a story, a neutral event, or a happening, our presence can be felt when we ask for more details. "Where were you when you heard this good news?" "Who was with you?" "What were you doing right before this happened?" (Chapter 4)

- Classroom Roles and Responsibilities: Assign or invite students to be the Kindness Keeper, Noticer, Researcher, Resource Manager, Neuroscientist, Artist, Architect, YouTube Creator, and Collaborator. (Chapter 4)

- More About Me and What I Need (Chapter 4)

Limit Setting: Never Go Public

In this preventive section, I want to address the power of emotional contagion. Our nonverbal communication is read in all moments and is acutely picked up by students who are feeling unsafe, rough, or agitated. One of the unspoken rules of adolescence is: "You can say or do anything, but NEVER CALL ME OUT IN FRONT OF PEERS!" I am learning that body language and facial expression can signal what we need from a child or adolescent. If I am noticing a pattern of escalating behavior, I will meet with this student in a mutual private time and ask for their help. For example, *"Trish, it feels that when we begin whole-group discussions, you seem to get frustrated and angry. Then I start to redirect you, and I end up raising my voice, and then we are both angry! What can we do to make this better? Would you like a break or some time before we begin the whole-group time? Maybe we create a hand signal that I will see and know what you need. What are your ideas?"*

This type of limit setting and subtle reminder are very beneficial when students begin to escalate and feel backed into a corner! Why? Students carrying in trauma and adversity can suffer from reluctance to admit fault. When the blame is pointed at them, they often feel their entire identity is under siege, when what has really occurred is only a correction of a specific behavior. What can we do?

- Create signals with students so that we can nonverbally address and redirect behaviors.

- Use Post-its instead of words to guide or redirect behaviors.

- Assign a classroom responsibility or leadership task to redirect behaviors.

Simple and Complex Incentive Systems

Simple incentive systems are designed for an entire class. Incentives work well as preventive discipline, and we teach, practice, modify, and adjust this approach throughout the school year. Simple incentive systems build safety and connection. These systems address how our routines and class rituals can build engagement, expanding upon whole-class success while emphasizing how essential it is for students to give one another support. This incentive system doesn't happen overnight. As a teacher or administrator, we understand that strengthening trust and relationships lies at the heart of this strategy. We meet and provide ideas and feedback for one another while we create classroom guidelines together. We build in an incentive at the end of a class period or school day to celebrate how we have supported one another and handled conflict throughout the period or day. These are a few of the questions we might discuss in group meetings as we are designing incentives.

- How should we structure the first hour or 20 minutes of the day or morning? Is there an opportunity during the first few minutes to create connections?

- What is our class challenge?

- What types of activities or free time at the end of the day or morning would we like to create?

- Which student could lead our brain intervals this week?

- How can we build in time for rejuvenation and service?

- How could we support each other when one of us is struggling?

Complex incentive systems are designed for individual students and can benefit from implementing the A SECRET template, which I explained in Chapter 3. This system is designed collectively by a student and a team of adults. It differs from a behavioral plan in that it addresses the sensations, feelings, culture, tasks, and experiences that are troubling for a student; and it replaces those troubling events with repairing experiences that lie beneath the behavior, allowing us to meet students where they are in brain state. When designing a complex incentive system, we agree to explore a student's interests, strengths, and the experiences that trigger or quickly escalate behaviors.

Following is an example of a new accommodation plan through a lens of adversity and trauma. This template does not replace an Individualized Educational Plan (IEP) or 504 documents, but it supports the student in every classroom or school environment to provide consistency and predictable opportunities that feel regulating and calming while preventing unnecessary escalations and conflicts. Next is an example of a template supporting students through an adversity and trauma lens.

A Comparison of Traditional Accommodations and Accommodations Using the Lens for Adverse Childhood Experiences (ACEs)

What do you need?

Many of our students who need emotional support and resources do not have an IEP, 504, or team of educators and staff available to consistently meet their social and emotional health needs each day. These students often come to school in a survival brain state, plagued by the adversities that have accumulated throughout the days, weeks, months, or years. This template is created collaboratively to support all students with significant Adverse Childhood Experiences. These supports and resources are for our children and youth who carry in pain-based behaviors. They need accommodations and possible modifications during the school day regarding their environments, regulation, and schoolwork. The template addresses the critical needs of attachment and regulation. Often, as students move to different classrooms and environments, we aren't consistent in providing a routine of two or three practices that students can implement to calm and regulate while building relationships with other adults or students throughout the school day.

What can we do to make it better?

Rather than adding more work to what we are already doing, we are intentionally and transparently handling this child or adolescent with care and understanding. We recognize that pain-based behaviors show up in disrespectful, defiant, or shut-down ways, and we offer accommodations that can occur naturally through our procedures, routines, transitions, and morning bell work and meetings!

How can I help?

We know that many of our roughest and most dysregulated students don't have these accommodations with accompanying accountability—or if they do, they aren't consistently available and monitored. As a district, school, department, classroom, or grade level, we need to create these accommodations so they are consistently implemented and discussed daily or weekly.

Why

If our social and emotional learning outcomes, programs, and competencies are to reflect the current brain research addressing the severe life disruptions and trauma occurring in our student populations across the country, we need to address specific areas of brain development with regard to acquiring these competencies. Brain development is complex, and even today, we know very little about how individual regions of the brain work collectively through neuronal connections and projections. We do know, however, that human brains are not complete at birth, but are designed to continue developing throughout a person's life. This development is intimately impacted by experiences. Because our students spend over 13,000 hours in school during their K-12 span, educators have the opportunity—and the obligation—to address the social and emotional skills and the competencies through creating the accommodations and adjustments needed for emotional, social, and cognitive well-being.

SCHOOL ACCOMMODATIONS

Traditional Accommodations	Accommodations Through ACEs' Lens
1. Seating at the front of the class	1. I need a seat where I feel safe and secure.
2. Graph paper to line up math problems	2. I need two adults in the building whom I can trust and a place to walk when I begin to feel triggered.
3. Multiplication table or use of calculator	3. I need a personalized routine of three practices that I can implement when I begin to feel anxious, angry, or negative (such as a sip of water, five deep breaths, drawing or creating with an art form for a few minutes).

Traditional Accommodations	Accommodations Through ACEs' Lens
4. Repetition and explanation of directions when needed	4. I need access to sensory area or table in our classroom for patterned repetitive activities to calm me down.
5. Preprinted classroom notes from the teachers	5. I need a personalized set of my accommodations given to all who work with me so that they can help me de-escalate, calm down, and become ready to learn.
6. Occupational therapy every Wednesday	6. I need a weekly meeting with my resiliency team (two or three individuals at school whom I trust).
7. One-on-one math tutoring twice a week during study hall	7. I need regularly scheduled, one-on-one check-in time with my pre-arranged mentor whom I can also go see to help me co-regulate as needed.

TEST ACCOMMODATIONS

Traditional Accommodations	Accommodations Through ACEs' Lens
1. Extended time on tests and quizzes	1. I need extended time to regulate if necessary and academic accommodations for my assignments when I am dysregulated.
2. Quiet testing room with small group setting	2. I need access to a quiet area when I need to regulate my nervous system via a routine of three options (such as taking my pulse, drawing or writing in my journal, or working in another classroom).

MY GOALS

Traditional Accommodations	Accommodations Through ACEs' Lens
1. Improve my mental math skills	1. Learn to regulate with an adult before I reach the tipping point
2. Get better at asking for help when needed	2. Lessen the number of times I need to use the resiliency team and the Amygdala Reset Area
3. Join a school club or activity	3. Create a journal of my ups and downs to track my progress

More About Me and What I Need:

1. **Strengths to Help Me With My Goals:** What skills and activities show my strengths with learning and service to others? For example:
   - I love to learn. I'm seen as a leader and good friend by others.
   - I have a great imagination.
   - I know how I feel and learn best!
   - I work quickly.
   - I notice everything.
   - I am good at sensing others and all nonverbal communication.

2. **Interests and Areas of Expertise:** What are my interests and areas of knowledge that I can share with my class, school, and community? For example:
   - I love art!
   - I am interested in animals, especially cats.
   - I have a pet-sitting service.
   - I am good at soccer.

3. **Triggers:** What are the experiences, events, sights, sounds, smells, relationships, and people who can unexpectedly trigger or activate anger, irritation, or worry? For example:
   - The angry sound of an adult shouting
   - The smell of frying onions
   - The sight of a dark green SUV covered with road dust

Behavioral Neuroplasticity Omission Process:
Individual Behaviors

When identifying behaviors that feel disruptive to learning, in-struction, and the class, we need to focus on one behavior at a time; otherwise, we can begin to feel overwhelmed by all the possible be-haviors we may have to address! All behaviors communicate a need, and each is a signal for us to look beneath the behavior. Relationships and regulation are at the core of the omission process, so when im-plementing this process, we choose a neutral calm time to meet with the student for exploring a specific behavior that we'd like to track together. Our objective is a mutual understanding of how we can slowly lessen this behavior through agreed-upon strategies. If a student shouts out 15 times a day, our goal is to aim for 14 times a day. We track this in a visual way, showing that we're both aware of and assessing the targeted behavior. This doesn't mean that there are no consequences, but rather that our focus is on creating "chunks" of time and noticing that we are moving in the right direction. Even if there needs to be a change in seating, redirection, or time spent in an area where the distraction is less, we still notice, work together on our goal each day, and make any necessary modifications. Pro-viding frequent feedback and checking with brain states are effective tools, especially when we use the template for brain state check-ins described in Chapter 3 and also included in the Resource Section of this book. Remember that behaviors change with patterned repetitive practices—and this change takes time. We need to assist our students in finding a mutually agreed-upon replacement behavior.

Behavioral Neuroplasticity Omission Process:
Class Behaviors and Emotional Contagion

Omission processes for group behaviors are addressed when we are tackling a challenge that the whole class is struggling to achieve. Some examples might be:
 • Shortening amount of time for bathroom breaks
 • Students constantly calling each other out

- Getting started on assignments
- Very little engagement because students are off task
- Completing work

As a class, we choose to focus on one behavior that we agree upon in a neutral time. We then decide how we will track this behavior and incentivize the process—because it *is* a process and it *will* take time! We've found that if we have students envision a container for collecting their worries, frustrations, and irritations, they can set it aside for later with the understanding that they can choose to share these concerns with someone they trust. We have also encouraged our students to use a sensory tool from the Amygdala Reset Area (as described in the Resource Section of this book) when they notice a sensation that signals anger or frustration, such as feeling hot, a racing heart, or shortness of breath. Our bodies tell us how we feel in every moment. When we learn to tune into the language of sensation, which is the language of our body experiencing discomfort and dysregulation, we can lessen that sensation with a sensory experience that feels calming to our nervous system. We provide a table of practices and strategies for regulating brainstem, limbic system, and cortex in the Resource Section of this book.

Small Backup Systems

Small backup systems provide immediate brain-aligned consequences that are natural, taught ahead of time as a procedure, modeled, and practiced with students. When students have made poor choices that result in infractions such as shouting out, getting out of their seat, refusing a directive, or displaying a type of disrespect that disrupts the learning process, we suggest that they take care of their brains in the Amygdala Reset Area. These areas are neutral and do not equate to time-out areas or a discipline procedure that calls students out or isolates in any way. It's very important that students have a significant role in creating these areas and that we use and model Amygdala Areas for celebratory purposes! For example, when I walk into my fifth-grade classroom, I share with the class about the great start to my day as I awakened early, did yoga, and had time to eat a little breakfast. I then tell them, "I am heading into the Amygdala Area for three deep breaths, a mint, and a sip of water, and then I will be ready for morning meeting!" We use this area to model what we can do when feeling anxious or overwhelmed. We also introduce prompts to remind students about this option: "What do you need that will help you when you return to your seat and begin working? How can I help?" They know through our previously taught procedures that they have the freedom and the choice to implement a routine of two or three regulation strategies to calm and regulate their nervous system—which they can initiate in this safe, welcoming space.

If students can regulate in the Amygdala Area for a few minutes, then there are no consequences. The only natural consequence is making sure that they make up any missed classwork, but we never tell the student this expectation until they are calm and regulated. The expectations of "making up work that was missed" is taught ahead of time, before anyone begins to access this Amygdala Area.

Medium Backup Systems: Co-Regulation

There are no words to really describe how very fundamental this system is with regard to this brain-aligned preventive discipline shift. A medium backup system is missing in almost every school across the country, and this is a significant gap in our discipline protocols with our most troubled students. We are learning every day that traditional discipline procedures, such as isolation, yelling, threatening, and throwing students out of school, simply escalate behaviors while reactivating the stress response systems of our children and youth. If you find yourself disagreeing with this statement, I encourage administrators and teachers to look at their discipline data. Most, if not all, of your students who are collecting class and office referrals and receiving in-school and out-of-school suspensions are the same students each day and week! We are not seeing a completely different group each week. Most of these students carry in pain, because the adversity and trauma in their lives have created a brain and body state that is bathing in an overwhelmed state of dysregulation. These students are constantly scanning the environment to see who they can trust and what experiences, people, or things can preserve their survival. When we reach the medium backup system, it's because our students are unable to regulate in the classroom. At this point, they need a trusted adult to co-regulate with them.

Let me explain and be very clear: *Co-regulation is not rewarding negative behavior, although it can seem this way if we do not deeply understand the science and story beneath the behavior.* Regulation, control, empathy, and kindness are a few of the skills that need to be taught and modeled just like math, reading, or any other academic subject. If a child isn't exposed to kindness, the circuits in the brain for kindness fail to develop; if a child isn't exposed to empathy, the circuits in the brain for empathy will not develop. Children from very tough places have learned to manipulate and control their worlds. From a child's or adolescent's viewpoint, manipulation is one of the greatest adaptations for self-protection, and the learned belief of control keeps him or her alive! We see control and manipulation when behaviors have escalated to the point at which we are in need of a medium backup system.

In the medium backup system, we provide students an opportunity to regulate with an adult they trust, which requires planning and preparation ahead of time. This is where we close the gap, and this takes time, planning, and leadership. *This shift to the medium backup system defines the differences between being a trauma-informed and a trauma-responsive school or district.* A teacher cannot teach a class filled with other children and co-regulate a dysregulated child at the same time. Schools will need to develop processes and predictable patterns of intervention that allow for adults who are available, and who have relationships with the children or adolescents they serve, to quickly come to a student's aid with the proper training and the skills to co-regulate a dysregulated student. Just as students don't become dysregulated by appointment, they need immediate response to regulate them safely and then reintegrate them back into their classrooms. This will require training and coordination by the school leadership and the entire school staff, as everyone in the school community will need to make the shift toward a culture that prioritizes connection and regulation at the core of its trauma-and-adversity discipline system.

Traditionally, when children become rough and dysregulated, most are sent to the large backup system also known as the school's office. A medium backup system, rather than being the office, is a safe place in the building. For a medium backup system to succeed, leadership and relationships are a priority. A medium backup system can look very different in every school, but the common goal is always modeling and teaching the behaviors that you want to see through co-regulation practices, the core of the medium backup system. Co-regulation requires an adult whom the student trusts, and who is somewhat "on call" that day, morning, or afternoon. It requires a structure and function that is prepared ahead of time by building administrators. In many schools where we are implementing this system, they've created a resiliency team, which is an on-call network of staff including one administrator and a variety of educators, such as counselors, social and emotional coaches, social workers, teachers, or a staff member who builds relationships with students and has a deepened understanding of the science of co-regulation.

A resiliency team can have many functions, but one of these roles is establishing a routine based on what is calming to the student, a space for regulation, and a procedure where children and adolescents can spend some time with a trusted adult when behaviors escalate.

Last year, we were working beside Chris, an eighth-grade student who was heading in the direction of his ninth suspension—and it was only early November! This stream of suspensions was spiraling into an unbroken and unwavering pattern. Chris was fighting constantly, running out of the classroom, punching lockers, and slamming class-room doors as he attempted to leave school. He had a history of significant adverse childhood experiences along with several foster home placements. The resiliency team in this Indianapolis Public School consisted of the assistant principal, the resource special edu-cation teacher, and the school counselor (and myself when I was in the building). On a Tuesday afternoon, following an outburst, Chris was in the resource co-regulation space with his teacher and me. We were not talking but simply sitting together in the quiet as I began thumbing through a few of the sensory tools in our Amygdala Area that were options for Chris. I discovered a hand warmer in the basket, the kind we place inside our gloves here in the cold Midwest winters, and I popped it open, holding and squeezing it until it began to warm. Chris saw what I was doing and asked if he could hold it for a minute. I handed it to him, and as he sat there squeezing it and moving it from hand to hand, we watched the anger and irritation literally begin melting away from his face and body. His posture changed and his face softened. The three of us sat together in the silence breathing deeply, sharing his moment as the heat from the hand warmer calmed him down. After a few minutes, we offered to walk with Chris, as walking was one of his pre-taught strategies for co-regulation. He agreed to walk with us as long as he could hang on to the hand warmer. Following a ten-minute walk, we returned to the resource room and Chris was ready to complete the work he had missed during the medium backup time. Chris' teacher was given a few minutes to regulate as the counselor took over her class for a few minutes when Chris was with us. This step of co-regulation is critical for the sustainable behavior changes, because the adults were modeling how to become calm before words were shared. Now it was time for the Dual Brain Sheet (which is shared, next). This template is filled out independently by both the student and educator who were involved in the conflict— at a later time when everyone has calmed down and focused. Following the completion of the Dual Brain Sheet, the team finds a time where the teacher and student can sit beside one another sharing their perceptions and creating a plan of action.

I must emphasize that the Dual Brain Sheet is *not* an activity that's just for the student. For the co-regulation strategy to be effective, the educator must complete this sheet as well and reflect upon it with the student. One of my colleagues, Principal Frank Kline, has added a "recovery bag" to this Dual Brain Sheet completion and ritual. The teacher and student complete their dual brain state surveys, connecting with a bottle of water, a stick of gum or a mint, and a notepad and pen inside each bag. This becomes a ritual that prioritizes connection through the conflict, and it is a process. We will need to focus on this recovery process because it is slow and needs patterned repetitive opportunities to create these shifts in brain state and behaviors.

Another role or responsibility of the resiliency team is taking over the class when the teacher needs to repair with a student following a disruption, allowing the student and teacher to spend time in a brain state that is conducive to listening, problem-solving, brainstorming, and collaborating.

What about consequences? Are they really consequences? To shift our lens of discipline, we'll need to redefine our understanding of the term "consequences." What if we replace that word with "experiences"? When a child is presenting emotional challenges, let us ask: What experiences would help this child begin to learn in a new way? This is the question that educators, administrators, and parents should ask continually when students shut down, refuse to work or follow a directive, or become explosive. Consequences are *never* delivered during the process of co-regulation. Consequences are a teaching tool designed to meet the needs of an individual student. Yes, there are consequences for disruptive behaviors, but they need to be experiences that are natural and delivered at a time when all parties are calm, providing the student with the best opportunity to learn from these disruptive behaviors. Below are some examples of consequential experiences that are brain-aligned, regulated, purposeful, and planned.

Name-calling:
- Create a poster or E-book of positive affirmations for the class.
- Assign this student the role of kindness keeper or noticer, having them focus on everything that is going well and right for a few days.
- This student could create a list of "kind words" and teach these words to a younger class.
- Validate the anger beneath the name-calling and help the student reframe the situation.

The following questions might be helpful.

Low-level physical aggression: All behavior is communication, and behaviors such as pushing, kicking, or hitting are a signal for a deeper need. Teachers should ask, "What is this behavior saying to me?"

- What does this student need? Do we need a new learning space in the room? (Implementing A SECRET could be very helpful with student feedback from this template.)
- Should we teach this student strategies to use their words? Should we begin to model an act of kindness or service for the person who the student hurt?
- What feels difficult?
- What could be the best possible outcome?
- What is the worst thing that could happen?
- Is the student's interpretation of this conflict true?
- How does the student know this?
- What is a first step in improving this situation?

Inappropriate school language: This calls for a discussion when both student and teacher are in a calm brain state. Sometimes the words that are inappropriate at school are used at home, so we need to understand the cultural context and have a discussion with the student. The Dual Brain Sheet is a significant first step, and this is part of the omission process discussed earlier in this chapter.

Incomplete assignments: We address this through one-on-one discussion of what this behavior is communicating. As the teacher, do you see patterns? Has something changed at home or school? Is there a lack of understanding? Do you notice a change in this student's organizational habits or patterns? After discussion, create a plan with the student and possibly a parent for making up the work that has been missed. Maybe the student would benefit from a mentor or an incentive plan to shorten assignments, shorten deadlines for completing an assignment, or tap into their interests, passions, and expertise.

Disruptive Behavior: Provide the students with opportunities to be a classroom leader in positive capacities.
- **Disrespectful**: This is challenging because disrespect is very personal and subjective, and because underneath feelings of

disrespect there is a disconnect in the relationship. Teachers should ask themselves, "What are my triggers? How am I feeling when I experience this tone and these words from the student? What am I misinterpreting or misunderstanding?" And when it's the student who feels disrespected, we need to be intentional about building connection.

- **Late/Tardy**: Ask the student, "What do you need? How can I help?" Solutions might include focusing the student on the building's reminder or warning bells, or giving them more time, an early release pass, a restroom break at the beginning of class to keep them more on task during passing periods, and storing their materials in classroom for quicker access. What patterns do we see and notice with this student?

- **Out of seat**: Allow the student opportunities to move and regulate as a part of their routine. When students are constantly out of their seat, we need to provide opportunities for movement following ten minutes on task or an agreed-upon amount of time that feels doable for everyone. If necessary, provide areas to stand during instruction. Notice when students are taking care of themselves, and thank them for it.

- **Destruction of property**: The student needs time to provide service and repair to property owner. You can also have them create videos, posters, or announcements about the importance of caring for property.

- **Walking out of the room**:
  - Offer the student agreed-upon breaks, passes for walks, or errands and responsibilities that let them work with another class, help out in the office or lunchroom, or share recess duty with another teacher.
  - Increase brain intervals throughout instruction. Ask students what they need during class and remind them of the three activities or routines that would assist them in staying focused and engaged for an agreed-upon amount of time. Start with

a few choices and small chunks of time so that so children and adolescents can meet with success immediately.

• **Impulse control:** Regulation activities are extremely significant as we develop a list of three routines with the student from the templates shared. Accommodations Through ACEs' Lens (see the chart earlier in this chapter) can also provide an opportunity for students to implement these strategies during class periods throughout their school day. These regulation routines should be taught ahead of time and modeled for and with the student. I provide a table of regulation routines at the end of this chapter.

Large Backup Systems

Large backup systems are our school's administrative offices and are traditionally used in punitive ways. These systems are implemented when students leave the class for an array of infractions, giving everyone a break from the chaos. We need large backup systems because the school administrators need to be involved with behaviors that have escalated to the point of feeling unsafe, unmanageable, and out of control. Sometimes students do need to be removed from school, and this requires a team effort from administration, teachers, parents, and the students themselves. The practical challenge in this time is that when our students are constantly removed from school without a backup plan, they return the next week, the next day, or even that same afternoon, and we end up repeating the same punitive procedures that exhaust everyone involved without yielding any real solutions.

Restorative justice practices are emerging as part of a large backup system, but for these practices and circles to be effective, adults and students need to be functioning from a regulated brain state. These practices in problem solving, reflection, and reintegration are successful when there is predictability and small doses of "felt control" by the student. Why? With the high-level disruptive and aggressive behaviors that require a large backup system, students in their survival brain state are expressing their need for manipulation and control, and all too frequently we misinterpret the fear and confusion that our most troubled students are silently (or loudly) conveying. All children manipulate and control to some degree, and we may be experiencing an increase in these students during times of increased stress or adversity.

As I have mentioned, when our children and youth from challenging adversities and trauma use manipulation, there is a part of them that believes they literally will not survive if they don't manipulate their current environment and experiences. *Our children and youth need appropriate levels of control and predictability to replace manipulation and an overwhelming need to control their worlds! What type of predictability and small doses of control can we give them to feel safe and to trust us in these moments of heightened dysregulation?*

In a large backup plan, these are the topics we need to be addressing, which is why Accommodations Through ACEs' Lens is a beneficial tool as we plan a student's reintegration into the school environment by creating connection and a felt sense of safety. Below are a few suggestions that we have implemented into the accommodations template for students who need more predictability and sense of control in their world. These accommodation plans will need modifications and changes based upon the needs, behaviors, and situations that arise in school.

1. Frequent feedback and check-ins (Brain State Reflection Surveys).
2. Frequent doses of small choices and more "yes" moments.
3. Space and time: We don't want to jump into words, lecturing, or a consequence before our students are ready to listen. We do want to make sure that we're providing some space and time before we demand a response, letting them know we are here if they need us.
4. Nonverbal assurance and validation through our facial expression, closeness or proximity, posture, tone of voice, and gestures.

The human brain is a social organ of adaptation.
As a social organ, human brains have evolved
to be linked to and learn from other brains
in the context of significant relationships.

DR. LOUIS COZOLINO

Dual Brain Sheet: Youth and Adult Working Together

A. Youth and adult will answer 1-5 independently.
B. Youth and adult will discuss and then complete 6-10 together.
C. Youth and adult will decide on additional questions to answer.

Youth
1. What was our challenge?
2. What led up to this challenge?
3. How did I handle this?
4. Could I have prevented this challenge or problem?
5. What are two adjustments that I will make the next time?

Adult
1. What was the challenge?
2. What led up to this challenge?
3. How did I handle this?
4. Could I have prevented this challenge or problem?
5. What are two adjustments that I will make the next time?

Both
6. What is our challenge?
7. What led to this challenge?
8. In the future, how can we handle this together?
9. Can we prevent this challenge or problem in the future?
10. What are two adjustments that we will make?

Additional Questions
11. What do you want?
12. How can I help you?
13. What feels difficult?
14. What is the worst thing that could happen?
15. What could be the best possible outcome?
16. Is your interpretation true, and how do you know this?

I would like to conclude this chapter with an account by Principal Karrianne Polk-Meek of Starr Elementary in Richmond, Indiana. As we weave together the concepts and practices of discipline as seen through a brain-aligned lens, Karrianne shares her journey as the administrator of a school embracing the challenges that mark the slow, arduous process of a sustainable discipline shift—and celebrating the eventual successes. Through this lens, we experience the frustrations, setbacks, moments of joy, and the effective behavioral shifts that promote student and staff well-being.

Discipline Through a Brain-Aligned Preventive Lens
Shared by Principal Karrianne Polk-Meek
Starr Elementary
Richmond Community Schools

No one becomes a principal to spend their days bogged down in student behavior and discipline. Yet I found myself in the fall of 2015 doing just that. As a first-year principal, I inherited an academically failing school (letter grade of D) with a free/reduced lunch rate of 95%. In past years, the school had been a magnet school bringing diverse groups of students through its doors to engage in business leadership and community building. That August, the magnet program ended abruptly, leaving a school staff full of questions and a new building leader with few answers for the teachers.

The neighborhood had changed significantly in the eight years since the school had become a magnet, and no one was prepared for the number of students with trauma that would walk through its doors. By the end of the 2015-2016 academic year, the school would experience a 100% increase in behavior referrals, and the faculty and staff would experience a fundamental change in the way they conducted the business of school.

How we changed the narrative is what brought you to this book and certainly why we sought out Dr. Desautels in October of 2015. I remember sitting in my office the day our district coach walked in with enthusiasm pouring from her after spending a day learning about neuroscience with Dr. Lori. This was the first moment I remember being offered an opportunity to really consider how our response to behavior could change it for the better. The key to implementing the framework is in believing we can change the brain states of our students.

While we had been tracking student behavior through PBIS (Positive Behavioral Intervention Supports) meetings and data tracking devices (SWIS) since August, we had not listened to the story that the behavior was telling us. Our team redesigned data meetings around strict protocol, keeping student names away from data sheets so that we made decisions based on what we could see, not what we believed about kids.

Because of these data meetings, we deliberately placed humans and resources in front of our students at peak times and days. We moved more adults to the lunchroom (behavior peaked at those times), and we started to reimagine what the resource room might look like. By December of that year, referrals went up exponentially and we felt like complete failures.

What we came to realize was that while we moved humans physically, we failed to move humans mentally and emotionally to help co-regulate students. It's significant to note that just having more resources is *not* a contributing factor for success. Traditional thinking holds that simply having more adults in the room will change behavior. We shifted to an understanding that having adults in the room who could co-regulate with students and who had training in neuroscience had a greater impact on their success. That required empowering adults to understand their own brain states first. PBIS meetings were increased to twice monthly after school. We created road maps for our staff to help guide them through student behavior. The district behavior coach and the principal modeled lessons for teachers and staff. The use of data was deliberate and focused at all times. We collected it continually and used it to redesign student days as needed. Conceptually, this may sound impossible. Seriously, how do you do this with 300 students, 16 teachers, eight support staff, and one principal? Again, students told us their story each day through their data. We could immediately see that mornings were *tough* for many of our students. With careful thought and planning, we could strategically place staff around the building during arrival to help co-regulate students coming in with acute need. This might mean they'd miss morning meetings in the classroom, but by the time they arrived they were ready to learn. We noted that some students were very hungry for a variety of reasons, but we tracked this and placed snacks into their day at strategic times so that they could regulate their brain states more easily.

If or when a student received three or more behavior referrals, they were immediately placed on a system of check-in, check-out aimed at teaching them ways to regulate their brain states and add layers of relationships to make them successful. We completed motivational assessments on these students and created clear, concrete behavior plans for each one that met their criteria — no IEP needed.

Students whose data showed a need for breaks outside of the classroom were given these breaks through our resource room. Breaks were never taken away, and our staff gradually began to see these breaks not as play but as a way for students to succeed through their day. Teachers began taking the strategies we were sharing and modeling to place them into their classrooms. They completed focused attention practices with their students, and classrooms were equipped with "brain" stations and opportunities for students to monitor and reflect on their own needs.

As a building leader, I became acutely aware of the needs of my staff and very familiar with my own brain state during the day. I openly acknowledged how my brain state changed, modeling ways that I managed my brain state for them. I started each day by checking in with our teachers before school and at midday during lunch. We started taking time before staff meetings to acknowledge our brain states. For example, prior to meetings I would ask our staff to move their picture above or below the line (to signal readiness to learn). Rather than looking at their referral data as something they were doing wrong, I started looking at their data as a means to support them. We found money for the resources they needed and encouraged them to take risks.

Over three years, our entire building became neuroscience-informed, and our school culture, practices, and discipline protocols were built around the framework. This could only occur because we continued to track and monitor our data directly and diligently. We never stopped learning or incorporating new brain-aligned techniques for our students. We branched out using community members for clubs such as CrossFit and offered parent courses designed to teach them how to use the framework in their own homes.

By the close of the 2018-2019 school year, Starr Elementary had decreased office referrals by over 70%, and academically we had gone from a "D" to a "B" by the State of Indiana's designation system, which rates public school accountability and assessment.

Educational neuroscience and the framework we built around it fundamentally changed behavior in our building because we proactively supported the needs of students, preventing the need to address as many behaviors after the fact. Our data tracking and deliberate use of resources created an atmosphere where students and adults could succeed both academically and emotionally.

Principal Karianne Polk-Meek
Starr Elementary
Richmond Community Schools

I'd like to end this chapter by emphasizing an idea discussed above, because I firmly believe this defines the difference between traditional regulation and brain-aligned preventive discipline: *What if we replaced the word "consequences" with the word "experiences"? When a child is presenting emotional and behavioral challenges, let us ask ourselves, "What experiences would help this child begin to learn a new way?"*

CHAPTER 6

Early Childhood Brain-Aligned Preventive Discipline

"Love is the greatest growth signal in the world."
DR. BRUCE LIPTON

In this chapter, written by my colleague, co-instructor, and former graduate student Ms. Courtney Boyle shares our work together in early childhood education during the past two years. We've spent several days each month working directly with early childhood educators and students at St. Mary's Early Childhood Center in Indianapolis. We've been modeling a variety of regulation strategies and touch-point practices to create and build relationships, promoting feelings of safety and trust with these young students. These practices embrace brain-aligned preventive discipline in early childhood and are integrated into day-to-day play and instruction. We've been intentional about morning routines that incorporate regulation practices with students as they walk into our classrooms.

Early childhood represents the miraculous years of neuroplasticity. Yet sadly, the attachment and discipline so critical to early brain development are becoming lost and distorted, greatly damaging our young children who must endure significant adverse childhood experiences. "Each year in the United States, thousands of preschool children are suspended or expelled from their early childhood care and education programs. Early childhood programs or settings are defined as programs that provide early care and education to young children birth through age five, including but not limited to private and public child care, Head Start, and public, private, and faith-based Pre-K/preschool programs. According to the National Association for the Education of Young Children (NAEYC), each year more than 8,700 three- and four-year-old children are expelled from their state-funded preschool or prekindergarten classrooms."[1] This heart-breaking statistic shows how uninformed many of us are with regard to early chronic adversity and its effects on the developing brain and body. Many of these children come from significant adversity and trauma. They are functioning in a survival brain state originating from early life experiences where secure attachments weren't always formed, generating disorganization in lower brain regions that has prohibited healthy brain development, which leads to dysregulation and chronic behavioral and cognitive challenges.

✦

In this time of early childhood, understanding brain development is critical in assisting how we address the neurodiversity of the developing brains in our young students. By implementing regulation, sensory, and movement practices as part of daily routines and transitions, we provide an opportunity for sustainable, flexible, and healthy changes in the developing brain. These predictable routines taught during the school day counteract the chronic unpredictability these children often face in their day-to-day experience. Our regulation routines have addressed a variety of rhythmic, body awareness, (vestibular and proprioceptive) sensory stimulation, along with breath, movement, and muscle stimulation associated with our fight-flight responses in the body.

We often overlook and dismiss how adversity- and trauma-filled experiences are changing how the brain develops structurally and functionally. Yet even the promise of trauma-informed programs often just scratches the surface, with the expectation of immediate results to complex problems. In other words, we keep looking for a "quick-fix" solution that will let us fix first and understand later. We see poor behavior choices and opt for compliance and obedience because, in the heated moments of conflict, even adults can fall back into a survival brain state where flight and fight overrule our cognitive and emotional strengths. We're quick to speak and slow to listen. We don't really "see" the children seated before us. Rather than ask what is wrong with these kids, we need to ask: What happened to them?

What is their story? What kinds of meaning are they deriving from their experiences?

Admittedly, we do have a national educational crisis. Our crisis, however, isn't centered on poor test scores. This crisis is rooted in childhood adversity and trauma. This crisis is severely affecting how our young people's brains develop, specifically how they form neuronal circuits based on experiences, relationships, and environments. As educators, we need to understand that many of our students who have experienced adversity and trauma sit in our schools and classrooms with a brain that is not functionally prepared to learn.

Brain development is complex, and even today, we know very little about how individual regions of the brain work collectively through neuronal connections and projections. We do know, however, that human brains are not complete at birth, but by design, continue to develop throughout a person's life.

From utero through the first two years of life, the brain is in its greatest phase of maturation. During this time, an infant's nervous system is also developing. Stimuli from the social environment enter the brain stem where attunement and attachment with a caregiver is critical for regulating the sensory and motor systems that are so important for emotional, social, and physiological well-being. According to Peter Levine, "The fetal period through the first two years of life creates the blueprint that influences every system in the body from immunity to the expression and regulation of emotion, to nervous system resilience, communication, intelligence, and self-regulatory mechanisms for such basics as body temperature and hormone production."[2]

The language of the brain stem is sensation. If sensations such as discomfort, hunger, touch, and exaggerated emotional responses are not buffered or addressed in those first few months or years of life, the child or adolescent may need to re-experience those critical earlier missed developmental steps and skills that occur in the brain stem. These include rhythm, movement, and sensory regulation. Rocking, balancing, fine motor activity, touch, and temperature regulation may need to be re-experienced later in life no matter the chronological age of the child or adolescent. These sensory and motor skills, which are developing in the brain stem, can lead to emotional regulation when a young brain is exposed to consistent and nurturing interactions with a caregiver. Before learning and cognition can be developed, children need patterned, repetitive, appropriate developmental experiences to assist them in meeting the needs of all lower brain regions.

Because the brain develops from the bottom up—from the brain stem to the limbic system and then to the cortex—children and adolescents who have been affected by chronic adversity may enter our classrooms with varying levels of brain development. As we see how many of our students come to school with high levels of adversity and trauma, we begin to realize that their levels of brain development have also been compromised by these experiences. Right now, we have an opportunity to attend to the neurodiversity of our students. We need to meet them where they are in their development and prime their brains for cognition and the healthy structures and functions required for appropriate growth and well-being.

The right-brain hemisphere develops earlier than the left-brain. The right hemisphere contains implicit memory, emotions, and visual images. It is the seat of the development for our core identity. In contrast to the right side, the left-brain hemisphere begins to develop language in the second year of life. While both sides of the brain are critical for brain functionality, the integration of hemispheres is foundational for healthy development.

Babies sleep long hours in the early days after birth as their sensory and nervous systems begin to develop. Infants cannot tolerate overstimulation as they adjust to the world outside the womb. In this stage of early development, the role of an attachment figure becomes so significant in helping co-regulation develop. An infant's underdeveloped sensory and nervous systems require gentle stimulation and a gradual progression of co-regulation techniques such as holding, rocking, healthy eye contact, and soft talking. During these processes, the infant is invited to explore new people, sounds, places, and experiences. Without a secure and steadfast attachment figure introducing these new stimuli, the infant experiences negative arousal. If this negative arousal becomes prolonged and chronic, the infant's brain begins to wire in a disorganized way. This affects the development of a healthy brain and nervous system.[3]

A Simple Expression of Love: Attachment and Co-Regulation in the Early Childhood Years

"It seems to me that the most essential element in the development of any creation must be love—a love that begins in the simple expressions of care for a little child, and, once received, goes on to mature into responsible feelings about ourselves and others."

FRED ROGERS[4]

Could there be a more perfect quote to begin a section focused on early childhood attachment and regulation? I can't think of one. Every time I read the words "a love that begins in the simple expressions of care for a little child," I break out in goose bumps thinking about the incredible opportunity that we have to work with our youngest learners. Now, if you've never worked with children in this age group, I would point you to the end of the phrase, "and, once received, goes on to mature." Attachment, the relationships we build with one another, and the regulation of our emotions and physiological states will affect us across our entire lifespan. So I would challenge anyone who doesn't believe this applies to them to keep reading, because where we have been matters just as much as where we will go.

Let's go back to where it all begins—not the first day of school or even the first day of life, but farther still. Attachment and regulation get their start in utero, as our little bodies miraculously grow and develop to the rhythm of our mother's heartbeat. At this stage, we are physically and emotionally attached to our mother. We can feel and sense an increase in her heart rate, we bathe in the same high levels of cortisol that pulse through her veins when stressed, and we respond to the sound of her melodic voice. After we try out our new lungs with that very first cry, the work of attachment and co-regulation takes off. As infants, we are completely helpless. We rely solely on our caregiver to meet our every need, not just food and shelter but also regulation and exploration of ourselves, our emotions, our psychological states, and our human condition. These first few years of life are crucial to brain development, as it is during this critical period that our neuro-foundation is laid. Through these earliest experiences, we create a template, an internal working model, on which every other life experience will be patterned. As Dr. Allan Schore says, "For the rest of the life span, attachment processes lie at the center of the human experience."[5] In summary, the first few years of life, beginning even before we are born, build the foundation of our brain architecture; but unlike a physical structure, our foundation is malleable and can be reworked and rewired across our lifetime. Now that we know the two key processes which are foundational to our development, we know exactly where our work begins: in attachment and co-regulation.

With our starting line drawn before us, the next step is to begin doing. What does attachment and co-regulation look like in the early childhood setting? We know that we can address these key processes at any age, but *how*? And by *whom*? Research in the area of attachment tells us that a caregiver is not limited to a biological parent, but rather can be thought of as an "older, stronger, and wiser figure in a child's life."[6] The title given to our role—whether it be parent, family member, teacher, clinician, day care provider, neighbor, or a host of others— does not matter. All that matters is that we are there, that we are consistent, attuned, and regulated. For the rest of this piece, I will be using the terms "educator" and "teacher" because these titles most accurately describe my current role in this work. But for all of you who may not identify with these terms, I implore you to substitute your own because this role truly applies to all of us. So, when I say "educator," substitute it with "mother." When I say "classroom," substitute it with "home." Make this work for you, for your context, and for the lives of the little human beings that you nurture, because at the end of the day we all have brains!

Now that the *whom* has been established, let's shift our focus to the *how*. Borrowing a phrase from Dr. Daniel Siegel, the ways in which we form and maintain attachments can be thought of as a "learned response."[7] Our ways of connecting with one another are not as innate as we once thought, but rather are learned from our experiences with relationships. For example, sometimes we classify people as "touchy-feely" and assume this is just part of who they are, but what if we expanded our thinking to include this as a learned behavior? Perhaps someone is "touchy-feely" because that is their internal working model built on what they experienced as a child. This has *huge* implications for our work, because the student who acts as if you are inconsequential to their existence doesn't act that way because of who they are but because of what they've learned. And let's remind ourselves that we are educators, the experts at learning—and this is something we can fix!

In the early childhood setting, play provides the most ideal and readily accessible environments for learning, and many of the experiences I will share next have taken place in this setting. Play allows us, whether educator or caregiver, to simply *be with* our children. In my experience, this state of *being with* provides the perfect opportunity to build authentic relationships, the core of attachment, and to introduce regulatory strategies. This is brain-aligned preventive discipline. These authentic relationships are based on shared experiences and individual understanding. It's not enough to simply say that we experienced something together—we must acknowledge that we processed it together. In other words, we must actively and intentionally sit beside our students in all situations, especially the challenging and uncomfortable ones. We must also overcome our own difficulties with these situations to better help our students make connections between the past, the present, and the future. Hindsight and foresight are not skills that we naturally inherit but must be taught, and they must be modeled and experienced by all. In the words of children's rights activist Marian Wright Edelman, "You can't be what you can't see." In addition to these shared experiences, we also are tasked with learning who our students are. This goes beyond remembering their names, whether they have pets, and what their favorite color is. We must understand the *why* of this student. What are the stories behind their names, pets, favorite colors, and so many other facts about them? Each of these is like a piece of a jigsaw puzzle. Alone, they may not seem like much but when we piece them together, they create a clearer picture. We do this by being active observers, by simply listening, noticing, and remembering. One of my go-to teacher tools is a journal. I always keep it with me to jot down notes to remember, because while we are tasked with so many huge responsibilities as teachers, we must not overlook the little things, those individual pieces of the puzzle.

Through my collaborative work with a local preschool, I have the fabulous opportunity to apply these assertions in real time. During my first visit, for example, I had an in-depth conversation with a young man about *The Lion King*. As the two of us colored together, we talked about the various films and television shows based on *The Lion King*, and we named the different characters. Being a fan of all things Disney, I eagerly shared that I had a shirt with Rafiki on it, and his wide-eyed response found me promising to wear it on my next visit. Knowing that it wouldn't be for a few weeks, I noted my promise in my journal so that I could intentionally follow through. I proudly wore my Rafiki shirt on my next visit, and words can barely describe his expression when he saw it—a mixture of excitement, astonishment, and pure glee! I easily could have forgotten to follow through, and offered a sincere reason for having done so, but I intentionally did not. This may seem like an inconsequential detail, yet not forgetting made all the difference. This step toward building authentic relationships and creating healthy, secure attachments is just one example of the millions of opportunities we're presented with each day, and while it may not seem like much by itself, without this one puzzle piece, the puzzle is not complete.

These "simple expressions of care," as Mister Rogers describes them, are literally everywhere. In teacher preparation programs, we often talk about building classroom community and relationships at the beginning of the school year, but opportunities for this crucial work continue far beyond August and extend further than our classroom walls. As a former special education teacher, I'm no stranger to the stress of not having enough time, so I took advantage of every second I had with my students. Walking to my room with my students became a key period in which I did this relational work. These moments were never planned. There was no activity to accomplish or lesson to be learned. We just walked and talked. This is a real-world example of *serve and return*, a term referring to the verbal and nonverbal interactions and communications between child and adult. Though he uses a slightly different term, Dr. Siegel describes this process as what happens when "a signal sent by the child is responded to by the adult with a signal sent back that matches, or is contingent, with what was initially sent."[8]

✦

Picture this: a three-year-old boy is gleefully prancing around a playground when he suddenly trips over his shoes. Upon hitting the ground, he immediately looks up and searches for his mother. During this search he shows no emotion; it's as if he hit pause. But this quickly changes once he locates mom and reads her response. If she responds with a smile and lighthearted, "You're OK! Shake it off!", then he'll most likely get up and return to his prancing, but if she responds with a look of horror and a gasp, he'll most likely burst into tears. This is serve and return. This is co-regulation. The beauty of this process is that it lives everywhere, especially in the world of early childhood. These experiences build brain architecture as the child learns to make sense of, communicate with, and navigate the world around them. This is brain-aligned preventive discipline.

While opportunities to engage in serve-and-return experiences are endless, it's important to note that the outcomes can be either positive or negative. Healthy serve and return experiences lead to what is often referred to as secure attachment, while the unhealthy ones lead to insecure attachments. To illustrate, let's revisit my story about the Rafiki shirt. I could have easily forgotten to follow through without the omission being earth-shattering to the child; but what if that child's interests had been repeatedly put down, ignored, or forgotten? What if most of his signals to adults hadn't been met with contingent responses? A few not-so-perfect serve-and-return experiences here and there aren't detrimental, but we know that patterned repetitive experiences shape our brain and specifically our internal working model of relationships. As teachers, we can't possibly know the specific details of each and every serve-and-return experience a child may have had, or of the repeating patterns of these experiences—and honestly, we don't need to know. When we offer opportunities for co-regulation (which is what healthy serve-and-return experiences are), there might be either of two potential outcomes: the experience is added to a pattern of healthy touch points which further solidifies it; or the experience is new, like nothing before, and therefore we've planted that first seed for other experiences to build on. It's a win-win!

It's also worth noting that not every experience will be perfect, and that in order to be authentic, we can't possibly plan these moments ahead of time. All we can do is be aware, be intentional, and try our best. I love the way Dr. Siegel describes this: "No parent is perfect, no relationship is without challenging moments. The key to security is not perfect attunement, but the intention for connection and the repair when our human lives encounter the unavoidable miscommunications."[9] During one of my visits to the early childhood center, I was struck by the simplistic beauty and power in these serve-and-return experiences and how naturally they erupt in our day-to-day interactions. All we require is an adult and a child—or in this case, an adult, three children, and a playground slide. As we played together, one of the little girls came gliding down the slide toward me. I instinctively knelt down, picked her up, whirled her around, and said, "I've got you!" That sounds very normal to adults who play with children, and perhaps even something we might overlook. But two other children saw this little interaction, and in a matter of seconds it had blossomed from my reaction with one child to an intentional game eagerly repeated for each child. I was blown away by how long this little game kept their interest as we repeated the pattern over and over—not to mention how sore I became as each round progressed. (They look so little, but after a few times you really start to feel the burn—as well as appreciate the impressive core strength of the average preschool teacher!) There were a few times when I altered my participation, once by standing instead of kneeling, and once by forgetting to say, "I've got you!" Of course, they quickly alerted me to my faux pas. They craved the patterned repetition of this activity and the serve-and-return process—the serve of their coming down the slide and the return of my physical and verbal response. What a better way to build trust and secure attachment than through such a natural, authentic, co-regulatory experience? The opportunities for these crucial brain-building moments are everywhere! These co-regulatory moments are touch points, connections that are the building blocks for healthy brain and body development.

Just as opportunities to model healthy touch points surround us, so do our opportunities to co-regulate. For me this is pivotal in our understanding of this concept and its application. I want to begin with a clear understanding of what this term "regulation" means. Simply put, it refers to the calming of the brain and body, and the return to baseline from a stressful situation. One only has to mention public speaking or taxes (the things that reliably upset most adults) and you can easily feel your stress response system kick into gear. Your heart rate increases, your blood pressure rises, you feel that knot in your stomach or lump in your throat, the muscles in your body tense, and all of a sudden, it's as if your brain is in a dense fog preventing you from thinking clearly or rationally. These are some of the physiological and emotional symptoms of stress. Regulation is like the antibiotic for stress, as it dampens the stress and allows us to physically and emotionally return to "a felt sense of normal." There are a million ways to regulate, but the most affective and brain-aligned ways include one or more of the following: breath, movement, sensation, and rhythm/pattern. Why these four? Our breath is the only part of our autonomic nervous system that we consciously control, so when we slow our breathing to long, steady inhales and even longer exhales, our heart rate naturally decreases and our blood pressure comes down. Movement allows us to feel unrestrained and to physically release the tension and stress pent up in our muscles. Sensations, not unlike movement, help solidify the brain-body connection that we need to feel whole. To understand how rhythm affects our bodies and brains, one only has to think back to how we developed in utero; the beat of our mother's heart was our first regulatory experience. This was also our first experience with co-regulation, because we weren't in control of our own regulation, relying instead on the regulation of someone else. Regulation is a lifelong process that begins with co-regulation and eventually expands to include self-regulation. During early childhood, we are still firmly in that co-regulation zone, meaning we need another human to help us regulate, and we need the help of a caregiver. This is where co-regulation begins to overlap with serve and return, but for now, I want to focus specifically on co-regulation.

When we talk about co-regulation in the school setting, we often picture something separate from our everyday activities. While adding, in time, to do yoga or meditate together is certainly effective, it's not always practical. In my experience, these activities are the first to go when we are searching for invaluable time. But science and common sense tell us that in order to access those cortical regions in the brain for logical thinking, problem solving, and reasoning, we need to be regulated first. During early childhood, these cortical regions are just beginning to come online, so we spend a lot of time working with the emotional and survival brain states—which means that a lot of co-regulating is needed! Just like with the ongoing touch points of serve and return, co-regulation builds and strengthens brain architecture while providing the foundation for those higher-level thinking skills. In the absence of a healthy foundation, we begin to see a disconnect or miswiring in those cortical regions, and this is one more reason that our work must begin in attachment and regulation. Play often provides the perfect environment to introduce and apply these strategies, which I have seen firsthand in my work with the early childhood center previously mentioned. To highlight the application of these concepts, I want to begin by including some of the strategies that I explored with Dr. Lori Desautels, and then share how these strategies were used in real-time through a few short narratives or vignettes.

Peaceful Brushing

This was one of the favorite calming and regulating strategies we recently began implementing. We used a variety of makeup brushes and sat in a circle as I modeled peaceful brushing circling my face and ears. I then brushed my arms, hands, and palms. After this, we took turns as I brushed areas on the children's faces, necks, arms, and hands. Many of the students did not want me to stop! This light touch was stimulating in a gentle way, and some of the children brushed their own peaceful spots. Brushing is a very effective strategy before naptime, during transitions, or when they first arrive at school.

This particular strategy had already been introduced to our preschool students when I began my work with them. As I visited each room, I noticed that these brushes were a huge hit, but not necessarily as "peaceful brushes" but as what they were—makeup brushes. On each visit, I was treated to a makeover with these brushes complete with eye shadow, blush, and even nail polish. A few times, I mentioned "peaceful brushing" and asked if they liked to do that or if they would want to show me what this strategy looked like, but I was usually met with one of two responses: they either ignored me and kept styling away, or they actually said no. In my neuroscientist(-ish) brain, I knew how regulating this particular strategy could be, especially for some of our roughest kiddos, but I also knew (in my teacher brain) that I needed to follow their lead and find a way to bridge the gap between the regulation and their own interests. Then the coolest thing happened. One day after one of our girls finished my makeup and nails, I asked her if I could do her makeup to which she eagerly said yes. (Regulation strategies and activities should always be a choice for the student.) I started by "painting" her nails—gently brushing down the tops of her fingers—and then, hoping to add some of the circular movements from the peaceful brushing strategy, I asked if I could add some "sparkle" to her hands. Using the same circular motion as mentioned above, I gently brushed the backs and palms of her hands. After this, I asked if she wanted "sparkle" on her cheeks and then repeated the same circular motions on her face. The beauty in this was that we did the peaceful brushing strategy but worded it in a different way that felt more engaging to her. I was very intentional about doing this in a calm and soft tone while taking some slow deep breaths myself. I didn't ask her to breathe with me, although I noticed that she naturally picked up on this and began mimicking the rhythm. As I brushed, I literally saw the tension melt away in her body and heard her begin speaking in a softer, slower voice. Co-regulation achieved!

During my next visit to a different room, I spent most of my time playing with one boy in particular. This little guy has faced some substantial trauma and adversity in his short life, and I really wanted to focus on how I could follow his lead in play but also interweave some co-regulation. Just before the end of my time, I asked him to get the brushes he'd used to apply my makeup earlier in my visit. I hadn't gotten a chance to try some peaceful brushing on him and wanted to give it one last go before I left. Once he brought me the brushes, I asked if I could do some brushing on him, and he quickly replied, "Boys don't do makeup!" I didn't mention that he'd done my makeup, but instead came back with a simple response. I have no idea where the words came from as I said, "These are not makeup brushes! They are superhero brushes, and we can use them to make you into a superhero!" That did the trick—he eagerly agreed! When I asked him what superhero he wanted to be, he chose "Super Bug." I'd been expecting something like Iron Man so that I could brush on the pieces of armor, but Super Bug proved to be a fun challenge. I did the same movements described in the peaceful brushing strategy but presented them a bit differently. For example, I gave him spider fingers as I brushed down the back of his hands and fingers, special spiderwebs while brushing his palms in a circular motion, and two extra bug eyes by brushing in the same motion on his forehead. Then I asked him what he wanted and so we added an antennae and special bug ears. He absolutely loved this and at one point he even softly closed his eyes as I brushed. We also shared lots of giggles and ear-to-ear smiles. What could possibly be more regulating than that?

I share these two stories because they beautifully illustrate the versatility in these strategies and the importance of getting to know your students individually. In both instances, we did the same things as detailed in the peaceful brushing strategy—the movements, patterns, and breathing—and I just changed the "packaging." And the beauty in this is that we can do it with any strategy! We keep the same core regulating components like breath, movement, sensations, and rhythm, but we change the way we present it to fit our students' interests. Both of these experiences happened during my second time with these students while I was still getting to know them, but I was able to draw from what I already knew to improvise on the fly. For my little girl, I knew that makeup interested her, and based on the content of our earlier play, I knew that my little boy really liked superheroes. The options on how to change the packaging of these strategies are endless. We just have to listen, notice, and give ourselves the space to try something different.

Animal Regulation Cards

Inspired by the true habits of animals, these cards have been designed to guide co-regulation activities based in sensory stimulation. After students become familiar with these exercises they can be used as self-regulation tools as well.

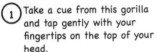

Monkeys

Did you know that monkeys use their voices, facial expressions, and movements to communicate? Gorillas beat their chests with open hands, not fists, to show their size and strength.

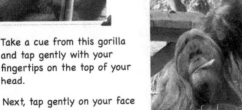

1. Take a cue from this gorilla and tap gently with your fingertips on the top of your head.

2. Next, tap gently on your face
   - on your eyebrows
   - on your temples
   - under your nose
   - on your chin

3. Raise your shoulders and arms and tap on your sides.

4. Finish by gently tapping on your chest making your best monkey sounds!

© 2019 Revelations in Education, Courtney Boyle

Elephants

Did you know that elephants create their own sunscreen by throwing mud onto their backs with their trunks?

1. Using your arm as a trunk, lift up as you inhale.

2. Hold for 3 seconds.

3. As you bring your trunk back down exhale through your mouth making a trumpet noise.

© 2019 Revelations in Education, Courtney Boyle

Koalas

Did you know that koalas can sleep up to 18 hours in one day? They tend to use most of their energy eating the leaves from the eucalyptus trees they live in.

1. Like a koala, curl into a little ball and take a few deep breaths (similar to a child's pose in yoga)

2. Laying down or sitting wrap your arms around your body and give yourself a hug

© 2019 Revelations in Education, Courtney Boyle

Dr. Lori and I created this deck of cards as a resource for teachers, a quick tool that they can use on the go. We featured many different animals, but I've included the monkey, elephant, and koala cards here because they connect directly to the following vignettes. I want to highlight two experiences in particular. The first one details how I introduced these cards to a small group of preschoolers, while the second looks at how we can use these strategies in the moment to support times of dysregulation—and stands as a practical application of brain-aligned preventive discipline.

During my second visit to Room 2, I set up what is often referred to as a provocation or a pondering question. In this instance, I brought out some animal figurines and asked a few students if they wanted to play with me. As we played and explored these animals, I asked questions such as, "What sound does that animal make?" and "Where does that animal live?" My intention was to establish their prior knowledge to use as a launching point for introducing the regulation strategies. This type of questioning often gives us indirect information about a child's perceptions and their world. After several minutes of playing, I asked if they'd like to see some videos of these animals. Of course, the second they saw my iPad they were all in!

Together we watched short clips of elephants, gorillas, monkeys, meerkats, a stork, and even some bats. As we watched the videos, we talked about what the animals were doing with specific emphasis on their movements. After watching, I invited them to move like the animals themselves. For instance, they tapped on their chest like the gorilla and gently swung their heads back and forth like the elephant. Through our play, a little routine organically emerged from our observations of the gorillas and monkeys, which coincidentally matched the tapping exercise noted on the monkey animal regulation card.

We started by imitating the small gorilla and tapping on our chests, later including tapping beneath our arms like a monkey, and finally tapping on the top of our heads, prompted by one of the animal figurines and a matching photograph of a gorilla doing the same thing. It's extremely important to point out that while I came to this experience with a rough idea of the activity, everything progressed naturally based on our play and conversation. I was intentional in the order in which I introduced the materials (figurines first, then videos), but beyond that, we moved seamlessly back and forth between the two. My "teacher" goal was facilitating an experience of naturally exploring the movements of animals and then connecting them to the cards. The power of this experience was how we naturally hit many of the activities outlined on the cards without actually looking at the cards. Following my visit, their teacher introduced the cards, and one of the children proudly shared our little routine with the rest of the class, which has since become a favorite of all the students.

This next experience took place during my second visit to Room 1. Unlike Room 2, the teacher in this class had already introduced a few of the animal regulation cards, so the students were somewhat familiar with these already. During my visit, I worked with a small group and shared my animal figurines, video clips, and the regulation cards. This experience was very different from the one I previously shared as it was free-flowing and didn't have the same intentional order of materials. However, what I want to share about this experience is how I used the cards to address some moments of dysregulation during our play.

During this time, I worked with three girls whom we'll call Lizzie, Louisa, and Hannah. As we huddled together looking at the animal videos, I noticed that Lizzie was becoming more and more dysregulated. She complained about not being able to see the iPad, started taking toys from the other two girls, and continually touched the iPad to change the screen or play the video. Unfortunately, my dinosaur of an iPad was painfully slow, which wasn't in line with this student's timeframe.

One thing that did keep her attention were the animal regulation cards. She looked at the pictures and sorted through them again and again. At one point, she got up to play with a boy who was pretending with the animal figurines just a few steps away, and when they began to argue, I decided it was time for a short break. I suggested to Louisa and Hannah that we put the iPad away and return to playing with the animals, which they eagerly agreed to. After promising the two girls I'd return to play, I asked Lizzie to take a little walk with me.

Bringing the animal regulation cards with us, we moved a few steps away but far enough to be out of earshot and feel private. I then asked if she wanted to pick a card and try the suggestions. She picked the koala. I shared that these animals sleep a lot and invited her to pretend we were koala bears and curl up like they did in the pictures. We each curled up into a ball (similar to child's pose or rock pose in yoga), and I said, "Let's pretend we're sleeping and take three deep breaths." I had a feeling that she wouldn't respond well to an invitation to just breathe, so I adapted the card a little and made my invitation more about pretending to be asleep. Next she picked the monkey card, and with a little support, she was able to tap on her head, cheeks, and temples. She told me that the tapping felt good, and I could see she'd loosened a bit of her tension, so we rejoined the other two girls.

A little later, as we built and played with the animals together, I noticed that Hannah was starting to become upset and slightly dysregulated. Then what she was building came crashing down, and she had hit her limit and began to cry. Thinking that a break was in order, similar to the one I'd taken with Lizzie, I asked Hannah to come sit with me. We backed up from the group but stayed in the same area, as I felt that Hannah wouldn't be as distracted or self-conscious about the others as I thought Lizzie might have been. Hannah climbed into my lap, and I slowly rocked side to side as I rubbed her back.

After a few moments, I asked if she remembered the video of a baby gorilla beating his chest that we'd watched earlier, and if she wanted to do that with me. As I started tapping on my chest, she gave me one of *those* looks, so I grabbed the little monkey figure whose one hand is placed on top of his head and asked if she wanted to try tapping on top of her head. I got a similar look in response, but she seemed a little more willing so I asked if I could tap for her, which she agreed to. After I did a little tapping, I asked her if she wanted to try. She did and even admitted that it felt good to her. We tapped on our chests like the baby gorilla and then under our arms. By this point, her smile was back and she was laughing again, so we rejoined the other two girls.

I share these experiences because I feel they demonstrate the importance of following the child and of how we can use play to either introduce co-regulatory strategies (as in the first vignette) or use them as in-the-moment tools for co-regulation (as in the second vignette). I believe the success of using these cards in the moment can be attributed to two factors. First, these strategies and concepts were introduced and taught in a neutral time, so the neural pathway had already been laid, making it easier to draw upon in moments of dysregulation. This is preventive discipline. I would highly discourage anyone from trying a new strategy in a moment of dysregulation, because we are just not in the clear state of thinking and processing that we experience at a neutral or regulated time. Secondly, I adapted the cards to fit the students' needs based on my knowledge and experience with them (even though this was only my second visit). For Lizzie, I adapted the koala activity based on what I felt would likely engage her more—pretending to sleep. For Hannah, I began by connecting back to a previous experience—watching the gorilla video— and then adapted the activity based on her responses. I think it's also important to note that the clips and photos I used with both groups were from my own travels, a fact that I openly shared with them. I find that when we can share pieces of ourselves, it not only increases engagement and meaning, but also offers an example of how we can share with one another. In a sense, when we build preventive brain-aligned procedures on the front end, we build trust.

Being With Me Is Healing Me!

In conclusion: 1) co-regulation does not have to be something separate from everything else but can be naturally interwoven into our daily work; 2) just because a strategy is written one way doesn't mean we cannot adapt and change it to work for us and our students; and 3) co-regulation and its effectiveness hinge on our relationships with students.

Returning to Mister Roger's wise words, I hope this chapter has helped you see the power in our simple expressions of care. Discipline is walking alongside our young people with care and connection. These practices apply not only to those early years, but also to all the years of our lives. We must begin with attachment and regulation as the new lens for discipline, because the beauty of the human brain is that it's constantly changing with experiences shared. We hope you've been able to see the vast opportunities that surround each of us to connect, grow, and learn, and that the most essential element needed in this work is love.

"The way we treat our children directly impacts what they believe about themselves."
ARIADNE BRILL

i think i might be

a nice place to land

RESOURCE SECTION

A. Brain-Aligned Strategies

B. A Secret

C. Animal Regulation Cards

D. Differentiating Amygdala Reset

E. Getting the Most Out of Your Amygdala Reset Station

F. Brain Deck (Brain Intervals and Focused Attention Practices)

G. "How Are You Feeling" Diagram

H. Brain Behavior Chart #1

I . Brain Behavior Chart #2

J. Accommodations for Adverse Childhood Experiences

K. Educator Brain State E-Book

L. Brain-Aligned Student Survey

M. Brain-Aligned Teacher Survey

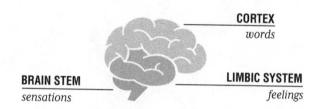

CORTEX
words

BRAIN STEM
sensations

LIMBIC SYSTEM
feelings

A. Brain-Aligned Strategies

Relational, Preventive Discipline

Meeting students and staff in brain state is critical for our emotional mental and physiological well-being! This chart shares regulation and connection strategies (touch points) that will be helpful in regulating and calming the student's nervous system so that they are able to learn, reason, create, and make choices that serve them well while building connections and relationships in our classrooms and schools.

Sensory Strategies:
The language of the **brain stem** is ... *sensations.*

Horse Lips	Loosen your lips and blow ... allow the air to wriggle your lips, and do these with a large inhale and even bigger exhale. We can laugh, too, as we calm the brain stem areas where the stress response begins!
Rhythm Circles	Rhythm circles take just a few minutes as the class mimics the leader in claps, snaps, stomps, or drumstick patterns. We use paint sticks from a local hardware store; students can decorate these and keep them all year long! We sometimes use music, sounds, or one another as we follow the lead of the designated drummer or rhythm maker. We can vary this drumming from soft to loud, slow to fast, and even move our bodies as we drum together.

Sensory Strategies:
The language of the **brain stem** is ... *sensations.*

Hand Massage	Once a day or as students walk in, pass out a drop of lotion, and for 90 seconds students give their hands and fingers a massage, noticing their palms, joints, fingertips, and any sensations that feel uncomfortable or stiff. Allow students to choose scented or unscented lotion.
The 7/11 Breath	Inhale for 7 seconds and exhale for 11.
Sensation Word Drawing	This is a great way of using imagery and art to activate the right hemisphere while integrating both hemispheres for cognition. Students choose a sensation word and draw an image of this word using size, shape and color, and possibly where they feel it on their bodies (tired, numb, tense, full, fuzzy, soft, open, flowing, teary, edgy, tight, etc.).
Hot Chocolate Breath	Imagine you are holding a cup of hot chocolate, feel the warmth of the mug in your hands, take a deep breath in, and then slowly blow out your exhale as if you are cooling down your hot chocolate.
Bi-Lateral Scribbling	• With two markers, begin scribbling vertically and then horizontally each for 15 seconds. • Take a marker in each hand, make two arcs at the same time across the page, and continue until there are several forming a rainbow shape. • Begin to make circles, with each circle becoming smaller until those turn into dots on the page. • Tracing paper is great for students to begin tracing their favorite objects and drawing around the perimeter of shapes.

Sensory Strategies:
The language of the **brain stem** is ... *sensations.*

Whack the Balloon	Foster eye-hand coordination by sitting across the table from child with a 12-inch balloon as the child holds a heavy cardboard tube about 1 inch in diameter. Move the balloon back and forth very slowly about 2 inches off the table and then pick up speed as the child tries to hit the balloon.
Drumming	Drum to different beats such as a piece of instrumental music, a song, or a metronome, drumming a pattern and mimicking the pattern back. Drum on your laps, with cups, with small drums, etc.
Temperature Sensations	Try using a change in temperature to regulate: • Ice chips • Heating pad • Cooling fan • Hand and toe warmers • Icy-hot
Draw the Beat	Children can listen to the beat of a piece of music and, with crayons, draw how they visualize and imagine the beat using colors, shapes, and different sizes.
Emotional Freedom Techniques (EFT) or Tapping	Gently tap on acupoints on the body. You can pair this tapping with positive affirmations said aloud or whispered.

EFT Tapping Points

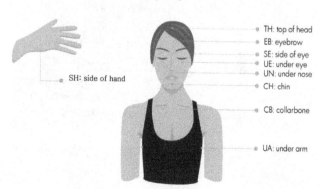

SH: side of hand

- TH: top of head
- EB: eyebrow
- SE: side of eye
- UE: under eye
- UN: under nose
- CH: chin
- CB: collarbone
- UA: under arm

Sensory Strategies:
The language of the **brain stem** is ... *sensations.*

Wake Up the Singing Bowl

Students listen to the sound that the bowl creates while collectively placing their fingers on their vocal chords and trying to match the singing bowl's tone. Follow this with three deep breaths, and then take turns waking up the bowl, matching the sound while increasing your breaths to five or six long inhales and exhales. Also, students can close their eyes and listen to the tone until it fades beyond their hearing. When this happens, have them raise their hands in the air. Some children may be sensitive to these sounds, so pay close attention to each child's response and adjust this activity as needed.

Taking a Sensory Bath

Gather a group of three or four children into an area of the room with a large beach towel, a bath-time luffa, a tube of lotion, and plenty of smiles and curiosity. Students can choose to take their own luffa and press it on their arms and legs pretending to scrub and clean; or they can choose an adult to give them the sensory bath. Model this activity as you begin by pretending to step into a warm, sudsy tub. Have everyone sit down together and sing in rhythm, "We're taking a brain bath, a brain bath, a brain bath, we're taking a brain bath to help us feel_____!"

Have students choose different words to fill in a sensation or feeling (happy, bubbly, fresh, clean, peaceful, etc.). Once everyone has patted the luffa up and down their arms and legs and on top of their heads, pretend to carefully step out of the tub. One at a time, wrap up each child tightly in the oversized beach towel while swaying and rocking back and forth, continuing to sing. This time, sing about drying off and feeling ready for the day. Students can then select a drop of hand lotion to massage on their hands, leaving the area with three deep breaths as they enter into their day of learning.

Sensory Strategies:
The language of the **brain stem** is ... *sensations.*

Ultra-Natural Pain Relief Gel

When we place a drop of pain relief gel in an area on our body that feels tense, anxious, tight, or uncomfortable, we teach our students how to pay attention to one particular spot and notice sensations. This is a great way to prime the brain for attention as we hold a quiet time for about 2 minutes while students place a drop on their hands, arms, neck, or shoulders, smell the aroma, and feel the texture. These 2 minutes integrate the senses, bring us to the present moment, and rejuvenate our frontal lobes so they are ready to learn!

Trauma and Tension Releasing Exercises (TRE)

Trauma and Tension Releasing Exercises (TRE) are intended to release pent-up stress and anxiety in the body. These exercises stimulate the body's innate tremor mechanism and target the psoas muscles, which are our fight-flight muscles in the pelvic region. Children's nervous systems are still developing, and these exercises are gentle enough to produce a bit of contraction and then release, allowing the child or adolescent to feel the sensations in their bodies.

Fast = Charge. Fast movements activate the nervous system, producing possibly pent-up energy.

Slow = Recovery. Slower, more intentional movements slow down our nervous system, activating a parasympathetic response.

Contracting and Stretching
1. We crunch and release our toes 5 times; then we rotate our ankles.
2. Standing, we rise up on our toes 5-10 times and then release. Recovery is sitting down and shaking out the calves.
3. We work our quads and hamstrings with a chair pose. We squat 5-10 times and then stretch by pulling our leg behind us.
4. We can place a ball between our legs, squeeze it tight, and then release to produce a charge and release.

Sensory Strategies:
The language of the **brain stem** is ... *sensations.*

TRE Foot Rolls   Spread your feet slightly wider apart than your shoulders and point them forward. Roll onto the sides of your feet rolling them in the same direction. You should be on the outside of one foot and on the inside of the other foot. Hold this position for a few seconds, then sway the body in the opposite direction and invert your feet. Continue swaying very slowly back and forth like this, 5-8 times in each direction. To end the exercise, shake out your feet.

TRE Tiptoe Raises   Place one foot in front of you and put all your weight onto the front leg. The back leg is on the floor just for balance. With the front standing foot, come up and down onto your toes, raising your heel as high as possible, then lower your foot to the floor. Repeat coming up onto your toes and back down about 5-8 times, depending on the strength and flexibility of your legs. If it becomes painful or begins to produce a burning sensation, stop the exercise! Come to a standing position on both legs and vigorously shake the leg you just exercised to eliminate any pain, burning, or discomfort. Repeat this same exercise with the other foot. When finished, vigorously shake the leg to relax the muscles.

TRE Hip Stretches   Keep your feet in the same position as the previous exercise. Place your hands partly on the lower back and the buttocks to support the lower back. Slowly push your pelvis slightly forward so that there is a gentle bow in your lower back. You should feel a stretch at the front of your thigh. This exercise is not about arching the back, but about pushing the pelvis forward so that the back naturally arches. This should be a gentle stretch according to your body's ability. Gently twist at the hips to keep the bowed position, looking behind you in one direction. Take three deep

Sensory Strategies:
The language of the **brain stem** is ... *sensations.*

TRE Hip Stretches *cont'd*	breaths. Turn again from the hips in the opposite direction, keeping the bowed position while looking behind you. Take three deep breaths. Return to facing forward, keeping the bowed position while taking three more deep breaths. To finish, release the bow and come to a normal standing position.
Peaceful Brushing	Using a variety of makeup brushes, model peaceful brushing as you circle your face and ears. Then brush your arms, hands, and palms. Let students choose whether they want to brush themselves or want an adult to brush them, and then have them take turns brushing faces, necks, arms, and hands. This light touch is stimulating in a gentle way, and students can brush their own peaceful spots.
Regulate With Another	Choose and partner. Without talking, find a rhythm in your own breathing with your partner. Change it up!
Vocal Cord Vibrations	Having everyone place fingers on their throats, the teacher begins the day with a sound, and then the students mimic the sound while feeling the vibration of their vocal cords. This gives everyone a chance to discover how different voice tones and volumes feel in the body. Students can also try mimicking different animals, instruments, and random classroom sounds such as papers crinkling.
Lotus Flower Breath	Place the fingertips of both hands together. With an inhale, pull your thumbs apart and bring them together on the exhale. Go through each finger with the same inhale, pulling the pair of fingers part and then exhaling the fingers together. On the last breath, pull all apart on the inhale, and then exhale your fingertips back together, fingers apart. Keep the heels of your hands together on this final breath, as if you're opening a flower.

Sensory Strategies:
The language of the **brain stem** is ... *sensations.*

Metronome Rhythms	• Draw to the beat of a metronome. • Clap, snap, or drum in time. • Exercise to the beat of a metronome. Try animal walks or moving your arms as you speed it up or slow it down.
Start With Art	Begin the day or period with 90 seconds of art and writing. Have students draw and paint with their eyes closed (if they choose) to bring their attention back to the present moment! Other than the 90-second count, there are no rules or guidelines for this activity.
Yoga Movements and Holding Postures	Yoga movements and holding yoga postures increase endorphins. Warrior is excellent, as are seated postures with twisting, and standing postures where we can see our environments. (Be aware that some postures can trigger feelings of trauma.)
Roller Coaster Ride Through Space	In this focused attention practice, we stand up with our feet shoulder-width apart, and bring our arms up to shoulder height, bending at our elbows. Standing like a scarecrow, we begin slowly twisting our upper body to the left and to the right, gradually picking up speed with our eyes closed. Our feet and legs do not move. As we move back and forth, we deeply inhale and exhale with each breath!
Parasympathetic Breathing	Initiate your parasympathetic nervous system by inhaling through the nose for 4 counts, and exhaling through the mouth with lips pursed for 8 counts.
Focused Sound Breathing	Focus on a sound as you slow your breathing, gently inhaling and slowly exhaling.

Sensory Strategies:
The language of the **brain stem** is ... *sensations.*

Spine Rocking	Have students rock along their spine to help them feel present in their bodies. This also provides a soothing rhythm that subtly grounds them with sensation and movement.
Feeling Your Breath	Place your fingers just an inch or two in front of your mouth. As you breathe in through your nose, inhale a shallow breath and feel the air, then exhale through your mouth. Now breathe in through your nose and exhale through your mouth as you blow up your belly with a deep diaphragm breath. Feel how much warmer this air is against your fingers
Belly Breathing	Place one hand on your belly and one hand on your chest. Breathe in and out normally, noticing which hand rises and falls. How do you normally breathe, deep or shallow?
Tongue Talking	Loosely place your tongue on the roof of your mouth and begin to speak without moving your tongue from this position. Create a class chant to say together. Since this can be an awkward exercise, the teacher should be prepared to go first, modeling the activity and breaking the ice!
Body Scan	Have students sit with their legs straight out and begin wiggling their toes and ankles, shaking knees and thighs, rotating shoulders, arms, and finally their heads, keeping all body parts moving at the same time. Then reverse the process and stop moving heads, arms, shoulders, and on down. This sequence also promotes working memory.
Drawing Emotions	Draw what happiness looks like! Draw what sadness is! Draw how anger feels and what it is! Now look at your art, then close your eyes and feel in your body if happiness, anger, or sadness are there. Where in your body are those feelings located?

Sensory Strategies:
The language of the **brain stem** is ... *sensations.*

Finger Raises

Inhale and lift the forefinger of your left hand, then lower this finger as you exhale. Go through these breathing movements raising and lowering each finger on both hands. You can use other parts of your body to match the inhale and exhale with 10 deep breaths, always exhaling a bit longer than the inhale.

Humming

There are so many ways to incorporate humming during a brain interval or at the beginning of the day! You could initiate a Simon Says, mimic me, name that tune, or move your arms and legs to the humming. This activity releases stress and blockages in the brain stem, flooding our systems with a norepinephrine release!

Scarf Dancing

Putting on music, give students old scarves and dance around the room together, waving the scarves and feeling the soft sensation as you dance and pass by one another. When the music stops, freeze. Notice your postures and the movement you interrupted by freezing. This strategy can be led by the teacher or a student to demonstrate that everyone can mimic a movement or create their own.

Double Scribble

With a different-colored marker in each hand, draw or scribble to the beat of the music for 30 seconds. When you finish, see if your drawing turned into anything familiar or strange. Share with a classmate and then give each other's drawing a name!

Stretch and Hold

Do some light stretching. Try holding a stretch while you breathe deeply.

Hold Your Cheeks

Place both hands on your cheeks. What do you notice? What do you feel?

Sensory Strategies:
The language of the **brain stem** is ... *sensations.*

Walking Labyrinth	Create a walking labyrinth using colorful tape. Students can then try to walk backwards or crawl. Add balancing a bag of rice or beans to make it even more challenging.
Funny Voices	Talk in a funny voice for 30 seconds. This voice could be deep, high, slow, drawn out, laughing, interspersed with hiccups, or anything else you can imagine. Let the students decide!
Kind Pressure	• Give yourself a bear hug. • Give yourself an arm or leg massage using gentle squeezes. • Give yourself a gentle neck massage.
Mannequin Freeze Challenge	Challenge students to hold a mannequin's pose, staying as still as they can. Gradually increase the length of time for holding these poses.
Lava Bottles	Have students create their own lava bottles to focus on while they breathe. You can find instructions here: https://awakeandmindful.com/how-to-make-diy-meditation-jar/
Brain Freeze	Stop with a sound! Ask students to show you how they might suddenly freeze, melt, moonwalk, or disappear.
Writing Switch-Up	Write your favorite word with your dominant hand four times, and then write it again with your other hand. How did it feel? Which hand was more difficult? Why? What happened in your brain when you wrote with your non-dominant hand? What would help your non-dominant hand to become stronger?

Sensory Strategies:
The language of the **brain stem** is … *sensations.*

Rectangle Breathing	Trace a rectangle with your finger, inhaling as you trace the short side and exhaling as you trace the long side.

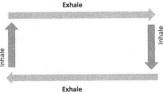

Create Heat	Rub both hands together as fast as you can until they feel hot. Then release.
Resistance and Tension	Create resistance and tension by having students do wall push-ups and squats.
Guess the Sound	Have students close their eyes for 30 seconds, mindfully listening to all the sounds they can hear in that time. Then students can share the sounds they captured.
Regulated Pacing	Create a pacing strip for students to use individually within the classroom. Many students feel calmer and more regulated when moving, and a strip of duct tape in a designated area of the room can be their pacing path to learning!
Tongue Stretch	With clean hands or a Kleenex, stick out your tongue and stretch it as far as it can go! This relaxes the throat, palate, upper neck, and brain stem. What could you add to make this exercise funny?
Track the Rhythm of Your Heart	Make pulse oximeters available in the classroom so that students can locate a resting heart rate, and then note and track the changes in their heart rates during the day. Name the sensations and feelings you experience in our bodies as your pulse rate rises and falls.

Sensory Strategies:
The language of the **brain stem** is ... *sensations.*

Mini Obstacle Course	Create a miniature obstacle course using a step stool, hula hoops, and other materials.
Building Regulation	Students can regulate through repetitive, patterned work. When we build and create with Legos, blocks, cards, magnetic shapes, or other objects, we find a rhythm to our activity as we repeatedly choose an object, balance, observe, add to ... until we finish and admire our creation!
Animal Walking	Have students do a crab walk or slithering snake.
Walk the Tightrope	Practice toe and heel walking along a designated line that we draw or create. We alternate walking the line on our toes and then on our heels, possibly moving back and forth with a heel toe movement every other step.
Safe Place Visualization	Walk your students to their "safe place." Have them close their eyes and with soft music playing in the background, and verbally take them on a journey to their own special place. In this focused attention exercise, they imagine colors, sounds, tastes, people, activities, places, and sensations! When they return from their "safe place" trip, reflect on your journeys! How did it feel? What was the best part? Who was with them? What did they see? What did they hear?
Invisible Jump Rope	Divide students into groups of 3. For 9 seconds, jump with an invisible jump rope. Students will take turns holding each end of the rope and jumping for equal amounts of time. Have fun with different jumps and combinations. Make sure those holding the rope are in sync with one another. Afterward, reflect on how this felt by writing down your jumps, the sequences of jumps, and if this exercise could really improve how you jump with a real rope! Why or why not?

Sensory Strategies:
The language of the **brain stem** is ... *sensations.*

Drawing Your Breath	Take a moment and notice how you breathe. Do you notice a rhythm? A pattern? A pace? Try to draw your breathing.
Regulating Sound	Sometimes it's helpful to provide background noise. White noise is regulating for some children and adults as it is a subtle, unwavering sound that can calm us while we work, play or sleep. Try using a noise machine or water element.
Calming Weight	The use of different weights can be regulating—and grounding as well. Have students carry weighted objects or do some heavy lifting. Add small weights to your Amygdala Reset Area.
Wriggle and Shake	Wriggle and shake out your tension, adding one body part at a time.
Textures	Different textures can be soothing to the brain stem, such as a weighted lap pad or blanket, soft yarn balls, or scented blankets.
Dancing Breaks	Incorporate dancing breaks throughout the day. You can even try chair dancing!
Eye Yoga	Take your right first finger and place it 12 inches in front of your nose. Without moving your head, follow the movement of your finger with your eyes—left, right, up, and down. The only part of your body moving is your eye and first finger.
Dancing Breaks	Incorporate dancing breaks throughout the day. You can even try chair dancing!
Blowing the Trumpet Breath	Take a deep inhale and then slowly exhale through your mouth, holding your hands as if blowing a trumpet, vibrating your lips until the end of the exhale.

Sensory Strategies:
The language of the **brain stem** is ... *sensations.*

Squishy Pillow Sandwich	This requires two large pillows. Laying one pillow on the floor, the child lies across the pillow on their tummy. Ask "What would you like on your squishy sandwich?" Use your hands to spread or sprinkle the requested ingredients with generalized touch and pressure along their back. Then lay the second pillow on the child's back, pressing gently to create the most delicious mushy sandwich!
Toothpaste Squeeze	The child lies on their stomach. Roll a large exercise ball from the child's feet all the way up to their head. As you roll the ball along the child's backside, narrate how you are very slowly squeezing the toothpaste out of the tube!
Vacuum Cleaner	Children lie on their backs with their arms behind their heads. The adult gently grabs their ankles swaying them back and forth to warm up the vacuum cleaner. Then the adult slowly scoots the child back and forth just as a vacuum moves along the carpet. This is a powerful sensory practice for calming the nervous system.
Sucking and Swallowing	The act of sucking and swallowing triggers a regulatory response of stimulating nerves connected to the parasympathetic nervous system. Use any of these methods: • Drinking warm water • Lollipops • Ice pops in paper cups, frozen grapes, or fruit juice • Sucking yogurt through a straw • Water bottles with straws or sippy cup lids
Regulating Essential Needs	Offering students a drink of water and a small snack helps to regulate their nervous systems. The brain cannot think straight when it is hungry or thirsty!

Sensory Strategies:
The language of the **brain stem** is ... *sensations.*

Chewing to Regulate	Rhythmic chewing helps to regulate the reticular activating system (RAS) in the brainstem. Crunchy foods in particular produce a stimulating reaction that enhances attention and alertness. Suggested strategies include: · Chewing gum · Crunching on Cheerios or crackers · Eating a chewy bagel
Clothespin Drop	Standing above a jar, try to drop clothespins into the jar without bending over. Add an extra challenge by raising your arms upward.
Sensory Discrimination	Sensory discrimination helps focus attention and creates associations that students can identify and therefore understand. We help children compare and contrast the way things look, feel, hear, and move! · Use visual discrimination techniques with white on black scribbling or drawing. · Promote tactile discrimination by having students feel different objects to see what they are.
Lavender Yarn Balls	Taking thick balls or skeins of yarn, show students how to wind these into balls. Then dab each yarn ball in a little lavender.
Blowing and Popping Bubbles	Sit in a circle. Using bubble fluid and a ring, take a deep breath and blow bubbles with a long, slow exhale, watching each one until it lands and pops. This strategy attends to breath, attention, and focus. Have children sit on their hands and pop the bubbles only with their eyes. This can be difficult, but by having them watch and not use their fingers, this strategy helps them create a pause, learning how to hesitate without immediately reacting!

Sensory Strategies:
The language of the **brain stem** is ... *sensations.*

Taco Roll	The taco roll is implemented for body awareness, rhythm, and some gentle but firm pressure. Children lie down on a blanket, and an adult slowly rolls them up, winding the blanket around them with a gentle pressure. When they're ready, unroll them with a little speed as they pretend to roll down a hill. This is also an excellent (and fun!) strategy for vestibular integration (balance information provided by the peripheral sensory organs).
Cloud Surfing	This is an exercise in body awareness, imagination, calming, and regulating through the sense of smell. Sit on beach towels and give each child a lavender-scented cotton ball representing a cloud. Talk about the sky and clouds, and imagine flying through them while smelling the cotton balls and moving your bodies to mimic flying and soaring. Then share what you saw.
Car Routine	This is an alerting strategy to prepare bodies and brains for the day! Begin this activity by sitting on the floor with legs stretched out. Start up your engines by wriggling legs and arms. As soon as your cars are warmed up, take off down the highway. Have students stand and follow the leader. We did this with our little animal buddies as our passengers, attached to the children's shoes to help them pay attention and focus, moving deliberately and carefully so their buddies would "stay in the car." This strategy attends to body awareness, focused attention, gross motor movement, balance, and motor and emotional regulation.
Roll Exercise Ball - Bounce On It - Repeat	Have children roll a huge exercise ball along a path and then stop, freeze, jump on it, and circle back around.

Sensory Strategies:
The language of the **brain stem** is ... *sensations.*

Merry-Go-Round   As a vestibular exercise for balance, have children stand and spread feet apart while holding out scarves in front of them. Have them move their upper body from side to side, either watching the scarves dancing in the air or closing their eyes.

Rock and Roll   For gross motor and vestibular activation, roll back and forth on your back, looking up to the sky and noticing everything around you! This is an exercise in core strength and rhythm activation, as many of our children have weakened or underdeveloped core strength.

Flying Swings   Take off running as if swinging high in the air. Then freeze for a few seconds while taking 3 deep breaths. Repeat these movements three times! This strategy focuses on attention, gross motor, breath, and movement.

Rocking Hammock   Double up a soft blanket. Children take turns lying lengthwise on the blanket. Others pick up the ends and gently swing the blanket back and forth, singing together a made-up song using the child's name. Gradually decrease the swinging motion to smaller movements and then slowly bump, bump, bump to the ground!

Amygdala Reset Areas   Create an Amygdala Reset Area with some of the following items:
- Balance board (kinesthetics, balance, movement)
- Exercise (or yoga) ball (kinesthetics, balance)
- Yoga mats (Trauma and Tension Releasing Exercises [TRE]/yoga) (kinesthetics, balance)
- Constellation night light (visual, focused attention)
- Liquid motion timers (visual)

Sensory Strategies:
The language of the **brain stem** is … *sensations.*

**Amygdala
Reset Areas**
cont'd

- Wood labyrinth table maze (movement, focused attention)
- Hoberman Mini Sphere (breathing, focused attention)
- Glitter wand (visual, focused attention)
- DNA Stress Balls (tactile, squeeze-release, TRE)
- Stacking cups (kinesthetic)
- Rain stick (auditory/tactile)
- *Your Fantastic Elastic Brain* book (neuroanatomy)
- *My First Book About the Brain* (neuroanatomy)
- *My Little Brain* book (neuroanatomy)
- *Rosie's Brain* book (neuroanatomy)
- Coloring books, crayons, colored pencils (tactile, visual)
- Bubbles (breath, visual, tactile)
- Play-doh (tactile, visual, olfactory)
- Relaxation music on a CD/MP3 player (auditory)
- Hand lotion (tactile, olfactory)
- Puzzles (visual, tactile)
- Motivational posters (visual)
- White board (visual)
- Water (hydration, gustatory)
- Snack crackers (Nutritive, gustatory)
- Gummi Bears or bubble gum (kinesthetic, gustatory, rhythmic chewing)
- Jump rope (kinesthetic)
- Essential oils (olfactory)

Connection Strategies:
The language of the limbic system is ... *feelings.*

2 by 10

For 2 minutes each day, 10 days in a row, teachers have a personal conversation with the student about anything the student is interested in (as long as the conversation is G-rated). Also try 1 by 30 and gradual release.

Catch Me!

"Catch" students doing or saying something kind! Notes of gratitude, messages of noticing, and stickers contribute to students' feelings of purpose and connection. This strategy can be used by teachers, aids, bus drivers, custodians, office staff, administration, etc.

Caring for Your Buddy

Take care of a staff member or another student through a Post-it, a smile, a question, or a talisman.

Partner Heart Rates

Measure your heart rate. Monitor and share with a partner.

Monster Drawing

With a partner, silently create a silly monster in one minute! Take turns adding to each other's drawing with shapes, lines and colors for one minute.

Newsletter, Website, Social Media

Create a classroom newsletter, website, or a social media account for sharing with parents to recognize the familial tribe of connection these students and this teacher have together! This could also be done in other communities such as a bus, a specials class, or an after-school group.

Journal

Try journaling with a personal diary at the beginning of a class period or day. Writing can be in the form of pictures or any type of art that feels good to express.

Connection Strategies:
The language of the limbic system is ... *feelings.*

**Noticing and
Noticing Sheets**

Noticing:
- New shoes
- Haircut
- How a student walked into class
- A smile
- A gesture

Noticing Sheets:

With older students, this noticing can be reciprocal with ground rules. (If you're noticing details, behaviors, and moods about your students, they can notice something about you, too!) Students love homemade worksheets from their teachers. Even during an off day with many challenges, we can always notice very specific behaviors, moods, or actions! This also allows us to track patterns of behaviors. It's a very simple yet effective daily activity! Even with 30 students, we can always jot down a quick note or even a "thank you!" when we see a positive.

Take Your Order

What do you need today?

- A break?
- Your favorite snack?
- Time to meet with another educator?
- A visit to another school?
- Time to yourself?
- An affirmation?
- Supplies?
- An ear and a heart that will listen?

Connection Strategies:
The language of the limbic system is ... *feelings.*

Touch Point Check-ins

Each morning and afternoon, students can check in with a chosen adult to share how they are feeling through a thumbs up, thumbs down, or neutral show of emotion. This is a great way for adults to notice patterns while students create a connection of trust! This strategy can be used by teachers, aids, bus drivers, custodians, office staff, administration, etc.

Safe and Calm Communities

Create a sense of safety and calm community by playing calming music, using call and response songs or chants, and creating a display of special projects or VIP work to recognize and accumulate successes. These strategies could take place in a classroom, on the bus, in after- or before-school care, in the cafeteria, etc.

Positive Referral Sheet

Cape Educational COMPACT
Positive Referral

Student Name _MATT HAYMAN_   Date _1/13/14_

Reporting teacher _MR BARRY_

The check mark indicates the area in which you exhibited exemplary behavior.

____ CARING — Student is sensitive to the beliefs, ideas, feelings, and experiences of others.
✓ LEADERSHIP — Student is a role model to others.
____ RESPECT — Student is considerate of the feelings and property of others and treats them without bias or judgment.
✓ RESPONSIBILITY — Student acts in a mature manner.
____ TRUSTWORTHY — Student is reliable and honest.

ACADEMICS
____ Excellent job on a major project   ✓ Finishes assignments on time
____ Improved participation   ____ Improved test scores
✓ Contributes significantly in class   ____ Academic improvement
____ Helps classmates learn   ____ High quality assignments

PERSONAL BEHAVIOR
____ Improved class behavior   ____ Sense of humor   ____ Consistent attendance
____ Less tardy   ____ Kind/warm   ____ Motivates students
____ Shows respect for others   ____ Courteous   ____ Cooperative
____ Emphasizes the positive   ____ Helpful   ____ Honest
____ Improved attendance   ____ Enthusiastic   ____ Conscientious
✓ Helps encourage others' positive habits
____ Does something good without being asked

SCHOOL/COMMUNITY SUPPORT
____ Super Do Gooder   ____ Helps train others at the gym
____ Helps maintain school's appearance   ____ School spirit
____ Leader on the basketball team

Administrator:

199

Connection Strategies:
The language of the limbic system is ... *feelings.*

Active Constructive Responding

This process means stepping into experiences with another person and responding with questions, details, and interest. It is a form of questioning that asks and focuses on details when another individual shares something about an experience, event, idea, or relationship.

- Where were you when you saw this or heard this?
- Who was with you?
- What were you doing right before this happened?
- What were you doing when this happened?
- What did it look like?
- What sounds did you hear?
- What was their reaction?
- What else did you notice?
- How did this feel?
- Now, how will this change things for you?

Power of Questions

This process offers two points for regulating and modulating feelings and emotions: in the moment and later.

- In the moment:
- What do you need?
- How can I help?
- What can we do to make this better?
- Is there anything you need right now that would ease your mind and your feelings?
- Is there another way you would like to talk about this other than words? I have paper, pens, crayons, and clay, or you could paint a picture.
- If you could list three or four people that you need right now, who would they be?
- Is there a place you would like to rest where you can feel safe until you feel a little bit better?
- Are there any objects or belongings I can find that would comfort you?

Later (once regulated):

Connection Strategies:
The language of the limbic system is ... *feelings.*

**Power of
Questions**
cont'd

· What are your resources?
· What feels difficult?
· What could be the best possible outcome?
· What is the worst thing that could happen?
· What is a first step in improving this situation?

Validation

When we validate a student, we rephrase the content of what they are saying, and we label the feeling behind the words we hear.

· That must have made you feel really angry.
· What a frustrating situation to be in!
· It must make you feel angry to have someone do that.
· Wow, how hard that must be.
· That stinks!
· That's messed up!
· How frustrating!
· Yeah, I can see how that might make you feel really sad.
· Boy, you must be angry.
· What a horrible feeling.
· What a tough spot.
· That must be really discouraging.
· I bet you feel disappointed.
· Yikes, I know how much that meant to you.
· Tell me more. (This response shows interest.)
· Wow, he/she must have made you really angry.

**Emotional
and
Academic
Designer**

This brain-aligned strategy taps into the student's interests, passions, and expertise. These techniques are implemented for students in a frozen stress response state to free up some of the negative emotions of helplessness and hopelessness. This brain-aligned strategy is process-oriented and builds over a one-, two-, or six-week time period. Many students walk into classrooms with a "shut-down" response which produces little to no homework or assignment completion and

Connection Strategies:

The language of the limbic system is ... *feelings.*

Emotional and Academic Designer
cont'd

engagement. These students are often referred to as internalizers. Their deep-seated anger and fear can look defensive, withdrawn, helpless, and disengaged.

At a neutral time, we suggest a variety of ways to complete small chunks of assignments. These might include drawing, painting, sketching, voice recording, video making, or another medium of the child or adolescent's choice. Chunking refers to shortening assignments so that completion feels possible and doable. Often, I've actually been the scribe who takes notes as the student speaks their thoughts. We begin with short, concise assignments that students feel comfortable in completing. We compromise and ask for their input, questions, and thoughts, and we agree to check in with one another during this process. The check-in isn't for evaluation or assessment, but instead for mutual feedback and dialogue. This strategy could also be implemented for a resiliency touch point.

Have a Cup of Coffee

Personal coffee cups for all students could be filled with water, hot chocolate, tea, or juice throughout the week. As the class shares a cup of coffee, we also share appreciations, apologies, and "aha!" moments. We can also take this time for our role and responsibility leaders to share what they have noticed. This is a great time for touch points! We can begin to incorporate Monday Brunch, Wednesday Game Day, and Friday Movie Afternoon. When we feel felt with a sense of purpose, we begin to flourish. Discuss these questions:

- Am I important to someone in here?
- Can I share my gifts with someone in here?
- Can I serve someone in here?
- How do I feel in here most days?

Connection Strategies:
The language of the limbic system is ... *feelings.*

Connection Buckets

At the front of the classroom/bus, there could be three buckets, each with a different label: 1) "What do you need today? Reach in and grab a pick-me-up!" 2) "What's on your mind? Let's work it out together!" 3) "Celebrations!" Each day, a student can reach for an affirmation, a book, a Sudoku, word search, coloring book, a cotton ball with lavender, some hand lotion, or other calming items. A "Celebrations!" bucket would be a wonderful way to incorporate daily or weekly successes, letting students take a leadership role announcing all the celebrations of students in their classroom (or on their bus) on a Friday afternoon!

Animal Totems

Have students choose an animal and invite them to draw, sculpt, create, etc., something to represent their animal. Ask them:
- What's one animal that you relate to, think about, or would like to have? Maybe it's an animal you don't like.
- How are you similar to this animal?
- How are you different?
- What strengths does this animal have? What weaknesses?
- What would this animal's home look and feel like?
- What superpowers would you give this animal?

Kindness Letters

Write a letter to someone who has been especially kind. This could be once a day, once a week, or whenever the time feels right. It doesn't have to be a fully written letter, just a few sentences that can be shared after they are written. Nothing moves us toward positive emotion more swiftly and steadily than gratitude!

The Load I Carry

Paint or draw the "load you are carrying."

Connection Strategies:
The language of the limbic system is ... *feelings.*

Painting With Imagery	This strategy can be a whole-class or one-on-one activity (we've used it both in morning meetings and as bell work). Using a symbol, image, or metaphor, paint lines, forms, shapes, and colors. We ask students to fill up the paper with paint. If a student describes their paper as messy, confusing, strange, and weird, we use those words to create questions for the student. • Do you ever feel confused, messy, or weird? • Can you paint the word confused? We can always help the student repair and heal an image they created but don't like! This, too, is a part of co-regulation.
The Things I Carry	In the front of the room is a backpack filled with five or six items, pictures, or words that I identify with or hold close to my mind and heart. As I model for my students the contents of my own backpack, I begin to share who I am as a person and not just an educator. This is a powerful way for not only getting to know your students, but also tying in the contents of the backpack with a class novel, science experiment, or any standard you are teaching by aligning these items to what students need to know! Students can guess what items might be in the backpack before they're revealed. Prediction is an effective brain state that increases the dopamine levels responsible for pleasure and goal- seeking behaviors.
Belief Systems	Understand that a belief system for a student with significant trauma and adversity might be filled with unlovable, shameful, and unworthy thoughts and feelings. To regulate, we have to give that student some space and time. Then, before giving a consequence, we need to validate the student's feelings. Our belief systems are our realities! Here is an example: • Teacher: "Jonah, I know this is going to be hard, but you're not able to go out to recess today because of what happened earlier."

Connection Strategies:
The language of the limbic system is ... *feelings.*

Belief Systems
cont'd

- Student: "That's not fair!"
- Teacher: "I know this cannot feel good to you!"
- Student: "But it wasn't my fault!"
- Teacher: "Why don't you and I sit over here and talk more about this so I can better understand your point of view."

Reflection Questions for Our Most Vulnerable Students

Questions to ask ourselves with our most vulnerable students:
1. What else is going on here?
2. What does this child need?
3. What keeps me looking only at the behavior and not at the child?
4. What is this behavior communicating right now?
5. What in the environment could be triggering this behavior?

Pockets of Brilliance

Neuropsychologist Dr. Ronald Federici states that many children and adolescents from adversity have "Pockets of Brilliance" because they've had to survive. Find their strengths in these areas. For example, if a student tells lies, how could we turn lying into strength? Understanding that lying is about self-preservation is the first step!!

Color Emotions

Have students fill their papers with colors. Then ask:
- What color is the largest? If it had a voice, what would it say?
- What color is the smallest? What might that color say?
- What advice would the large color give the smaller color?
- What color is in charge?
- What color would like to hide? Where would it go?
- Divide the paper in half. Label one half "Where have I been?" and the other half "Where am I going?" for a fun snapshot of the student's present and future life.

Connection Strategies:
The language of the limbic system is ... *feelings.*

Post-It Worries   Write out worries on Post-it notes.

Outline of Me   Create a life-size cut out of the outline of "you" (each individual student) or "us" (one life-size person to show how we are "one" in the classroom). After cutting out this life-size model, color code different places in the body where we experience feelings, and then draw some coping strategies that would help lessen the negative feelings.

Meet Our Buddies   Give students small stuffed animals to care and attend to while at school. They can give their buddy a name, care for their buddy throughout the day, and take their buddy with them whatever they do. Discuss what their buddies might need to feel peaceful and calm. Many children will project their own lives onto their buddies, providing adults with a source of effective perceptual data.

Cortical Strategies:
The language of the cortex is ... *words.*

Talking to Ourselves	Talking to ourselves can be very calming and helpful when we feel anxious or stuck with a problem or challenge. By talking to ourselves, we're actively reaching out to a friend (ourselves). What you can name, you can tame ....
Regulation Routines	Create short routines of 2-3 regulation strategies. These can also be thought of as preventive dosing. Try creating personal prescription pads for dosing and routines:

    1. Five dragon breaths
    2. Pacing for one minute while humming your favorite song
    3. Three rounds of finger tapping

Coping Strategies Wall	Create a wall of experiences that trigger your students and coping strategies to calm them.
Create Brain Maps	What would our map of safety look like? What about our map of experiences that feel scary or fearful?
E-Story	Create an electronic story of personal and school life. In this E-Story, students have the opportunity to let you know who they are through their dreams, goals, and stories. These E-Stories will change much like a time capsule, which is great for reflection, feedback, and relationship building! They will also encourage personal narratives, research, and a free form of creative writing and reading ... literacy made fun!
Dopamine Increasing Activities	Write down goals or lists of things you'd like to accomplish in an hour, a morning, or a day. Begin with incremental benchmarks that are doable, and maybe select a partner who will help you with accountability. Create a visual winning streak of accomplishments, processes, or efforts. Seeing is believing!

Cortical Strategies:
The language of the cortex is ... *words.*

Classroom Roles and Responsibilities
Choose a classroom role for the week.

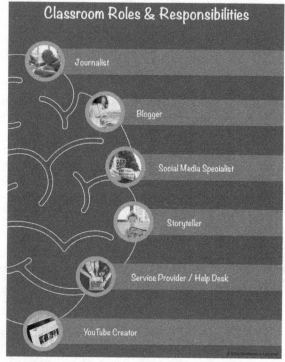

Cortical Strategies:
The language of the cortex is ... *words.*

10-Word Story   Write or draw a 10-word story on a specific topic that you're teaching. Or have students write a 10-word story describing their strengths and expertise. Those who don't want to write could create an infographic.

My Wise Self   Guided imagery is a powerful healing technique. Start with these questions:
· Who is the "Wise Self" soothing, comforting, and accepting you—or the younger version of you that still lives inside?
· Is this a person? What do they look like? Is this an animal? What would your Wise Self do to calm you and bring you joy? What words of comfort do they share?

Chance to Lead   One of the most effective ways to regulate negative emotion is by providing students with leadership opportunities. Older students could act as mentors for the younger students by modeling focused attention practices (such as how to take deep breaths) or helping them redirect negative emotion through a healthier channel (such as drawing, coloring, or creating a new solution to a problem)!

DIY Commercials   Choose a short TED Talk or documentary and watch the first minute. Following this one-minute presentation, students will predict two or three outcomes as to how this presentation will end. This can relate to the subject matter you've been teaching, or it could be a motivational video that addresses social and emotional skillsets.

The Garden of My Brain   Let's plant a garden in our classroom and in our brains and watch it grow! Our gardens need water, sunlight, and good soil. They may need shade and a protective fence. Using a journal, which is a touch point, keep track of and share some of the following provocations or pondering questions:

Cortical Strategies:
The language of the cortex is ... *words.*

The Garden of My Brain *cont'd*	• Who watered you this week? • Who is your sunlight? Who can see the best and brightest in you when you or others cannot? • What places help you to feel safe? What people? • What sounds help you feel safe? What types of rooms or outdoor areas? • Who protects you? What do you do to self-protect?
Allowing for Choice	Give choices every day with regard to assignments, consequences, homework, and activities. These are choices you can live with as a teacher. Without compromising any higher-level work or negative behaviors, you can empower students with minor everyday choices for things like Do Nows, quantity of materials used, color of paper, using a full or half sheet of paper, doing something before or after a five-minute break, etc. There are so many possible ideas!
Brain-Aligned Organic Consequences	What types of consequences will be experiences that can help our students to learn new behaviors? • **Not following directions:** Students support creating classroom expectations. When students aren't following, it's time to sit down and have a conversation and connect with the student. "What can we both agree to do the next time?" • **Not turning in assignments:** Connect. What's making it difficult to turn in assignments? Create a plan together and monitor. • **Disruptive:** Provide opportunities to be a classroom leader in positive capacities. • **Disrespectful:** Connect. Build a relationship and understand how that student is feeling in class. • **Late/tardy:** "How can I help?" Suggestions may include warning bells, more time, early release pass, restroom break at the beginning of class to eliminate stopping during passing, and storing materials in classroom for use.

Cortical Strategies:
The language of the cortex is ... *words.*

Brain-Aligned Organic Consequences *cont'd*

· **Out of seat:** Allow students opportunities to move and regulate without punishment. Thank students for taking care of themselves. Provide areas to stand during instruction.

· **Doing nothing:** Connect. "What do you need? How can I help?" Offer students choices.

· **Destruction of property:** Give the student time for providing service to property owner. Have them create videos, posters, and announcements about the importance of caring for property.

· **Physical altercations:** Use Restorative Justice practices (involving students, families, and teachers).

· **Verbal altercations:** Use Restorative Justice practices (involving students, families, and teachers).

· **Walking out of room:** Offer options for breaks, passes for walks, and brain intervals throughout instruction. Ask students when during class they'd like a break.

· **Impulse control:** Propose regulation activities throughout the learning block, fidgets, mind-wandering time, focused attention practices, and mindfulness exercises.

· **Dress code:** Identify a trusted adult or a safe space in the building that would provide a change of clothing.

· **Procedures:** Have students practice or repeat procedure until they learn to follow it.

Escape Stories

These could be written out, drawn as cartoons, or expressed with symbols and words. At some time, we've all had to escape from something or someone that didn't feel good to us. Maybe your escape story is true or make-believe. Either way, share where you were, what happened, and how you escaped. Do you have a plan for next time? What would you do differently? What was the best part about this plan? Who are the people that could help you escape? After drawing or writing the Escape Story, students could color code different parts of their scenes with this chart.

Cortical Strategies:
The language of the cortex is ... *words.*

Escape Stories
cont'd

Blue - sad
Orange lines - nervous
Yellow polka dots - happy
Black - feeling numb or frozen
Purple curvy lines - energetic
Red - hot and angry or mad
Brown - tight and tense

Adversity and the New Story

Reframing a negative experience can provide new sensory associations for the child. This could take place in the heat of the moment or in reflecting with a student who has already experienced this adversity but would benefit by telling a new story to reframe the positive aspects, creating new sounds, smells, sights, and tastes for this adversity.
   · What were you doing when this happened?
   · What did it look like?
   · What sounds did you hear?
   · Who was with you?
   · What was their reaction?
   · What else did you notice?
   · How did it feel?

Co-Teaching

Every week, students take turns signing up to co-teach with you. They'll help in planning lessons, designing assessments, and doing research! Nothing is more motivating than when students take the lead with their own expertise and build confidence in their abilities to lead, share, and design. In middle school, this might be best to do with partners—peers are everything in these years!

Trees Are Like Our Brains!

Trees are like our brains!
   · What do you notice? The tree's roots are like our nerves.
   · What do trees need to grow? What stresses a tree?
   · How would your tree look? Does your tree have many branches or just a few? Describe the trunk of your tree.
   · Finish with a tree pose!

Cortical Strategies:
The language of the cortex is ... *words.*

Ideas for Your Superhero!

Ideas for Your Superhero!
• What is your superpower?
• Where do you live?
• How will your schoolwork change for the better with this superpower?
• What could be different about the brain of a superhero?
• Do you have a secret identity?
• Who is your real-life superhero?
• Do superheroes have neuroplasticity?
• Do superheroes use their amygdalae and frontal lobes? How and when?

Belief Commercials

Using images, words, colors, or technology, design an infomercial promoting a strong belief that you hold. This can be a personal belief, one that's developed through recent experience, or a long-held belief that you're now questioning.

Reinventing Gum

Place a piece of Trident gum and five notecards on every desk as students walk in. Have students design five new inventions for chewing gum. They can share and compare at the end of the Bell Work.

Meeting of the Minds

Students will select characters from a book, historical figures, or any author, inventor, scientist, or individual they've been studying. Given a 21st-century challenge, how would these individuals solve it? What would their discussion look like and how would they relate to one another?

Invent a New Language

Either individually or with a partner, create a new language that we need today! This language could be one of feelings, kindness, service, or just a silly language that we make up by adding or deleting words, parts of words, vowels, or consonants.

Cortical Strategies:
The language of the cortex is ... *words.*

The Traveling Pants

Place an old pair of trousers or blue jeans on a table in the front of the room. Use them to prompt a variety of questions and activities. Where have these pants been? Where would you travel if you wore them? Describe three places you'd travel or goals you'd accomplish with these pants. What will it take for you to get there? How can you begin creating these destinations or goals today?

Writing Blindfolded

Wearing a blindfold or with your opposite hand, write a short review paragraph about a topic that will be on the upcoming test or that needs to be remembered. Following the activity, trade papers with a classmate and see if they can read and understand what was written.

Dream Interviews

When students enter the class, they choose a half sheet of colored paper with a set of instructions displayed on the smart board. In the front of class is an empty chair and maybe some props to create a comfortable setting. The question: "If you could choose any person in the world to spend 15 minutes discussing, questioning, and sharing with, who would this be and why?" The students can write or draw their responses. They have a choice to share responses following the exercise. When I implemented this experience with middle school and undergraduate students, the sharing and empathy in the room was palpable! I learned so much about the emotional and social profiles of these students!

Cortical Strategies:
The language of the cortex is ... *words.*

Dual Brain Sheet

Youth and Adult Working Together

    A. Youth AND adult will answer questions 1-5 independently.

    B. Youth AND adult will discuss and then complete 6-10 together.

    C. Youth AND adult will decide on additional questions to answer.

<u>Youth</u>

1. What was our challenge?
2. What led up to this challenge?
3. How did I handle this?
4. Could I have prevented this challenge or problem?
5. What are two adjustments that I will make the next time?

<u>Adult</u>

1. What was the challenge?
2. What led up to this challenge?
3. How did I handle this?
4. Could I have prevented this challenge or problem?
5. What are two adjustments that I will make the next time?

<u>Both</u>

1. What is our challenge?
2. What led to this challenge?
3. In the future, how can we handle this together?
4. Can we prevent this challenge or problem in the future?
5. What are two adjustments that we will make?

Additional Questions:

    · What do you want?

    · How can I help you?

    · What feels difficult?

    · What is the worst thing that could happen?

    · What could be the best possible outcome?

    · Is your interpretation true, and how do you know this?

B. A SECRET: Guiding Questions

A = Attention

What experiences, things, people, or processes hold this student's attention?

What types of attention feel good to them?

What do they enjoy?

What experiences, interests and activities do they discuss often?

S = Sensory

What sensory needs is behavior communicating?

Troubling Sensations	Repairing Sensations
Yelling, loud noises, abrupt movements, harsh tones	Headphones, quiet area, more predictable transitions
Crowds, too many people	Space, a buddy, create chunks of time in large spaces
Sitting still	Movement
Hot, angry, sweaty	Ice pack, portable fan, a walk outside
Jumpy, irritated	Rhythm, weighted pad, an errand, stationary bike, lifting heavy objects or weights

E = Emotions

What are the dominant emotions beneath the behavior, and what can we provide?

Anger/ Irritated	Validate, "notice me," more space, less talking
Sad	Touch, connection, warmth, pressure, questions of service

Edgy	Deep breaths, movement, Focused Attention Practices
Worried	Active Constructive Responding, validating
Anxious	Journaling, Focused Attention Practice, EFT practices

---

C = Culture

Where and when is the behavior occurring?

Was the behavior activated or triggered in the cafeteria, hallway, recess, bathroom, classroom, or school bus?

What does the student need? (A different space, less noise, improved smells, etc.)

Does student need a different adult or a different relationship with the adult currently in charge?

Does the student need different arrangements of classrooms, time, or space?

R = Relationships

Who does the student trust?
Who does the student need?

If that adult is unavailable in the moments of distress, consider a phone call or text, drawing a picture, writing a letter, and preparing to send it.

E = Environment/Experiences

What is happening in the environment to activate the growing stress?

Consider the student's neuroception (their current relationship with both their inner and outer environment). Is the student experiencing a lack of structure, routine, predictability, or rituals? Do they need more predictability, increased routines, or more clearly defined structure? Who does the student need?

What does the student need in the environment? A different place to work? Co-regulation? Three practices built into a routine?

T = Tasks

What task is difficult?

What work feels overwhelming?

Is it difficult to get started?

Is it difficult staying focused? Is it too easy to be distracted?

What can we do with these challenging tasks?

Some solutions: Dosing chunks of challenging assignments into shorter assignments, rearranging the timing of a task, offering frequent feedback and validation, allowing the student to incorporate movement into the task

A SECRET – Protocol/Pre-Op

This protocol can be used while thinking of a specific student and situation, or after observing a specific scenario.

1. Reflecting on the situation/scenario of focus, use the guiding questions to fill in the first column of the pre-op chart. What did you see? What did you notice?

2. In the second column, use the guiding questions to create alternative accommodations/supports. What could we do in the future? What proactive strategies can we put into place?

Observations/Reflections	Pre-Op
A = Attention	A = Attention
S = Sensory	S = Sensory
E = Emotions	E = Emotions
C = Culture	C = Culture
R = Relationships	R = Relationships
E = Environment/Experiences	E = Environment/Experiences
T = Tasks	T = Tasks

A SECRET – Example Chart

The following chart was filled out by a grade-level of educators after watching the *Listening Skills* Life Space Crisis Intervention video.

Observations/Reflections	Pre-Op
A = Attention • Returning to class: "Can I go back?" • Behavior point sheet	**A = Attention** • Validate instead of telling, and begin to use waiting time. • Use a fidget or sensory tool to shift focus. • Provide more physical space.

S = Sensory
• Tired
• Woke up at 2 AM to "go to work"
• Did not want to be sitting
	S = Sensory
	• Different seating options:
	  ◦ Large exercise ball – movement
	  ◦ Bean bag – provides noise in the silence, low to the ground to encourage a feeling of being grounded
	• Softer lighting options
	• More open space

E = Emotions • Anger • Irritation • Wants someone to "notice me"	**E = Emotions** • Validation • Active Constructive Responding
C = Culture • Oppressive • Resembles an interrogation	**C = Culture** • Change in arrangement of seating • Choices of seating • Fewer adults, 1-on-1

A SECRET – Example Chart   *cont'd*

Observations/Reflections	Pre-Op
R = Relationships • No obvious secure, sustainable relationships in the building	**R = Relationships** • Finding touch points • Is there anyone here at school you would like to spend some time with? • Who do you need? • If it is not someone at school can we write them a letter? Email? Text? Call them on the phone?
E = Environment/Experiences • Closed in space • Lack of co-regulation	**E = Environment/Experiences** • Open space • New experiences: help him create a pause with a visual reminder (object, rubber band)
T = Tasks • Behavior point sheet: overwhelming, goal seems out of reach	**T = Tasks** • Create more opportunities for success in the task

C. Animal Regulation Cards

Inspired by the true habits of animals, these cards have been designed to guide co-regulation activities based in sensory stimulation. After students become familiar with these exercises, they can be used as self-regulation tools as well.

CARD 1

Pigs

Did you know that pigs cannot sweat? They roll around in mud and water to cool off. Pigs also love to snuggle with each other!

Using a blanket or towel, roll yourself up nice and snug like a pig. (Students can do this themselves, or a teacher can help. If a teacher is helping, gently pat the student clean with light pressure.)

Take 3 short inhales by snorting through your nose like a pig. Then slowly exhale through your nose.

CARD 2

Monkeys

Did you know that monkeys use their voices, facial expressions, and movements to communicate? Gorillas beat their chests with open hands, not fists, to show their size and strength.

Take a cue from this gorilla and tap gently with your fingertips on the top of your head.

Next, tap gently on your face:
- on your eyebrows
- on your temples
- under your nose
- on your chin

Raise your shoulders and arms and tap on your sides.

Finish by gently tapping on your chest making your best monkey sounds!

CARD 3
Dogs

Did you know that dogs don't only shake to dry themselves off? The also shake after they get up from a nap, and even "shake it off" when they are stressed.

Can you shake off your stress or worries like a dog?

After a nap, many dogs stretch as they do their own version of the Downward Dog Pose in yoga. Let's stretch, too!

CARD 4
Cats

Did you know that cats arch their backs to stretch their "sleepy" muscles after a cat nap?

On "all fours," arch your back up like a cat and hold it for 5 seconds.

Then slowly bring your chest and tummy down as you lift your head. Hold this stretch for 5 seconds.

Repeat these cat stretches 2 more times.

CARD 5
Elephants

Did you know that elephants create their own sunscreen by throwing mud onto their backs with their trunks?

Using your arm as a trunk, lift up as you inhale.

Hold for 3 seconds.

As you bring your trunk back down, exhale through your mouth making a trumpet noise.

CARD 6

Flamingoes

Did you know that a flamingo's legs can be longer than their entire body? The knot that looks like a knee is actually its ankle!

Begin by balancing on one leg.

Slowly lift your leg while lowering your head.

Can you imitate this flamingo?

CARD 7

Koalas

Did you know that koalas can sleep up to 18 hours in one day? They tend to use most of their energy eating the leaves from the eucalyptus trees they live in.

Like a koala, curl into a little ball and take a few deep breaths (similar to a Child's Pose in yoga).

Lying down or sitting, wrap your arms around your body and give yourself a hug.

CARD 8

Crocodiles

Did you know that crocodiles can go underwater with their mouths open? They have a special valve that closes their throats, so they won't accidentally swallow or breathe in water.

Using your arms like the jaws of a crocodile, inhale through your nose as you open your arms.

Exhale through your nose as you close your crocodile jaws in slow motion. Finish with a big clap!

D. Differentiating the Amygdala Reset Station

As educators we all know, without a shadow of a doubt, that every child is unique, and that this uniqueness extends far beyond their personalities. It spreads into their life experiences, their learning styles, their needs, and even their brain architecture. This is what makes our job so complicated, and at times frustrating, because we all know that what works for Joe does not necessarily work for Thomas, and what works for Kayla this morning might not work for Kayla this afternoon. Our kiddos are unique, plain and simple. As educators we also know, whether through experience or training, the importance of differentiating our instruction. So if we know that our students are unique through and through, then differentiation must be applied to every situation through and through.

When thinking about an Amygdala Reset Station, we often default to this idea of a calming corner or designated spot located somewhere within one's classroom. But the reality is that our amygdala does not fire only in a classroom but everywhere—in the hall, in the lunchroom, in the bathroom, even at recess. In addition, we know that emotions are contagious, meaning there is a high probability that more than one student might need to reset their amygdala at the same time, and the last thing we want to do is put two firing amygdalae together! If the true purpose of an Amygdala Reset Station is to reset our amygdala, then we might want to expand our vision of what this resource looks like, where it is located, and how it is used. All of these factors can and should be differentiated based on the needs of those who use it.

It's All in How You Look at It ....

There's nothing wrong with an Amygdala Reset Station that fits the default idea mentioned earlier, so if this works for you and your students, by all means keep calm and carry on! For some students a designated spot in the room with a yoga mat, lavender-scented pillow, and flashcards outlining breathing exercises might not do the trick, so here are some alternate ideas:

- Instead of creating an entire corner or area, think about utilizing a basket or bin. The materials of an Amygdala Reset Station can be thought of as just that, materials, so don't be afraid to house them as you would other materials, like crayons and markers, clipboards, books, base ten blocks, etc. If we want students to use these materials as any other learning material, then the way in which we house them should reflect that, too.

- We can also think about the materials in our Amygdala Reset Stations as tools, and where do tools belong? In a toolbox! Create an Amygdala Reset Toolbox where students can grab a regulation tool and take it back to their seat just like they would grab a screwdriver or hammer from a toolbox to use on a building project.

- Our brains love imagery and making associations, so for younger students learning about regulation, try creating an Amygdala First Aid Station. Use a doctor's bag or first aid kit to house your materials. By doing this, we communicate to our students that these materials can help and heal us. In addition, it also communicates that everyone, not just the little guy screaming, can use the Amygdala Reset Station because everyone needs a Band-Aid or an ice pack from time to time.

Location! Location! Location!

Having a designated space in a classroom or even a designated room in a school is a great place to start when creating Amygdala Reset Stations, but don't let that limit you! As mentioned before, our amygdala might need to reset beyond the classroom, so here are a few ways to make sure that all amygdalae can reset in all situations:

- Since the *look* of an Amygdala Reset Station might not fit all students, *where* we keep these stations might not work for everyone, either. For some students the act of physically moving to a spot clearly known as a place of regulation might be too noticeable or garner unwanted attention. One thing you might try is creating mini Amygdala Reset Stations at students' desks or work places. That way, they can use the tools in a less overt way.

- The above idea raises another important factor to consider: one Amygdala Reset Station may not be enough! If you find that a couple of smaller stations are needed, you can place them strategically around your classroom. This is also a fantastic way to model the importance of choosing a regulation strategy that fits with one's environment. For instance, you may have a station in your whole-class meeting area and another in your class library, and while thinking putty or a small piece of Play-doh might be appropriate during whole-group instruction, it may not be appropriate for silent reading ... imagine trying to peel dried putty or Play-doh from the pages of a Dr. Seuss classic!

- Let's say that students cycle in and out of your room each period because you are a specials teacher, middle school teacher, or high school teacher. You might try having a basket of tools at the doorway where students can grab tools as they walk in and put them back as they walk out.

- Or perhaps you're a special education teacher, a reading interventionist, or another educator who moves from room to room throughout the day. You may want to create a portable Amygdala Reset Station that travels alongside you.

- It is also advantageous to think about the spaces beyond the classroom, like hallways, lunchrooms, recess yards, etc. How many of us have sent a regulated student to the bathroom only to have a dysregulated student return? What if we created environmentally specific Amygdala Reset Stations?

- For instance, a bathroom Amygdala Reset Station might include a variety of scented lotions with visual instructions posted for hand massages. Or instead of covering the inside of the stalls with engraved names, numbers, and unmentionable words, we could post a few quick breathing exercises on the back of the stall doors.

- A recess-friendly Amygdala Reset Station might include rain sticks, balls to bounce in rhythm, or even bubbles.

- And don't forget about the hallways, which provide one of the richest environments for regulation! Not what you expected to read, right? But seriously they do, since hallways tend to have the most powerful regulation tool of all: other people. Treat your hallways like a giant Amygdala Reset Station where you are the tool! Remember, emotions are contagious, so use your time in the halls to spread a smile, a laugh, a wink, or even a high five. This station is not only filled with tools of the teacher variety but includes students, parents, administrative staff, custodians, and any other members of your community. Everyone can be encouraged to take part in co-regulating one another!

Use it or Lose it!

Just as we might differentiate how an Amygdala Reset Station looks or where it is located, we can also differentiate how it is used. As we begin to think about the different ways we can use these stations, we must remember one thing: using an Amygdala Reset Station is a personal choice, not a requirement or a place to be sent. Forcing students to use these stations or even certain tools within them removes the "self" from self-regulation, which is what these stations are designed to promote.

- Keeping this purpose in mind, it's important that we use this space for all types of regulation, not just those viewed negatively. Just because we need to reset doesn't mean that we're resetting from a "bad" place. Ever heard the expression "I need a vacation from my vacation"? Even the fun, joyful, exciting moments of life warrant a little reset afterward. When we use amygdala resets only to reset negative feelings and behaviors, the space itself takes on a negative connotation. Emotions are contagious, after all!

- It's also important to remember that these tools aren't just tools for students—they're for us, too! Fire up those mirror neurons and model for students what an amygdala reset can look like. We've all done a read-aloud or two in our days as teachers, but what if you tried an amygdala reset think-aloud? Consider the impact for everyone by using this space for your own resetting, too! Move past just *showing* how to use it and actually *use* it. Even the teacher's amygdala needs to be reset every once in a while. Monkey see, monkey do, right?

- The last section presented the idea of a mobile amygdala resets, but if the station itself can be mobile, perhaps the tools can be, too. Some tools might need to be used at their station but there are plenty of others that could travel within the classroom or even the school.

- Remember, we strengthen neural pathways by utilizing them over and over and over, so if we want those self-regulation pathways to become the road more travelled, we have to use it or lose it! If you aren't using your Amygdala Reset Station, it might warrant some self-reflection, or a class discussion focused on why the station isn't being used and how you can change it to be more beneficial.

As you create your Amygdala Reset Station, remember to make it your own. These resets should be designed not only around a general understanding of the brain, but also around a specific understanding of your students' brains. Don't be afraid of changing things to better meet the needs of you and your students. Think beyond the ideas mentioned here, and the sky is the limit! The power of an Amygdala Reset Station is not in the station itself, but in how we use it.

E. Getting the Most Out of Your Amygdala Reset Station

"I know that I've taught a successful lesson when my students never use what was taught again!" said no teacher ... EVER! We all strive and work our fingers to the bone creating lessons and experiences that will impact our students well beyond the classroom. One of our main goals as educators is to set our students up for success, to prepare and equip them with the understanding and the tools needed to reach their greatest potential long after they leave us. We can apply this goal to all areas of our teaching, whether it be math, reading, writing, or even behavior, so it would only make sense that we apply this goal to the Amygdala Reset Station as well. Let's face it—Amygdala Reset Stations take a great deal of time and money, both of which teachers tend to be running low on, so we want to get the best bang for our buck! And we get that bang when we set our students up for success in using that Amygdala Reset Station.

The How and When of Regulation

How is this accomplished, you might ask? Well, we need to start with a common understanding of an Amygdala Reset Station's purpose: regulation. Notice the broad use of the term "regulation." This is intentional because these stations can house many different forms of regulation, including both co-regulation and self-regulation. Overall, self-regulation is the long-term goal here, but this isn't where we begin. When we teach a child to read, we don't walk them over to our class library, give them a little tour by pointing out the different types of books and options for places to read, and then leave them there expecting the reading to just magically happen. We start at the basics, and we sit beside them. The same approach should be taken when teaching our students how to use an Amygdala Reset Station. We start with the basics, controlling our breathing, and we sit beside them, modeling how we control our breath. Horse trainer Monte Roberts once said, "To blame the horse [for their instinctual behavior] is like blaming the night for being dark." When we blame students for not being in control of their emotions, feelings, and responses, we are blaming them for their own biology, which is far beyond their control. Regulating our emotions, feelings, and physiology is something that must be taught, and just like reading or arithmetic, we have to start at the basics and sit beside students as they learn. We must recognize that it will take a lot of intentional work and support, but trust me—the payoff is worth it!

While the *how* of introducing and setting up an Amygdala Reset Station is important, so is the *when*. We all know that regulation strategies are to be used when we are dysregulated, but that doesn't mean they should be taught when we are dysregulated. Quite the contrary, regulation strategies must be introduced and practiced during neutral times, times when our amygdalae are not triggered and when we're able to think and function in our cortex. Now, when I say "we," I mean both teacher and student.

This is where the beauty of neuroplasticity comes in! We know that our brains can create new neural pathways, but to create pathways that become hardwired circuits producing emotional well-being and sustainable learning, we need patterned repetitive opportunities that help to create brain states of relaxed alertness—which means *these pathways have to be created when we are in a state of calm, relaxed alertness.* Furthermore, if we want these pathways to be used, especially when they are needed most, then we have to make sure that they're well travelled. This occurs through patterned, repetitive experiences— in other words practice, practice, practice! Remember, practice does not make perfect, so be prepared for bumpy roads and setbacks, but just keep on keeping on. This continued practice is no different from a fire drill which, contrary to popular belief, isn't just a way to get out of teaching that hard math concept or our principal's way of keeping us on our toes.

We practice fire drills so that in case of a real fire, we know where to go and what to do. Practicing regulation strategies is exactly the same thing! We practice these strategies at times when we can go slow and get it right, so that when an emergency does arise and our amygdala fires, we know exactly what to do and where we can go. Setting your students up for success when self-regulating means giving them the tools, instruction, and support they need, not *at* the times when they need it the most, but *for* the times when they need it the most.

The Three Dysregulators

When creating and using Amygdala Reset Stations, we spend a great deal of time talking and thinking about what actually regulates the brain, but we often leave out what dysregulates the brain. Honestly, this is just as important, if not more so. You can't know right from wrong if you never identify the wrong; thus you can't know regulation if you never identify what causes dysregulation. Before we set off on an unending journey to identify all the things that might set one's brain off, we really need to remember only three stressors: chronic unpredictability, isolation, and restraint. The brain is an amazingly adaptable organ, but it does have limits. It simply cannot take these three stressors—even one of these conditions can compromise healthy brain functioning. So we must address these dysregulating factors when creating, introducing, and implementing an Amygdala Reset Station. By teaching regulation strategies and how to use the Amygdala Reset Station on the front end, during neutral times, we've already begun to remove unpredictability. Sitting beside our students in this work, truly co-regulating, takes away isolation, therefore giving our students the tools to succeed in understanding and coping with their emotions and feelings while removing restraints. As with anything, though, we have to remain vigilant in case the Amygdala Reset Station starts creeping toward these three dysregulators as we use of them day to day. It's extremely easy for these stations to become places of dysregulation if we're not continually asking: Is the station or how we use it unpredictable? Is it isolating to anyone? What restraints might it place on those who use it? Just as we continually self-reflect on our teaching habits, we need to continually reflect on our regulation habits. Following are additional questions that can help us avoid these three stressors of dysregulation.

Chronic Unpredictability	Isolation	Restraint
Do all my students know how to use the Amygdala Reset Station?	Is this a place where students can choose to go, or am I sending students there?	Who decides when students leave this space or discontinue their use of a tool? Is it always me?
Do they all know what it is for?	Am I actively using this space and its tools to co-regulate with my students?	Do students understand how to tell when they are finished?
What procedures and routines can we put in place to remove any unpredictability?	Do my students know that the Amygdala Reset Station can be used as a place of co-regulation with a trusted adult or friend?	Do the tools in our station allow for a variety of ways to regulate, or does it cater to a specific way?
Is the Reset Station always accessible to those who need it? Even if I am not there?	Who tends to use our station the most? Why is that? Is that a good thing?	
How can I proactively plan for times when my students have a guest teacher?	What can we do to make sure this is a resource utilized by all?	
	How can I use this station to build connections with students?	

So as you can see, the Amygdala Reset Station involves far more than setting up a yoga mat and a basket of putty and fidgets. These stations take a great deal of planning, require thoughtful and intentional introduction, and need continuous attention and reflection. This is not easy, but neither is teaching a kiddo how to read. Just as we set our students up for success in reading or math, we can set them up for success in regulating. At the end of the day, we have to remember that we are teachers, and that tackling the seemingly impossible is in our job description.

F. Brain Deck (Brain Intervals and Focused Attention Practices)

Dance It Out!

"Chicken Noodle Soup"
Kidz Bop
Dance along to this fun video!

Find it on YouTube:
https://www.youtube.com/watch?v=16CsjIlfwQc

Tap Your Head and Rub Your Tummy

Take one hand and tap it up and down on your head.

Take the other hand and rub it in circles on your tummy. Once you've gotten the hang of it, try to switch motions!

Grab Ear and Nose

Take your right hand and grab your left ear.

Take your left hand and touch your nose.

Now switch; take your left hand and grab your right ear. Take your right hand and touch your nose. Switch back and forth.

Clap, Lap, Clap, Miss

While sitting, clap both hands. Then hit your lap with both hands. Clap both hands once more, and then miss a clap. Repeat faster and faster each time.

The Flamingo

Put your right hand on your left hip and balance on your left foot. Hands together. Put your left hand on your right hip and balance on your right foot. Hands together. Then repeat with left hand in the air.

Fish & Snake

Move your right hand up and down in a wave-like motion. Now move your left hand side to side in a snake-like motion. Try performing it at the same time and then try switching hands.

Color Breather

Dim the lights and find a restful position. Close your eyes and take 3 deep breaths. As you breathe in, breathe in your favorite color. As you breathe out, imagine your least favorite colors flowing out of you along with any worries that you have. Repeat.

Take a Breather

Dim the lights and find a restful position. Close your eyes and take three long deep breaths. As you breathe in, imagine a happy memory from the past week. As you breathe out, imagine a worry leaving your body with your breath. Repeat.

Animal Noises

Pick a partner. One person makes an animal noise while the other tries to guess what it is. It's OK to be creative, so try something like an ostrich or hyena noise! Take turns making sounds and guessing.

Pen Revolution

Each person takes out a pen. Throw the pen into the air and catch it after it revolves once. Then try two revolutions. Now, find a partner and practice throwing pens to each other in one revolution, then in two. Repeat the whole sequence with each person favoring the opposite hand.

Tip of the Tongue

This one is silly! Find a partner. Have one partner try to tell the other a story while keeping your tongue on the top of your mouth. Then have the other partner try to guess what you are saying.

Pinky Thumb

With your right hand, hold up your pinky. With your left hand, hold up your thumb. Now switch and hold up your left pinky and your right thumb. Switch back and forth as fast as you can go!

Jumping Jacks

Stand up from your desk and do 10 jumping jacks to get the blood flowing. Now do 5 more while going in a circle. Turn in the opposite direction as you do the last 5 for a total of 20 jumping jacks.

Body Math

Assign numbers to certain parts of the body (ex: nose=1, ear=2, shoulder=3). Have one partner make an equation while the other partner has to figure out the solution. Try to add and subtract.

Create a Handshake

Find a partner to work with. With your partner, invent a cool new handshake that you can both enjoy. Use claps, snaps, fist bumps, or anything you can think of!

Create a New Language

Find a partner. Between the two of you, create a language by using patterns or sounds. Make up new words with new meanings.

Create a Rhythmic Pattern

Create your own rhythmic pattern by using a series of as many taps, claps, stomps, and other noises as you want. Share with everyone!

Thumb Wrestling

Find a partner and grasp their hand with yours. With your thumb, try to pin your partner's thumb for 5 seconds.

Arm Wrestling

Find a partner. Each puts an elbow on the table and grabs their partner's hand. Gently try to pin your partner's arm against the table.

Tic Tac Toe

Find a partner and play Tic Tac Toe with them. Try to get three in a row before your partner does.

I Spy

Think of an object somewhere in the room. Have a partner try to guess what object you've picked.

Rock, Paper, Scissors

Find a partner. Play rock, paper, scissors. Rock beats scissors; paper beats rock; scissors beat paper.

Imaginary Double Dutch

Find a group of 3 people. Have 2 stand on the ends and pretend to swing 2 jump ropes. The third person has to jump in and pretend to jump when the jump rope hits the ground.

Hangman

Start a hangman game with a partner or a group. Pick a category and have your partner(s) attempt to guess the word or phrase.

Words in a Word

Have someone pick a word—any word. Then have everyone else try to find smaller words within that word. (ex: "rad", "den", "are" in "garden"). See who can find the most words.

Picture in the Air

Find a partner. The first person draws a favorite place in the air. The other person tries to guess what the first person is drawing. Switch and repeat!

Charades

Split up into groups. Have one person act out a motion. All the other group members must try to guess what action is being performed. Whoever is correct can act out the next motion.

Yoga

Have one person lead everyone in yoga. Try the Downward Dog, Sun Salutation and many others. Find the poses online if needed. Slowly breathe in and out as you do them.

Mirror, Mirror

Find a partner and face each other. Have one partner be the leader. The other partner must move like a mirror image of the leader. Try to move arms at exactly the same time.

Dance Your Name

Have everyone in the class make up a small dance move. Going around the room, have everyone say their name as they do their dance move. Then everyone repeats the dance move.

Conga Line

Place hands on the shoulders of the person in front of you. Once music begins, move forward in a line, kicking your legs to the right and then to the left as you move.

Pantomime

Find a partner. Have one partner act out the movements of a person in a certain location. The other partner must try to guess the location. Switch.

Air Band

Perform a silent song with invisible instruments. Have a guitarist, pianist, lead singer and anything else you can think of!

Telephone

Have everyone stand in a line. Have someone make up a sentence and whisper it to the person on the left. Repeat the sentence down the line. At the end, see if the sentence changed or stayed the same.

Statue Imitation

Have someone put a picture of a statue up on the board. Everyone else should imitate what the statue is doing. Switch images and repeat.

Seat Switch

Have everyone stop what they are doing and find another person's seat to sit in. Repeat 5 times. You cannot sit in the same seat more than once.

Would You Rather?

Find a partner. One partner must make up "would you rather" questions, and the other partner has to pick one of the two. "Neither" is not an option.

Four Corners

Pick one person to stand in the center of the room with eyes closed. Have everyone else choose a corner.
If the middle person points to your corner, you are out. Continue until one remains.

Class Wave

Have everyone stand up. Start the wave with hands going up and then down from one side of the room, moving the wave all the way around the room.

Book Balance

Take out one of your light textbooks. Place it on top of your head and try to balance it. Now try to walk with the book still balanced on your head.

Heads Up, Seven Up

Have all students lay their heads down without peeking. Have a few volunteers choose students to stick their thumbs up. Those with thumbs up will try to guess who tapped them.

Class Story

Create a story by starting with one word. The next person adds a word, and so on. The words form sentences, and the sentences form a short story. Have fun and be creative!

Categories

Have someone pick a category (ex: food items). Have everyone else write down as many food items as possible. See who can write down the most (no repeats) in a set amount of time!

Alphabet Game

Find a partner. Switching back and forth with each letter, partners must go through the entire alphabet naming things by first letters. (ex: Apple, Bear, Car, Donkey, Ear...)

First Letter

Using the first letter of your name, think of an animal whose name also begins with that letter. Then have everyone go around and say their animals' names. Try to remember each name!

First Thought

Have someone start singing or humming a favorite song. Everyone else must draw a picture that describes what they hear and think about when they listen to the song.

Position Switch

Turn your seat around and use the desk behind you. If you sit in the back row, move all the way to the front seat, but facing the back of the room.

Rhyme Me

Have someone pick a word—any word. Then have everyone else try to come up with as many words as possible that rhyme with the chosen word. Set a time limit to make it more fun!

Draw by Words

Sit back to back. Have one student draw a picture and describe what he or she is drawing. The other person has to draw at the same time while listening to the description by the first person. Compare results!

G. How Are You Feeling Diagram

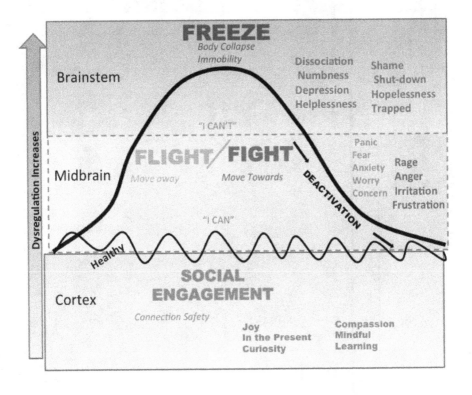

H. Brain Behavior Chart #1

NEUROCORTEX
Higher-order thinking

LIMBIC SYSTEM
Emotions

BRAIN STEM
Survival

DAILY BRAIN REFLECTION/FEEDBACK REPORT

NAME _____   DATE _____

TARGETED CHALLENGE	Morning Mtg 8:30 – 8:50	Subject Time 2	Subject Time 3	BREAK 4	Subject Time 5	Subject Time 6	Subject Time 7	Subject Time 8	Subject Time 9	BREAK 10	Subject Time 11	Subject Time 12	Subject Time 13
	1	2	3	4	5	6	7	8	9	10	11	12	13
Completing Work	Green Red Blue	Green Red Blue	Green Red Blue	Green Red Blue	Green Red Blue	Green Red Blue	Green Red Blue	Green Red Blue	Green Red Blue	Green Red Blue	Green Red Blue	Green Red Blue	Green Red Blue
Taking Care of Business With Regard to Myself and Others	Morning Mtg 8:30 – 8:50 — 1	Subject Time 2	Subject Time 3	BREAK 4	Subject Time 5	Subject Time 6	Subject Time 7	Subject Time 8	Subject Time 9	BREAK 10	Subject Time 11	Subject Time 12	Subject Time 13
	Green Red Blue	Green Red Blue	Green Red Blue	Green Red Blue	Green Red Blue	Green Red Blue	Green Red Blue	Green Red Blue	Green Red Blue	Green Red Blue	Green Red Blue	Green Red Blue	Green Red Blue

Goal =

I. Brain Behavior Chart #2

Green = **NEUROCORTEX** = feeling peaceful, calm
Red = **LIMBIC SYSTEM** = feeling angry, irritated, sad
Blue = **BRAIN STEM** = feeling shut down

Higher-order thinking

LIMBIC SYSTEM
Emotions

BRAIN STEM
Survival

DATE _____

NAME _____

DAILY BRAIN REFLECTION/FEEDBACK REPORT													
TARGETED CHALLENGE	Morning Mtg 8:30 – 8:50	Subject Time	Subject Time	BREAK	Subject Time	Subject Time	Subject Time	Subject Time	Subject Time	BREAK	Subject Time	Subject Time	Subject Time
	1	**2**	**3**	**4**	**5**	**6**	**7**	**8**	**9**	**10**	**11**	**12**	**13**
Completing Work	Green Red Blue	Green Red Blue	Green Red Blue	Green Red Blue	Green Red Blue	Green Red Blue	Green Red Blue	Green Red Blue	Green Red Blue	Green Red Blue	Green Red Blue	Green Red Blue	Green Red Blue
Kind feet, hands, words (no aggression with others)	Morning Mtg 8:30 – 8:50	Subject Time	Subject Time	BREAK	Subject Time	Subject Time	Subject Time	Subject Time	Subject Time	BREAK	Subject Time	Subject Time	Subject Time
	1	**2**	**3**	**4**	**5**	**6**	**7**	**8**	**9**	**10**	**11**	**12**	**13**
	Green Red Blue	Green Red Blue	Green Red Blue	Green Red Blue	Green Red Blue	Green Red Blue	Green Red Blue	Green Red Blue	Green Red Blue	Green Red Blue	Green Red Blue	Green Red Blue	Green Red Blue

Goal Met? ☐ Not Yet ☐ Getting there

Goal = _____

©LORI L. DESAUTELS

Green	Red	Blue
CORTEX	**LIMBIC SYSTEM**	**BRAIN STEM**
Peaceful, Calm	**Angry, Irritated, Sad**	**Shut down**
HIGHER-ORDER THINKING	*EMOTIONS*	*SURVIVAL*
Safe and Calm	Angry or Irritated	Shut Down
Ready to Talk	Worried or Sad	Numb or Frozen
Problem Solver	Ready to Yell, Fight, or Run	Disengaged

J. Accommodations for Adverse Childhood Experiences

A Comparison of Traditional Accommodations and Accommodations Using the Lens for Adverse Childhood Experiences (ACEs)

What do you need?

Many of our students who need emotional support and resources do not have an IEP, 504, or team of educators and staff available to consistently meet their social and emotional health needs each day! These students often come to school in a survival brain state, plagued by adversities that have accumulated throughout the days, weeks, months, or years. The following template is created collaboratively to support all students who come to school with significant Adverse Childhood Experiences (ACEs). These supports and resources are for our children and youth who carry in pain-based behaviors and need accommodations and possible modifications during the school day regarding their environments and schoolwork. These supports will address the critical needs of attachment and regulation. Often, as students move between different classrooms and environments throughout the school day, we are not consistent in providing a routine of two or three practices that they can implement to calm and regulate while building relationships with other adults or students.

What can we do to make it better?

We are not suggesting that we add more work to what we are already doing. Instead, we are intentionally and transparently handling this child or adolescent with care and with the understanding that pain-based behaviors show up in disrespectful, defiant, or shut-down ways. We propose accommodations that can occur naturally through our procedures, routines, transitions, bell work, and morning meetings!

How can I help?

We know that many of our roughest and most dysregulated students don't have these accommodations with accompanying accountability ... or if they do, the accommodations are not consistently available and monitored. As a district, school, department, grade level, or classroom, we need to create these accommodations so that they're consistently dispersed, discussed, and implemented each day.

Why

If our social and emotional learning outcomes, programs, and competencies are to reflect the current brain research addressing the severe life disruptions/trauma occurring in our student populations across the country, we need to address specific areas of brain development with regard to acquiring these competencies. Brain development is complex, and even today, we know very little about how individual regions of the brain work collectively through neuronal connections and projections. We do know, however, that human brains are not complete at birth, but are designed to continue developing throughout a person's life. This development is intimately impacted by experiences. Because our students spend over 13,000 hours in school during their K-12 span, educators have the opportunity and the obligation to address their social-emotional skills and competencies through creating the accommodations and adjustments needed for emotional, social, and cognitive well-being.

School Accommodations

Traditional Accommodations	Accommodations Through ACEs' Lens
1. Seating at the front of the class	1. I need a seat where I feel safe and secure.
2. Graph paper to line up math problems	2. I need two adults in the building whom I can trust and a place to walk when I begin to feel triggered.
3. Multiplication table or use of calculator	3. I need a personalized routine of three practices that I can implement when I begin to feel anxious, angry, or negative (such as a sip of water, five deep breaths, drawing or creating with an art form for a few minutes).
4. Repetition and explanation of directions when needed	4. I need access to sensory area or table in our classroom for patterned repetitive activities to calm me down.
5. Preprinted classroom notes from the teachers	5. I need a personalized set of my accommodations given to all who work with me so that they can help me de-escalate, calm down, and become ready to learn.
6. Occupational therapy every Wednesday	6. I need a weekly meeting with my resiliency team (two or three individuals at school whom I trust).
7. One-on-one math tutoring twice a week during study hall	7. I need regularly scheduled, one-on-one check-in time with my pre-arranged mentor whom I can also go see to help me co-regulate as needed.

Test Accommodations:

Traditional Accommodations

1. Extended time on tests and quizzes

2. Quiet testing room with small group setting

Accommodations Through ACEs' Lens

1. I need extended time to regulate if necessary and academic accommodations for my assignments when I am dysregulated.

2. I need access to a quiet area when I need to regulate my nervous system via a routine of three options (such as taking my pulse, drawing or writing in my journal, or working in another classroom).

My Goals:

Traditional Goals

1. Improve my mental math skills

2. Get better at asking for help when needed

3. Join a school club or activity

ACEs' Lens Goals

1. Learn to regulate with an adult before I reach the tipping point

2. Lessen the number of times I need to use the resiliency team and the Amygdala Reset Area

3. Create a journal of my ups and downs to track my progress

More About Me and What I Need:

---

1. **Strengths to Help Me With My Goals:** What skills and activities show my strengths with learning and service to others? For example:

   · I love to learn. I'm seen as a leader and good friend by others.

   · I have a great imagination.

   · I know how I feel and learn best!

   · I work quickly.

   · I notice everything.

   · I am good at sensing others and all nonverbal communication.

2. **Interests and Areas of Expertise:** What are my interests and areas of knowledge that I can share with my class, school, and community? For example:

   · I love art!

   · I am interested in animals, especially cats.

   · I have a pet-sitting service.

   · I am good at soccer.

3. **Triggers:** What are the experiences, events, sights, sounds, smells, relationships, and people who can unexpectedly trigger or activate anger, irritation, or worry? For example:

   · The angry sound of an adult shouting

   · The smell of frying onions

   · The sight of a dark green SUV covered with road dust

IV. *Members of this student's resiliency or support team*

1.

2.

V. Key Adult Mentor(s) assigned to this student:

1.

K. Educator Brain State E- Book

Educator Brain State
A guide to regulation strategies for teachers based in applied educational neuroscience.

For teachers, by teachers.

This guide was created by the Applied Educational Neuroscience Certification 19/20 cohort at Butler University's College of Education. The hope of this collaborative booklet is to provide teachers, administrators, related service providers, counselors, social workers, building staff, and anyone else who works with our youth with a resource filled to the brim with practical, everyday strategies that address our brain states.

It all starts with you.

If we want to make a lasting change in the lives of our students, we must first begin within ourselves. Neuroscience shows us that a dysregulated brain cannot learn, that our emotions are contagious, and that we are equipped with special structures to mirror and empathize with the world around us. Thus, we are the epicenter of this change. We must practice these regulation strategies ourselves not only to serve as a model, but also to show our students that regulation is important for all of us, and that personal well-being is just as important as math, reading, and writing.

Where to begin?

Sensory Strategies: This first section focuses on regulating the brain stem using the language of sensations.

Feelings, Touch Points, and Connection Strategies: This section focuses on regulating the limbic system, the emotional center of the brain using the language of feelings and connection.

Cortex Strategies: This final section focuses on regulating the cortex using the language of words, self-reflection, and communication.

Sensory Strategies

Movement

- Take a walk. Partner up with a co-worker and use a tap-out or tag-out system when you need a break.

- Bring in a stationary bike to pedal out the stress or worry.

- Stand up and get water from a different area to give yourself a breather and take some time for yourself.

- Have comfortable seating that allows you to either feel involved with the whole class or even boxed off when alone time is needed.

- Do some stretching. This could be whole body stretches or just wrist circles.

- Incorporate exercise. You can do this as a class or simply throw in a few lunges, jumping jacks, or push-ups when you need them.

- Intentionally move around your space, perhaps standing and looking out the window for a few moments.

Breath

- Practice meditation and calming breaths.

- Take a moment for intentional breathing (e.g., long, slow, deep breaths that reach into our bellies).

- Take a few deep breaths extending the exhale.

- Do a superwoman (or power) pose when nervous. Taking a deep breath and doing a motion, such as putting your hands on your hips, can help you quickly regulate or calm down.

Touch

- Make your own sensory table or space. Try running your hands through uncooked rice, pebbles, beads, marbles, sand, etc.

- Create a personal calming space for yourself at school. This could be in the corner of your room, in your car, a building Amygdala Reset Room, or any area that works for you. Know what helps you regulate, try different sensory tools, and place what works best for you in that area.

- Give yourself a hand massage with some lotion (scented or unscented). Focus on your breath as you rub in the lotion.

- Practice EFT or tapping.

- Use a fidget for your hands or a weighted blanket for your lap or shoulders.

- Practice tension and release by squeezing various levels of therapy putty, a squishy ball, or resistance bands.

- Place an outline of hands on the wall and push on them.

- Hug someone who seems to need a hug.

- Take off your shoes.

- Designate a comfortable place to sit other than a desk chair.

Scent

- Use an aromatherapy diffuser, switching out the oils depending on what is needed, such as lavender for calming, citrus for energy, or peppermint for focus.

- Utilize essential oils.

- Use scent sticks with caps.

- Have some lavender-scented lotion handy.

Sound

- Create your own playlists with themes, such as getting the morning started, peaceful tranquility, wake up after lunch, joy, motivation, calm down, energizer, and one with your favorite songs or genre.

- If classroom setup makes it available, soft and rhythmic music can help you track breathing and can deliver a calming effect.

- Listen to music with the sound adjusted in order to feel the vibrations.

- Play soft music in the background.

- Pop some bubble wrap or click a pen.

Taste

- Drink water.

- Chew gum (the rhythmic motions of chewing are regulating to the body). You can also suck on a mint.

- Organize a food truck visit.

- Keep a stash of candy just for you.

- A hot cup of coffee or tea can go a long way.

Visual

- Take a brief visual break focusing on sand art or a bubble timer.

- Do some adult coloring. The rhythmic movements used and the patterns and predictability of what you are coloring are especially calming to the brain.

Feelings, Touch Points, and Connection Strategies

Feelings

- Wear your favorite comfy clothes.

- You get to wear your favorite pair of jeans whenever you choose.

- Create a recess duty pass.

- Ask yourself, "What's the story in my head?"

- Have a family photo spot in your room.

- Take a moment to look closely at framed pictures of your family and friends and send a silent affirmation to each one.

- Make a to-do list to help you feel in control and organized.

- Practice a brief 1-3-minute meditation.

- Meditate with students, practicing positive affirmations or reading a light text. This gives you and your students time to regain balance and just breathe.

- "It's OK" to take a break, tap-out or tag-out, etc.

- Instead of having to ask for a reset, break, or tap-out, create recommended teacher resets. These resets can be supported by an administrator or teaching colleague who recognizes the need and offers to cover a class while the teacher taps-out for a few minutes. This way the teacher does not always have to ask for a break.

Touch Points

- Designate an accountability partner, someone like-minded that you can be open and honest with and receive feedback from. If your partner sees you flipping your lid, using negative language, shaming, etc., they can kindly intervene and co-regulate with you. This person could also serve as someone to brainstorm with and offer encouragement to you through work challenges.

- Seek out a friend that you can "vent" to for five minutes before moving on to identify positives and problem-solving solutions. Having someone listen is co-regulation!

- Use the 2x10 strategy with colleagues and staff, especially support staff who often feel disconnected.

- Text or write your coworkers notes with light-hearted messages to provide a humorous break throughout the day.

- Develop relationships with other students beyond your own classroom, and check in with them during the day or week. This offers a break to the usual teacher-student relationship as you do not have to worry about discipline or pressures of curriculum.

- Go to younger students' class to play. Visit a kindergarten room!

- Visit the playground and play with students, not just watching but actually playing alongside them. Find you inner child again!

Connection

- Eat lunch with your colleagues.

- Create an accountability team.

- Begin a daily shout-out or recognition of the work your peers are doing.

- Create a shout-out board or staff praise email that staff can add to throughout the week, and can then be emailed out to everyone on Friday.

- Have a community circle with staff every morning or at the beginning of the week to check in. Try to focus on personal well-being and connection. You might challenge everyone to keep the "shop talk" to a minimum.

- Plan schoolwide (all staff) social events throughout the year (e.g., raise a glass).

- Create a corner of the staff lounge where teachers can use sticky notes to post their triggers, see a list of helpful regulating strategies, and have access to their own reset tools to use in the moment.

- Set up a teacher brain check-in (e.g., Above or Below the Line) in the staff lounge for those who wish to participate.

- Make a card with "likes" in the lounge or workroom to share with other staff members. "Make a day" based upon the input on the card.

- Designate a trophy (something formal, meaningful, or silly) that is passed along weekly to spotlight a teacher and/or class.

Cortex Strategies

Perspective

- Practice positive self-talk. Incorporate your breath as you think or say positive affirmations.

- Use positive reframing. For example, if you find yourself saying that a student is attention seeking, reframe that as connection seeking.

- Take a quick step into the doorway, allow the temperature to change around you, and take a few deep breaths. This allows you to still manage the classroom, but separates yourself for a couple of seconds or minutes at a time.

- Need to focus? Do a focused attention practice! They are not just for students!

- Do not forget to laugh! Lighten yourself up with humor and you may lighten up the whole mood of the school. (Just be sure to respect the appropriate boundaries for students and teachers.)

- Create a regulation jar in the lounge for teachers to draw from when needed.

- Keep a special box of positive reminders or pick-me-ups to read from when needed. You might include funny cartoons, thank you notes, positive notes from colleagues/supervisors/parents/students, daily devotionals, etc.

- Practice self-care by being mindful of your diet, sleep, and exercise.

- Encourage self-care in others by creating a lending library with self-help, inspirational, and motivational resources.

Communication

- Set the tone by sending a complimentary message, email, or note to a colleague, student, or parent.

- Add a daily quote, food for thought, strategy, song lyric, joke, etc. to your email signature.

- Keep your camera ready throughout the day to snap pictures that move you. Appropriately share on social media to contribute to a positive school culture.

- Have a visual item for students to know when quiet time is needed; for example, a hat or a certain necklace. Consider using another item for signaling to students those times when you, as their teacher, need a small gap of quiet to focus on yourself because you are feeling dysregulated.

- Outside your classroom or office door, hang a picture of a suitcase where students, visitors, and you can touch it on the way in

CONNECTIONS OVER COMPLIANCE

to signify leaving one's baggage at the door. You could even find a big old-fashioned suitcase and have students and teachers drop in a written worry, concern, or anything they don't need or want to bring along with them.

- Create a Google Form that can be sent out to teachers with questions inquiring what their triggers might be and how the administration or staff could best support them. This can help administrators become more aware of how they can provide support that will be best received by individual teachers. This would be especially helpful when becoming familiar with new teachers and staff each school year.

- Create a wall in the staff lounge or workroom to chart thoughts, post quotes, and communicate triggers.

- Make a weekly video that encourages staff to reflect on their brain states. Increase engagement by using both educational and motivational content.

Planning Ahead

- Create a set of rituals or routines (e.g., passing period).

- Organize or clean your immediate space and prioritize tasks.

- Plan ahead for various outcomes (e.g., if this happens, then I will do ...).

- The rhythm and repetition of cleaning and organizing your space can help dampen the stress response system.

- Make a list of things to do and intentionally check them off.

- Set a timer or reminder for the last 2-3 minutes before the bell rings or your prep period ends to give yourself time for a mindfulness or regulation activity. (See the Sensory Strategies section for specific ideas.)

Reflection

- Take a moment of gratitude and jot down two things you are thankful for.

- Pause and quickly draw your brain state. What do you notice?

- The difference between a good teacher and a great one is the ability to self-reflect. Take a break and journal about your day.

- Grab a pen and paper to write and/or draw your thoughts and process through situations. Practice writing out your thoughts before responding in the moment. This can build your reflexes for quickly and effectively defusing tension in an escalating situation.

- Fill out your own SUDS (Subjective Units of Distress Scale) to gauge your brain state and mark how you can achieve or avoid certain levels.

- Create your own brain map and check in throughout the day asking: "Where am I?" "Am I reaching to teach/love my students?"

- Take a personality test online to learn more about yourself. Self-awareness helps us identify our reactions and be better prepared to regulate.

L. Brain-Aligned Student Survey

Assessing AEN Through the Lens of the Student

1. This school is a safe and secure place.

   AGREE___   DISAGREE___

2. I can get to school every day safely.

   AGREE___   DISAGREE___

3. I feel connected to a few of the teachers in my building.

   AGREE___   DISAGREE___

4. I feel everyone is treated with respect, even though we all make mistakes occasionally.

   AGREE___   DISAGREE___

5. I feel everyone in the classroom seems relaxed and we are learning.

   AGREE___   DISAGREE___

6. There is a lot of laughter and smiling in this classroom.

   AGREE___   DISAGREE___

7. I feel my school teaches me about my brain, stress, and how I can best learn.

   AGREE___   DISAGREE___

8. My school recognizes how I learn best and makes sure I feel my best, too!

   AGREE___   DISAGREE___

9. My teacher and the other adults in my school make sure that I am feeling successful, and when I am not, they help me!

   AGREE___   DISAGREE___

10. There is a lot of movement in my classroom and school!

    AGREE___   DISAGREE___

11. My classmates are excited about what they are learning and talk about what they are learning.

                      AGREE___   DISAGREE___

12. Everyone can drink water in this classroom when they want it.

                      AGREE___   DISAGREE___

13. There are many visuals used for all kinds of learning within this school.

                      AGREE___   DISAGREE___

14. In our school we are taught focused attention practices, using our breathing, sounds, tastes, or other ways to focus and become calm.

                      AGREE___   DISAGREE___

15. Music is used in this classroom during classwork time.

                      AGREE___   DISAGREE___

16. We get to move around and use rhythm during the day.

                      AGREE___   DISAGREE___

17. Our classrooms are active, and novelty is used to increase engagement, yet students know the routines and procedures. Things are buzzing but not chaotic.

                      AGREE___   DISAGREE___

18. In our school we are given choices during the school day.

                      AGREE___   DISAGREE___

19. In my school our teachers emphasize our strengths and pay attention to our interests. They want to know what I like and what I am good at!

                      AGREE___   DISAGREE___

20. My class and school give us brain intervals when we are bored or feeling restless!

                      AGREE___   DISAGREE___

21. My class and teachers usually build in fun and engaging ways to begin our class and end the class.

          AGREE___   DISAGREE___

22. My teachers make sure I understand what I am learning, and they give me time and lots of feedback.

          AGREE___   DISAGREE___

23. In our classroom we have projects or days where we serve other people, classes or other people.

          AGREE___   DISAGREE___

24. My school emphasizes and demonstrates caring, kindness, empathy, and compassion to everyone and the community.

          AGREE___   DISAGREE___

25. My school and teachers pay attention to how I feel and that I feel safe and connected to others when I am at school.

          AGREE___   DISAGREE___

M. Brain-Aligned Teacher Survey

Before the brain can attend to cognitive learning, students must feel physically safe and emotionally secure. Emotion is a strong force, and when learners experience strong negative emotions, the limbic system kicks in and shuts down cognitive processing. In other words, "reflex" trumps "reflection" when negative emotions occur.

A positive learning environment increases endorphins in the bloodstream, which generates a positive feeling and stimulates the brain's frontal lobe to support memory of the learning objective and of the positive situation. A negative learning environment leads to increased cortisol in the bloodstream, which raises the learner's anxiety level, shuts down processing of what it perceives to be low-priority information (the lesson content), and focuses the brain on what it perceives to be high-priority information (the situation causing the stress) so that the stressful situation is remembered rather than the lesson content. Please read the following survey questions and answer to the best of your ability. "Brain-aligned" describes school cultures, environments, strategies, and techniques that capitalize on the way the human brain learns naturally.

Rate each item for an individual classroom, or according to your perception of the school environment as a whole.

Use the following scale to rate each item:
Strongly agree - 1
Somewhat agree - 2
Somewhat disagree - 3
Strongly disagree - 4

Environments That Create a Sense of Belonging and Attachment:

All long-term learning takes place in the context of relationships.
MAURICE ELIAS

1. ____Adults know students by name and students all know the adults within the school.

2. ____ The school is a safe and secure place.

3. ____Children and youth can get to the school safely and without threat of harm.

4. ____The school intentionally connects children and youth with an adult in the school who serves as a source of support.

5. ____The school provides food, clothing, and other assistance to students living in unstable home environments.

6. ____Everyone in this classroom is treated with high levels of dignity and respect regardless of behavior or attitude.

7. ____Everyone in the classroom seems relaxed, yet alert.

8. ____There is much laughter and smiling in this classroom.

9. ____The school intentionally avoids the use of coercion to motivate and discipline young people.

10. ____The school intentionally trains its staff to avoid humiliation, shaming, sarcasm, ridicule, or other forms of attack with regard to students' personalities, achievements, or behaviors.

11. ____The school intentionally gathers perceptual data about its programs and services from all its constituents, including its students.

Environments That Create a Sense of Mastery and Achievement:

Children are defeated by failure.
Children who are depressed or angry can literally not learn.
SANDI REDENBACH

12. _____The school formally teaches social and emotional skills to its students.

13. _____The school intentionally recognizes and uses each student's unique learning style and recognizes multiple forms of intelligence.

14. _____The school establishes practices to ensure that all students experience success in the classroom and that no one is left to fail and flounder.

15. _____There is frequent movement in this classroom.

16. _____Students in this classroom are talking about what they are learning.

17. _____Everyone in this classroom is able to drink water when they want it.

18. _____There are many visuals being used for all kinds of learning within this school.

19. _____ Children are being formally taught to visualize at this school. Patterns and conceptual models are used to form connections.

20. _____ Music is being used in this classroom during classwork time.

21. _____ Children are moving and using their bodies to learn content in this school.

22. _____Classrooms are active and novelty is used to increase engagement, yet students know the routines and procedures. Things are buzzing but not chaotic.

23. _____Children and youth can demonstrate their mastery of material in a variety of ways that allow them to use their learning styles and strengths.

24. _____Collaborative groups, as well as independent work, are used throughout the day.

25. _____The school regards—and uses—a student's mistakes simply as opportunities for new learning.

Environments That Create a Sense of Independence and Autonomy:

When possible, engage and maintain students' attention by providing opportunities for them to set their own pace, select the hook that will connect them to the topic, and have some choice in the way they learn the information.
JUDY WILLIS, M.D.

26. _____The school recognizes that the primary purpose of evaluating a student's work is to determine what type of instruction or resources that particular student needs next.

27. _____The school provides many developmentally appropriate choices to its students.

28. _____The school emphasizes teaching students about their strengths and their gifts through the use of "strength discovering" assessments.

29. _____The school offers an array of electives for all students, and every student can find something they enjoy doing at school.

30. _____The school encourages developmentally appropriate risk taking and discourages a focus on simply taking courses and ranking students by grades and GPAs.

31. _____When teaching, the school staff recognizes that learners ask two critical questions prior to learning for long term memory: (1) Do I understand it? and (2) What's it got to do with me?

Environments That Create a Sense of Generosity and Altruism:

Our higher needs include making full use of our gifts ...
Such needs are fulfilled in an atmosphere of the five As by which
love is shown: Attention, Acceptance, Appreciation, Affection, and Allowing.
DAVID RICHO

32. _____The school provides a menu or opportunities that allow students to experience serving others.

33. _____The school provides a sense of optimism and hope through established rituals that involve all students.

34. _____The school culture emphasizes and demonstrates caring, kindness, empathy, and compassion to all its members. It extends these to the outside community in a variety of ways.

35. _____The school culture promotes wellness in body, mind, and spirit.

i think that's when
i learned to trust myself

GRATITUDES

This book contains the journeys and experiences of so many educators who pour their hearts and minds into their work with children and youth every day, and I am eternally grateful to learn from them. I want to specifically thank all of my colleagues who have contributed and enhanced this book and our endless work together with children and youth who have experienced significant adversity as we are continually generating trauma-responsive discipline protocols that move away from traditional and punitive experiences to ones that are relational, brain aligned, and preventive.

Thank you, Dr. Anita Silverman, for sharing your brilliant and creative ways of connecting with our youth and children who come to school very relationship reluctant. Your touch points with many of our most troubled adolescents will always be felt and appreciated in their growing experiences and lives.

Principal Frank Kline, it has been an honor to work beside you these past two years learning about Abbett Elementary and the vulnerable population of children who walk through your doors each day! Your compassionate presence is felt by all staff, children, and parents who share their deep emotional and social needs and celebrations with you every hour of the day! Jamie Rice, I am so grateful to have worked beside you and Frank these past two years and a memory that will be encoded in my brain forever is the individual greetings you give each student in every hall as they beam with joy from your kind loving presence!

Karrainne Polk-Meek, your leadership in the Richmond Indiana schools gives us all hope as we re-imagine collective neuroplasticity that is possible when an administrator is intentional about co-regulation, touch points, staff brain and body states, and teaching your student body about their neuroanatomy! Thank you for providing such inspiration with your shared story.

Courtney Boyle, you have been by my side for the past three years as a former student, graduate assistant and now co-instructor and colleague. Your work with early childhood is remarkably instinctive and so brilliantly shared in chapter six. Thank you for your loving guidance with all those you encounter and for the collaboration in our courses at Butler University, St. Mary's Early Childhood Center, and in our work through Revelations in Education. Your contributions to this book—your observations of working with me in schools in chapter six, the animal regulation cards, and the two sections on the amygdala reset stations—are immeasurable.

I want to give a special thank you to Michael McKnight for the kind, loving introduction and for teaching me through your quiet, powerful, and compassionate presence over the past seven years. It was lonely writing this book without you but your words, mind, and heart shine through!

I could not do this work or could not have written this book without the ongoing academic and heart-felt contributions of our Revelations in Education collaborators: Michael Cox, Jon Guthrie, Jennifer Wittrup, Dr. Shelia Dennis, Sara Midura, Mary Kate Daniels, Joe Bowman, and Gaby Fisher.

Sarah Desautels Dorsey, thank you for essential creative input on the cover of this book, as it has captured the miraculous synaptic possibilities that are achievable when our brains and bodies intentionally begin to rewire new feelings, thoughts, and perceptions. Your art as the inspiration speaks to the potential and reachable overall well-being for so many of our children and youth whom we have labeled disordered, disturbed, and dysfunctional when in reality, our most troubled children are functioning from a despairing and survival brain state.

Regan Desautels, thank you for creating the beautiful images that elegantly, yet simply, represent the themes, challenges, and the resiliency possible when we strengthen relationships and attune to a child's innate gift of emotional regulation, desire for safety, and his/her capacity to love deeply.

Alan Lipton, I literally could not have written this book without you. As my editor for the past several years, and my partner in writing this book, you know my heart, educational journeys, mind, and the twists and turns I abruptly write. Thank you for always listening, validating, noticing, and guiding my thought processes so skillfully and authentically! Thank you for the last-minute changes, questions, suggestions, and rewrites through this entire process. I am forever grateful!

Nancy, my heartfelt thank you for always believing, supporting, and creating a platform of perfection in book publishing for this educational work. Your positivity is uncontested, and the professional and personal partnerships you develop with your authors produces genuine and superior outcomes for all those who write, read, and reflect upon the experiences we embrace and ponder across the world! Thank you for another opportunity to sit beside Wyatt-MacKenzie as you highlight and share the brilliance, pain, and growing emotional challenges our children and youth carry into our schools. Thank you for shining a light on the patience, emotional availability and the consistency it will take from us all as we plant the seeds of hope and possibility into the lives of our future world citizens.

Thank you to the Butler University College of Education for providing a precipice for this work and for understanding the importance of preparing our pre-service educators in becoming trauma responsive through the lens of discipline that is the most critical subject area we could teach.

Michael, Andrew, Sarah, Matt, and Regan, thank you for always supporting me and understanding how this work in education is my soul's purpose and journey in this time. I love you and thank you from the bottom of my heart!

ENDNOTES

Sources for Prefaces

1. Sarah Al-Arshani, "9 large metro police departments reported 'double-digit percentage jumps' in domestic violence 911 calls as more people shelter at home." *Business Insider,* April 6, 2020, https://www.businessinsider.com/as-the-coronavirus-pandemic-grows-so-does-domestic-violence-2020-4.

2. Ibid.

3. Bonnie Badenoch, *The Heart of Trauma* (New York, NY: Norton Publishing, 2018), 13.

4. Ibid., 19.

5. Ibid., 10.

6. Bruce Perry and Maia Szalavitz, *The Boy Who Was Raised as a Dog: What Traumatized Children Can Teach Us About Loss, Love and Healing* (New York, NY: Basic Books, 2006), 231.

7. Bruce Perry, "Columbine, Killing, and You," Available at: https://www.scholastic.com/teachers/articles/teaching-content/columbine-killing-and-you/.

8. Laurie Zephyrin, M.D., David C. Radley, Yaphet Getachew, Jesse C. Baumgartner, and Eric C. Schneider, M.D., "COVID-19 More Prevalent, Deadlier in U.S. Counties with Higher Black Populations," https://www.commonwealthfund.org/blog/2020/covid-19-more-prevalent-deadlier-us-counties-higher-black-populations?gclid=EAIaIQobChMIoeGdqua26gIVBNvACh1KtQWGEAAYASAAEgKbwPD_BwE.

Sources for Chapter 1

1. Gregg Doyel, "I thought I was too late. Take the time to thank a life-changing teacher now." *IndyStar,* May 2, 2019, https://www.indystar.com/story/sports/columnists/gregg-doyel/2019/05/02/doyel-dont-do-what-did-take-time-thank-teacher-week-teacher-appreciation-week/3549380002/.

2. Children's Defense Fund, *The State of America's Children 2017* (Washington, D.C.: The Children's Defense Fund, 2017), 1-79. Available at: http://www.children'sdefense.org/library/state-of-americas-children/2017-soac.pdf.

3. Thom Garfat, "The Inter-personal In-between: An Exploration of Relational Child and Youth Care Practice," in *Standing on the Precipice: Inquiry into the Creative Potential of Child and Youth Care Practice,* eds. G. Bellefueille and F. Ricks (Edmonton, Canada: MacEwan, 2008), 8-9.

4. Allan N. Schore, "Effects of a Secure Attachment Relationship on Right Brain Development, Affect Regulation, and Infant Mental Health," *Infant Mental Health Journal* 22, no.1-2 (2001): 7-66. Available at: http://www.allanschore.com/pdf/SchoreIMHJAttachment.pdf.

5. Dr. Bruce Perry, "Bonding and Attachment in Maltreated Children," adapted in part by The ChildTrauma Academy from *Maltreated Children: Experience, Brain Development and the Next Generation* (New York, NY: W.W. Norton & Company, 2013).

6. Christine R. Ludy-Dobson and Bruce D. Perry, "The Role of Healthy Relational Interactions in Buffering the Impact of Childhood Trauma," in *Working With Children to Heal Interpersonal Trauma: The Power of Play,* ed. Eliana Gil (New York, NY: The Guilford Press, 2010), 26-43. Available at: https://7079168e-705a-4dc7-be05-2218087aa989.filesusr.com/ugd/ aa5lc7_810aa7b06ff74efe9b9d6833ff78a7f6.pdf.

7. Larry K. Brendtro and Nicholas J. Long, "Punishment Rituals: Superstition in the Age of Science," *Reclaiming Children and Youth: Journal of Emotional and Behavioral Problems* 6, no. 3 (1997): 130-135. Available at: https://eric.ed.gov/?id=EJ562330.

8. Ibid.

9. Ibid.

10. "Juvenile InJustice: Charging Youth as Adults is Ineffective, Biased, and Harmful," Human Impact Partners, February 2017, https://humanimpact.org/hipprojects/juvenile-injustice-charging-youth-as-adults-is-ineffective-biased-and-harmful/; Elizabeth T. Gershoff and Sarah A. Font, "Corporal Punishment in U.S. Public Schools: Prevalence, Disparities in Use, and Status in State and Federal Policy," *Social Policy Report* 30, no.1 (2016). Available at: https://www.ncbi.nlm.nih.gov/pmc/articles/PMC5766273/.

11. Marilyn Odendahl, "Juvenile waiver bill stirs controversy at Statehouse." The Indiana Lawyer, April 2, 2019, https://www.theindianalawyer.com/articles/49861-juvenile-waiver-bill-stirs-controversy-at-statehouse?utm_source=il-in-this-issue& utm_medium=newsletter&utm_campaign=2019-04-03; Richard E. Redding, "Adult Punishment for Juvenile Offenders: Does It Reduce Crime?" Villanova University Charles Widger School of Law Working Paper Series (2006). Available at: https://digitalcommons.law.villanova.edu/cgi/viewcontent.cgi?article=1047&context=wps.

12. Perry and Szalavitz, *The Boy Who Was Raised as a Dog,* 79-80.

13. Children's Defense Fund, *The State of America's Children 2017,* 1-79.

14. Centers for Disease Control and Prevention, "America's Drug Overdose Epidemic: Data to Action," accessed March 24, 2020, https://www.cdc.gov/injury/features/prescription-drug-overdose/index.html.

15. Nicholas J. Long, Frank A. Fescer, William C. Morse, Ruth G. Newman, and Jody E. Long, *Conflict in the Classroom: Successful Behavior Management Using the Psychoeducational Model* (Austin, Texas: PRO-ED Inc., 2014), XV.

16. Center on the Developing Child, Harvard University, "Toxic Stress," accessed April 29, 2020, https://developingchild.harvard.edu/science/key-concepts/toxic-stress/.

17. Ibid.

18. Ibid.

19. Ibid.

20. Jane Ellen Stevens, "The Adverse Childhood Experiences Study—the largest, most important public health study you never heard of—began in an obesity clinic." *ACEs Too High News,* October 3, 2012, https://acestoohigh.com/2012/10/03/the-adverse-childhood-experiences-study-the-largest-most-important-public-health-study-you-never-heard-of-began-in-a n-obesity-clinic/.

21. Ibid.

22. "Philadelphia Urban ACE Study," Public Health Management Corporation, last accessed July 30, 2018, https://www.phmc.org/site/97-press-releases/2015/1055-phmc-s-research-and-evaluation-group-conducts-second-survey-on-adverse-childhood-experiences-on-urban-communities.

23. Wendy Ellis and Bill Dietz, "A New Framework for Addressing Adverse Childhood and Community Experiences: The Building Community Resilience (BCR) Model," *Academic Pediatrics* 17, no. 7 (2017), 586-593.

24. Kristin Turney and Christopher Wildeman, "Mental and Physical Health of Children in Foster Care," *Pediatrics* 138, no. 5 (2016): e20161118.

25. Kenneth V. Hardy, "Healing the Hidden Wounds of Racial Trauma," *Reclaiming Children and Youth* 22, no. 1 (2013), 25-28.

26. Melissa T. Merrick, PhD, Derek C. Ford, PhD, Katie A. Ports, PhD & Angie S. Guinn, MPH, "Prevalence of Adverse Childhood Experiences From the 2011-2014 Behavioral Risk Factor Surveillance System in 23 States." *JAMA Pediatrics* 172, no. 11 (2018). Available at: https://jamanetwork.com/journals/jamapediatrics/fullarti-cle/2702204.

Sources for Chapter 2

1. Schore, "Effects of a Secure Attachment Relationship on Right Brain Development, Affect Regulation, and Infant Mental Health," 7-66.

2. Bruce D. Perry, "The Brain Science Behind Student Trauma: Stress and trauma inhibit students' ability to learn," *Education Week,* December 13, 2016, https://www.edweek.org/ew/articles/2016/12/14/the-brain-science-behind-stu-dent-trauma.html.

3. Larry Brendtro and Scott Larson, *The Resilience Revolution: Discovering Strengths in Challenging Kids* (Bloomington, IN: Solution Tree, 2006), 26.

4. Nicholas Long and Frank Fescer, *Life Space Crisis Intervention: Managing Troubled and Troubling Students in Crisis* (Hagerstown, MA: Life Space Crisis Institute, 2000), 34-35.

5. Nicholas Long, "Why Adults Strike Back: Learned Behavior or Genetic Code?" *Reclaiming Children and Youth* 4, no. 1 (1995):15.

6. Bessel van der Kolk, *The Body Keeps the Score: Brain, Mind, and Body in the Healing of Trauma* (London, U.K.: Penguin Books, 2015), 122.

7. Brendtro and Larson, *The Resilience Revolution,* 26.

8. Parker Palmer, *The Courage to Teach* (San Francisco, CA: Jossey-Bass Publishing, 1997), 11.

9. Dan Siegel, *Mindsight* (New York, NY: Bantam Books, 2010), 62-63.

10. Lori Desautels, "Activities That Prime the Brain for Learning," *Edutopia*, April 15, 2019, https://www.edutopia.org/article/activities-prime-brain-learning.

11. Brady Wilson, "Want To Bounce Back Better? Here's What Resilient People Do To Get Back In The Game," *Inc.*, October 19, 2016, https://www.inc.com/brady-wilson/want-to-bounce-back-better-heres-what-resilient-people-do-to-get-back-in-the-gam.html.

12. Shefali Tsabary, *The Conscious Parent: Transforming Ourselves, Empowering Our Children* (Vancouver, Canada: Namaste Publishing, 2010), 5.

13. Mona Delahooke, *Beyond Behaviors: Using Brain Science and Compassion to Understand and Solve Children's Behavioral Challenges* (Eau Claire, WI: PESI Publishing, 2019), 107.

Sources for Chapter 3

1. Delahooke, *Beyond Behaviors*, 11.

2. van der Kolk, *The Body Keeps the Score*, 111.

3. Nicholas J. Long et al., *Conflict in the Classroom: Successful Behavior Management Using the Psychoeducational Model,* 7th ed. (Austin, TX: PRO-ED, Inc., 2014), 35.

4. Ibid., 34.

5. Ibid., 34.

6. van der Kolk, The *Body Keeps the Score*, 116.

7. Children's Defense Fund, "Overview of *The State of America's Children 2017*" (Washington, D.C.: The Children's Defense Fund, 2017). Available at: https://www.childrensdefense.org/wp-content/uploads/2018/06/state-of-americas-children-overview.pdf.

8. Allan N. Schore, "Attachment, Affect Regulation, and the Developing Right Brain: Linking Developmental Neuroscience to Pediatrics," *Pediatrics in Review* 26, no.6 (2005): 204-217. Available at: http://allanschore.com/pdf/_SchorePediatricsInReview.pdf.

9. Allan Schore, *The Science of the Art of Psychotherapy* (New York, NY: Norton and Company, 2011), 238.

10. Schore, "Attachment, Affect Regulation, and the Developing Right Brain," 204-217.

11. Donna Jackson Nakazawa, *Childhood Disrupted: How Your Biography Becomes Your Biology, and How You Can Heal* (New York, NY: Atria Publishing Group—Simon & Schuster, 2015), 49-50.

12. Sierra Health Foundation, *Adverse Childhood Experiences, Toxic Stress and Implications for Juvenile Justice* (San Francisco, CA: Center for Youth Wellness, 2015), 1-21. Available at: https://www.sierrahealth.org/assets/pyji/-CYW_PYJL_Guide_July_2015.pdf.

13. U.S. House of Representatives Committee on Education and Labor. *Written Statement of Dr. Nadine Burke Harris Surgeon General of California Before the Committee on Education and Labor United States House of Representatives Full Committee Hearing: Trauma-Informed Care in Schools, September 11, 2019.* Nadine Burke Harris. 091119. Education & Labor Committee: 2019. Available at: https://edlabor.house.gov/imo-/media/doc/BurkeHarrisTestimony091119.pdf.

14. Bruce D. Perry, MD, PhD, "Maltreatment and the Developing Child: How Early Childhood Experience Shapes Child and Culture," *The Margaret McCain Lecture Series* (London, Canada: The Centre for Children & Families in the Justice System, 2005), 1-6. Available at: https://www.gvsu.edu/cms4/asset/903124DF-BD7F-3286-FE3330AA44F994DE/maltreating_and_the_developing_child.pdf.

15. Perry and Szalavitz, *The Boy Who Was Raised as a Dog,* 138-139.

16. Perry, "Maltreatment and the Developing Child: How Early Childhood Experience Shapes Child and Culture," 1-6.

17. Badenoch, *The Heart of Trauma,* 1.

18. Delahooke, *Beyond Behaviors,* 15.

19. Lucy Jane Miller, *Sensational Kids: Hope and Help for Children with Sensory Processing Disorder (SPD),* rev. ed. (New York, NY: TarcherPerigee-Penguin Books USA, 2014), 105.

20. Amy Gaesser, "Emotional Freedom Techniques: Stress and Anxiety Management for Students and Staff in School Settings," in *Promoting Mind-Body Health in Schools Interventions for Mental Health Professionals,* eds. Cheryl Maykel and Melissa A. Bray (Washington, D.C.: American Psychological Association, 2020), 283.

21. Ibid., 285.

22. Stephen W. Porges, PhD, "The polyvagal theory: New insights into adaptive reactions of the autonomic nervous system," *Cleveland Clinic Journal of Medicine* 76 (Suppl. 2), S86-S90 (2009). Available at: https://www.ncbi.nlm.nih.gov/pmc/articles/PMC3108032/.

Sources for Chapter 4

1. Perry and Szalavitz, *The Boy Who Was Raised as a Dog,* 79-80.

2. Rebecca Lewis-Pankratz, "The Absence of Punishment in Our Schools," *ACEs in Education,* March 10, 2020, https://www.acesconnection.com/g/aces-in-education/blog/the-absence-of-punishment-in-our-schools?fbclid=IwAR18fVvTVTZU9B8eucyZrQ1MUL_DApSWsSjXu3FmKnn8BZ5e11u8fqNSyNE.

3. Porges, "The polyvagal theory."

4. Joanna Moorhead, "How dealing with past trauma may be the key to breaking addiction," *The Guardian*, November 24, 2018, https://www.theguardian.com/life-andstyle/2018/nov/24/joanna-moorhead-gabriel-mate-trauma-addiction-treat.

5. John Seita and Larry Brendtro, *Kids Who Outwit Adults* (Bloomington, IN: Solution Tree, 2005), 10.

6. Ibid., 13.

7. Ibid., 15.

8. Ibid., 27.

9. Ibid., 16.

10. Ibid., 37.

11. Perry and Szalavitz, *The Boy Who Was Raised as a Dog*, 135.

12. Ibid., 38-39.

13. Seita and Brendtro, *Kids Who Outwit Adults*, 39.

14. Ibid., 48.

15. Meg Anderson and Kavitha Cardoza, "Mental Health in Schools: A Hidden Crisis Affecting Millions of Students," *National Public Radio*, August 31, 2016, https://www.npr.org/sections/ed/2016/08/31/464727159/mental-health-in-schools-a-hidden-crisis-affecting-millions-of-students.

16. James Redford and Karen Pritzker, "Teaching Traumatized Kids," *The Atlantic*, July 7, 2016, https://www.theatlantic.com/education/archive/2016/07/teaching-traumatized-kids/490214/.

17. Bruce L. Wilson and H. Corbett, *Listening to Urban Kids: School Reform and the Teachers They Want* (Albany, NY: State University of New York Press, 2001), 91.

18. TeachThought Staff, "52 Of Our Favorite Inspirational Quotes For Teachers," *TeachThought*, February 3, 2020, https://www.teachthought.com/pedagogy/52-favorite-inspirational-quotes-for-teachers/.

19. Shelly L. Gable, Harry T. Reis, Emily A. Impett, and Evan R. Asher, "What Do You Do When Things Go Right? The Intrapersonal and Interpersonal Benefits of Sharing Positive Events," *Journal of Personality and Social Psychology*, 87, no. 2 (2004): 228-245. Available at: https://labs.psych.ucsb.edu/gable/shelly/sites-/labs.psych.ucsb.edu.gable.shelly/files/pubs/gable_et_al._2004.pdf.

20. Raymond J. Wlodkowski, *The M.O.S.T. Program: Motivational Opportunities for Successful Teaching* Leaders' Guide, (Phoenix, AZ: Universal Dimensions, 1983).

21. Daniel Vollrath, "A De-escalation Exercise for Upset Students," *Edutopia*, January 14, 2020, https://www.edutopia.org/article/de-escalation-exercise-upset-students.

22. *Edutopia*, "Making Sure Each Child Is Known," October 27, 2017, https://www.edutopia.org/video/making-sure-each-child-known.

23. *Edutopia*, "A Daily Support System for Students," February 5, 2018, https://www.edutopia.org/video/daily-support-system-students.

24. Ludy-Dobson and Perry, "The Role of Healthy Relational Interactions in Buffering the Impact of Childhood Trauma," 26-43.

25. Nakazawa, *Childhood Disrupted*, 192-193.

26. Lori Desautels, "The Key of Connection," *Edutopia*, January 29, 2014, https://www.edutopia.org/blog/the-key-of-connection-lori-desautels.

Sources for Chapter 5

1. Gershoff and Font, "Corporal Punishment in U.S. Public Schools: Prevalence, Disparities in Use, and Status in State and Federal Policy."

2. Murray A. Straus with Denise A. Donnelly, *Beating the Devil Out of Them: Corporal Punishment in American Families and its Effects on Children* (New Brunswick, NJ: Transaction Publishers, 2009).

3. Jack P. Shonkoff, MD, "Stress, Resilience, and the Role of Science," *Center on the Developing Child, Harvard University*, March 20, 2020, https://developingchild.harvard.edu/stress-resilience-and-the-role-of-science-responding-to-the-coronavirus-pandemic/.

Sources for Chapter 6

1. Dolores A. Stregelin, PhD, "Preschool Suspension and Expulsion: Defining the Issues," *Institute for Child Success*, December 2018, https://www.instituteforchildsuccess.org/wp-content/uploads/2018/12/ICS-2018-PreschoolSuspensionBrief-WEB.-pdf.

2. Peter A. Levine and Maggie Kline, *Trauma through a Child's Eyes: Awakening the Ordinary Miracle of Healing* (Berkeley, CA: North Atlantic Books, 2007), 34.

3. Ibid., 80.

4. Fred Rogers, *Life's Journeys According to Mister Rogers: Things to Remember Along the Way*, (New York, NY: Hachette Book Group, 2019), 42.

5. Judith R. Schore and Allan N. Schore, "Modern Attachment Theory: The Central Role of Affect Regulation in Development and Treatment," *Clinical Social Work Journal* 36, no. 1 (2008): 9.

6. Daniel Siegel, *Pocket Guide to Interpersonal Neurobiology: An Integrative Handbook of the Mind* (New York, NY: W.W. Norton & Company, 2012), 20-4.

7. Ibid., 21-9.

8. Ibid., 20-2.

9. Ibid., 20-3.

ABOUT THE EDITOR

Alan K. Lipton spent over five years as an editor with the George Lucas Educational Foundation, lending his support to both the Edutopia platform and Lucas Educational Research's curriculum development initiative. He's also worked on education-themed books by Abe Feinberg and Brian Sztabnik, served as a media consultant at Center for Inspired Teaching, edited many blog posts for Vicki Davis' Cool Cat Teacher and Leoni Consulting Group's edtech-focused clients, and advised a number of other educators sharing their written insights and experiences. Alan is honored to work with Lori Desautels on *Connections Over Compliance*, helping to distill her knowledge, compassion, and enthusiasm into a book that can truly revolutionize how our schools teach our most vulnerable children.

ABOUT THE AUTHOR

Lori L. Desautels, Ph.D. has been an Assistant Professor at Butler University since 2016 where she teaches both undergraduate and graduate programs in the College of Education. Lori was also an Assistant Professor at Marian University in Indianapolis for eight years where she founded the Educational Neuroscience Symposium.

Currently, the Symposium is in its eighth year, and now sponsored by Butler University College of Education. Through these conferences and symposiums, educators, parents, and the community learn to implement the tools to help our students be successful and feel a sense of purpose and connection as they walk into their classrooms. Because of her work, Lori has been able to attract the foremost experts in the fields of educational neuroscience, trauma and adversity, which significantly grow the conference each year.

Lori has created a nine-hour graduate certification at Butler University in Applied Educational Neuroscience/Brain and Trauma. This certification has grown from 6 graduates in its pilot year in 2016 to 70 graduate students in its third cohort. The certification is open to students around the world as it has transformed into a distance learning, hybrid format. The Applied Educational Neuroscience Certificate, created by Lori in 2016, is specifically designed to meet the needs of educators, counselors, and administrators who work beside children and adolescents who have, and are, experiencing adversity and trauma.

Lori's passion is engaging students through the application of neuroscience as it applies to attachment, regulation, and educator brain state, and teaching students and staff about their neuroanatomy, thus integrating Mind Brain Teaching learning principles and strategies into her coursework at Butler. Lori has conducted brain institutes and workshops throughout the United States, Canada, Costa Rica, and Dubai on Mind Brain Teaching and Learning. She has created webinars for educators, clinicians, and administrators illustrating how educators and students alike must understand their neuroanatomy to regulate behavior and calm the brain.

Lori is co-author of the social and emotional competencies for the State of Indiana published in January 2018. She also has authored a series of articles for "Inside the School," an online publication providing strategies to administrators and educators alike. Lori's articles are published in *Edutopia, Brain Bulletin,* and *Mind Body Spirit* international magazine. She also was published in the *Brain Research Journal* for her work in the fifth-grade classrooms during a course release partnering with the Washington Township Schools in Indiana.

Lori continues her work in the Pre-K classrooms and is currently co-teaching in fifth grade and working with St. Mary's Early Childhood Center in Indianapolis for the second consecutive year. Lori has met with hundreds of school districts across the country, equating to more than 60,000 educators, with much more work to be done!

Lori taught emotionally troubled students in the upper elementary grades, worked as a school counselor in Indianapolis, was a private practice counselor and was coowner of the Indianapolis Counseling Center. Lori was also a behavioral consultant for Methodist Hospital in Indianapolis on the adolescent psychiatric unit where she learned that emotional and mental illness can be so challenging for youth, but the brain can repair and heal, and resilience rests at the core of human nature and our well-being.

Find Lori's work, presentation videos, and latest research on her website revelationsineducation.com. Her first book, *How May I Serve You, Revelations in Education*, was published in March of 2012. Her second book, coauthored with educator Michael McKnight, entitled *Unwritten, The Story of a Living System*, has been used as a foundation to create curriculum across the country. Lori's third book, *Eyes Are Never Quiet*, was published in January of 2018.

Lori graduated with a BS in Special Education from Butler University, an MS in Counseling Education from Indiana University, and earned her Ph.D. in Philosophy with an emphasis in early adolescence/thought formation from Indiana University and American Institute of Holistic Theology.

Lori resides in Indianapolis, Indiana, with her husband, Michael. She has three grown children, Andrew, Sarah, and Regan, and four rescue fur babies.